CU00821379

The Book of Government

The Book of Government or Rules for Kings

The Siyar al-Muluk or Siyasat-nama
of NIZAM AL-MULK

Translated from the Persian by
HUBERT DARKE

Routledge
Taylor & Francis Group

LONDON AND NEW YORK

First published in 1960
Second edition published in 1978
This edition published in 2002
by Routledge
2 Park Square, Milton Park, Abingdon, Oxfordshire OX14 4RN
711 Third Avenue, New York, NY 10017, USA

First issued in paperback 2015

Routledge is an imprint of the Taylor and Francis Group, an informa business

© 2002 Persian Heritage Foundation

British Library Cataloguing in Publication Data
A catalogue record of this book is available from the British Library

Library of Congress Cataloguing in Publication Data
A catalogue record for this book has been requested

ISBN 13: 978-1-138-96488-4 (pbk)
ISBN 13: 978-0-7007-1228-1 (hbk)

Publisher's Note
The publisher has gone to great lengths to ensure the quality of this reprint but points out that some imperfections in the original may be apparent

Contents

Introduction

The book which is here offered to English readers was described
by E. G. Browne as 'one of the most valuable and interesting
prose works in Persian'. It was written by Ḥasan ibn 'Alī of Ṭūs,
entitled Niẓām al-Mulk, who for thirty years, first under Sultan
Alp Arslan and then under his son Malikshāh, as their chief
minister directed the administration of the great empire of the
Saljuqs. These Saljuqs were the ruling family of a tribe of wild
Turkish nomads who, coming from the steppes of Central Asia,
asked persmission from Sulṭān Maḥmūd of Ghazna to cross the
Oxus in search of fresh pastures for their flocks in Khurāsān. They
came and flourished, and soon became so strong that they were
able to take Khurāsān from the Ghaznavids. The rise to power of
the Saljuqs and the period of their ascendancy coincided exactly
with the lifetime of Niẓām al-Mulk. He was born, according to
two good authorities, either in 408 A.H./1018 A.D. (*Mujmal-i
Faṣīḥī*) or in 410 A.H./1019–20 A.D. (*Tārīkh-i Baihaq*); he died,
as we know, in 485/1092, murdered by one of the assassins of the
Isma'īlīs whom he denounced so fiercely in this book; thus he
lived, and remained working, until a ripe old age. After his death,
even to some extent because of it, the empire of the Saljuqs went
into decline.

Not much is known about his early life. His father was a native
of Baihaq, which is the old name for the town and district of
Sabzvār; he had come to Ṭūs as a tax-collector in the service of
the Ghaznavids. In the *Asrār at-Tauḥīd,* which is a collection of
anecdotes about the famous mystic, Shaikh Abū Sa'īd ibn Abi'l-
Khair, there are some glimpses of Ḥasan in his boyhood: on two
occasions the Shaikh saw him and prophesied that he would become 'the khwāja of the world'; one was at Ṭūs, when Ḥasan
was a small boy, and the other was later when he was on his way
to Marv to further his studies and stopped at Maihana to visit the
Shaikh. He retained a great faith in the Shaikh and remained a
nominal disciple all his life; he used to say that to him he owed
all his success. Though not inclined to mysticism himself, in his
later life he founded several hospices for the Ṣūfīs, and continued

to support them financially. Politically more important was his promotion of orthodox religious education; he founded madrasas or colleges of higher learning in several cities; they were known as Niẓāmiyyas after him, and the most famous of them were at Baghdad and Nishāpūr.

When Khurāsān fell to the Saljuqs with the defeat of Sulṭān Mas'ūd in 431/1040, Ḥasan's father went to Ghazna, taking his son with him. Ḥasan probably worked in the Ghaznavid administration for a time, but after a few years he left there and went back to Khurāsān to enter the service of the Saljuqs. Meanwhile, the Saljuq brothers, Tughril Beg and Chaghri Beg, had divided the dominion between them, Tughril taking the western half with his seat at Baghdad, and Chaghri remaining in the east with his headquarters at Marv. When Chaghri died in 452/1060 Tughril became paramount ruler and Chaghri's son, Alp Arslan, succeeded him as governor of Khurāsān. Niẓām al-Mulk had for some years been adviser to Alp Arslan during the period that the latter had served his father in a subordinate command in eastern Khurāsān; he was now retained by Alp Arslan as his right-hand man, and thus, until the death of Tughril in 455/1063, he was responsible for the administration of the whole of Khurāsān. It was during this period that enmity grew up between him and Tughril's vazir, 'Amīd al-Mulk al-Kundurī. Tughril had no male heir, and Kundurī had persuaded Tughril to designate Sulaimān, Chaghri's younger son, to succeed him, knowing full well that if Alp Arslan, the elder son of Chaghri, became great sultan, it would be Niẓām al-Mulk who became 'khwāja of the world' rather than Kundurī himself. Eventually Alp Arslan's succession was secured and Kundurī was sent into exile and a little later executed, no doubt on the orders of Niẓām al-Mulk.

During the reigns of Alp Arslan (455–65/1063–73) and his son Malikshāh the Saljuq power reached its zenith and Niẓām al-Mulk was at the height of his career. The empire covered a vast territory extending from the borders of Afghanistan to the shores of the Mediterranean, and as head of the administration Niẓām al-Mulk acquired great authority and prestige. When Malikshāh came to the throne he was only eighteen years of age and at first he relied heavily on his vazir. Thus Niẓām al-Mulk was able to have his own way for a number of years, and there is no doubt that he directed affairs with great skill and efficiency. However, his manner was not without arrogance; his habit of putting his friends and relations into the best posts began to arouse resentment, and his opponents were able to gain the ear of the sultan. As the sultan increased in maturity he asserted himself more vigorously, and there were times when he was on bad terms with his vazir. Perhaps it was at such a moment, when he was dissatisfied with the state of things in his kingdom and tempted to consider ways of replacing him, that he commanded Niẓām al-Mulk and several others to compose treatises on the art of government. What the others wrote, if anything, we shall never know; what survives is the book before us – the memorial of a great Iranian statesman.

The Nakhjivānī MS of Tabrīz

Until the discovery of this MS it could be said that the text of this book had been badly preserved. Not one of the dozen or so extant MSS gave a satisfactory text; not only did they contain incongruous material which cast doubt upon the authenticity of the whole book, but the copyists had been guilty of every conceivable aberration – interpolation, alteration, omission; and only by comparing a number of these could a readable text be produced. The Nakhjivānī MS, which was used to prepare the text (published by the Royal Institute of Translation and Publication in 1968 and soon to be re-issued with corrections) from which this translation was made, was copied in 673/1274, and not only is it older than all other MSS, but it far surpasses them in correctness. Part of this virtue of credibility and authenticity can be attributed to the fact the scribe, to judge from his manner of writing and the nature of the mistakes he did make, was almost certainly illiterate; letters are sometimes confused, dots are often omitted and misplaced. But the MS is absolutely free of those gratuitous alterations and interpolations which abound in other MSS; erroneous omissions are few and short and can generally be ascribed to lipography. Archaic words and forms and unfamiliar place-names are preserved, which were ruthlessly modernized or changed by later copyists; attention is drawn to some of these in the notes. But the outstanding feature of the text of this MS is that those passages in previous texts (chapter 40, paras 33 and 34, and Chapter 41, para. 22) in which Niẓām al-Mulk is referred to in the third person and sultans are mentioned who ruled after Niẓām al-Mulk's death are completely absent. The author's prologue appears in a form which previously it was possible only to adumbrate, while the epilogue with its reference to 'Muḥammad the copyist' (only in one MS is he called 'Maghribī') is absent altogether. So it seems highly probable that here we have a text closely descended from the author's autograph and that the composition of an epilogue, the adaptation of the prologue and the interpolation of two spurious passages were all the work of 'the copyist'. By extreme good fortune, a single copy of Niẓām al-Mulk's original text survived to be copied directly (or at one or two removes) into the Nakhjivānī MS, while all the other extant MSS (except that of the Majlis library in Tehran, which is demonstrably a direct and recent copy of the Nakhjivānī) derive from an edited version. The Nakhjivānī MS is remarkably well preserved, and consists or consisted originally of 147 folios; unfortunately, however, it has a lacuna; folios 29 to 40 are missing; here the previous synchretistic text has been used to fill the gap. With the strong internal evidence of the authorship of the book in chapter 21, para. 5, where in one of his all too few personal reminiscences the author relates a conversation in which other parties refer to him as 'the vazir of Sultan Alp Arslan', we can be more confident overall that the book is the genuine composition and compilation of Niẓām al-Mulk.

Title

Since Charles Schefer published the Persian text (1891) and the French translation (1893), this book has been generally known in Europe as the *Siyāsat-nāma,* and accordingly the present translation retains the title 'The Book of Government'. However, all MSS give the title as *Siyar al-Mulūk* (literally 'Manners of the Kings') and the book has been known in Iran and quoted in Persian literature down the centuries by this name. Of early references the one in *Tārīkh-i Ṭabaristān* is indisputable and that in the *Naṣīḥat al-Mulūk* of Ghazzālī ('Counsel for Kings', 70–71) is virtually certain, for there Ghazzali quotes the story (our book, chapter 3, paras 19–21), in which 'Amr-i Laith tempts Ismā'īl ibn Aḥmad with an offer of the Ṣaffārid treasure. The same story is found in *Tārīkh-i Guzīda* (72) and *Jawāmi' al-Ḥikāyāt,* in both of which books the *Siyar al-Mulūk* is listed as one of their general sources. An internal allusion to the title comes in chapter 43, para. 6,

where we find the words *dar in kitāb-i siyar*. The only evidence
for a name embracing the word *siyāsat* is to be found in an epilogue
(absent in our MS), where some MSS read *in ast kitāb-i siyāsat*.
Indeed Niẓām al Mulk seems to have set a fashion (himself modelling his title on the *Kitāb at-Tāj fi Akhlāq al-Mulūk* – 'Le livre de
la couronne') whereby Persian 'Mirrors for Princes' were given
titles of the style ... al-Mulūk; Ghazzālī was next in the line, and
there were many more after him.

Numbering of chapters

All MSS shew confusion in the numbering of chapters in the body
of the text; this is resolved by referring to the list of contents at
the beginning of the book. Errors crept into the text when scribes
came to the heading of a fresh section within a chapter (such as
chapter 27, para. 2) and numbered this as a new chapter. Even our
own MS in chapter 40 numbers para. 18 as chapter 41 and para. 19
as chapter 42, and does not come back into line until chapter 47.
The corrected numbering agrees very well with the Librarian's
Note at the beginning, which states that Niẓām al-Mulk first composed thirty-nine chapters, and later 'because of his anxiety on
account of enemies of the dynasty' added a further eleven chapters.
The subject matter of chapter 40 exactly suits the beginning of a
new section; so we are justified in indicating the division of the
book into two parts accordingly.

Hajjī Khalīfa, the great eleventh/seventeenth century Turkish
bibliographer, gives a description of the book which is faulty in
some details; the entry in his *Kashf aẓ-Zunūn* runs as follows:

> *Siyar al-Mulūk,* Persian, of the vazir, Niẓām al-Mulk Ḥasan ibn
> 'Alī of Tūs (died 485); he composed it during his vazirate in 469
> for Malikshāh, the Saljuqid, in 39 chapters; then al-Yamīnī
> made it 51, and arranged all the chapters in his own order,
> different from the author's.

Ḥajjī Khalīfa probably had only inferior MSS at his disposal, and
we cannot accept his figures against the evidence of the Nakhjivānī MS.

It is practically as certain that the second part was never seen by
Malikshāh; this can be inferred from the Librarian's Note. The
Librarian would hardly have dared to present such outspoken

criticisms to the sultan, and he had no opportunity to do so anyway, because Malikshāh himself died soon after arriving at
Baghdad, just a month or so after Niẓām al-Mulk was assassinated
on the journey.

Date of composition

According to one group of related, and late, MSS the book was
composed, or rather the order for its composition was given, in
484/1091. In our MS (supported by one late MS, not that of
Majlis library) the prologue is written in the name of Niẓām al-
Mulk himself and he says that in 479/1086 Sulṭān Malikshāh
invited him and several others to write a book. This does not
mean that the book, that is the first part of it, was necessarily
written in that year, but composition was probably not delayed
as late as 484/1091. Niẓām al-Mulk's stories about his own times
mostly concern incidents in the reign of Alp Arslan; the only
reference in Part One to an event in the time of Malikshāh is in
chapter 35, para. 2, where he says –'on that occasion when we
went to Samarqand and Ūzgand'. If, as is historically most likely,
the author is referring to the campaign of 481/1058–482/1089,
then either Part One was written after 481/1058, or this passage
was added at the time of the revision mentioned by the Librarian.
So as far as Part One is concerned, we can only say that it was
written between the years 479/1086 and 484/1091, sooner rather
than later. The date given by Ḥājjī Khalīfa must be regarded as a
mistake resulting from a misreading of figure 7 as figure 6.

However, it is quite possible that 484/1091 was the year of
composition of Part Two. Indeed two things happened in the
year 483/1090 which could have prompted Niẓām al-Mulk to take
up his pen again. One was his quarrel with Sultan Malikshāh, and
his fall from favour, if not from office (the *Rāḥat aṣ-Ṣudūr* does say
that he was replaced by Tāj al-Mulk); and this would account for
the tone of bitterness and frustration which pervades these chapters. The other circumstance, which could have been responsible
for his outcry against heretics, the Ismaʿīlīs in particular, was the
return of Ḥasan-i Ṣabbāḥ from Egypt in this year, when he
occupied Alamut and commenced his activities in Persia.

After the deaths of Niẓām al-Mulk and Sulṭān Malikshāh in the
year 485/1092, the country was thrown into confusion by the

struggle for power between Berk-yaruq and Muhammad, and we can well believe the Librarian when he says that he did not dare to reveal the book while the troubles lasted. Stability was restored when Muḥammad became undisputed sultan in 498/1105, and it is surely this sultan to whom the Librarian refers in his note. Ghazzali composed his *Naṣīḥat al-Mulūk* before 505/1112, and since he probably had the *Siyar al-Mulūk* in his hands at the time, we can say that the *Siyar al-Mulūk* was published, bearing in mind the limited circulation of books in those days, between 498/1105 and 505/1112.

Materials and sources

The book is put together like a patchwork from pieces, longer or shorter, gathered from various sources; these materials can be classified as follows:

Advice. Apart from chapters 1 and 2 which are introductory and deal with the theory and theology of kingship, and chapters 44–7 which consist of historical narrative, introduced by chapter 43, every chapter opens with a passage offering practical instruction on some aspect of the functions and duties of the monarch. This advice material is very original, having been written for a particular sultan at a particular time, and it is derived hardly at all from the old *pand-nāma-ha* ('books of counsel') which were the foundation of more abstract treatises. It may be that because the author had no model before him, the advice is sometimes crudely and vaguely expressed; this is particularly the case with some of the very short chapters consisting of only a few lines. A different reason for obscurity is to be seen in those chapters which criticize the royal master or offer unwelcome advice, and here we may imagine that measured words and equivocal language were deliberate.

Quotations, Traditions and Sayings. The material under this head belongs to a great corpus of quotations from the Qur'an, traditions of the Prophet and his Companions and sayings of famous men, generally only a few lines in length, which was drawn upon freely by the composers of Arabic and Persian ethical treaties. Doubtless authors often culled them from the works of their predecessors rather than from original sources – witness the number of consecutive passages from this book (especially chapters 7 and 8) which Ghazzali incorporated into his *Naṣīḥat al-Mulūk*.

Anecdotes. In this class are included the numerous short stories, of about one or two pages in length, relating to some historical ruler or minister. The source of these would be earlier books in which writers gave the stories at first hand and the 'Collections of Tales' (see page 25, note 2 and *Counsel for Kings*, 94), which developed later into such a massive collection as the *Jawāmiʿ al-Ḥikāyāt*. These anecdotes were common literary property; examples from the *Siyar al-Mulūk* are to be found, sometimes with modifications, in many other books, such as *Counsel for Kings* (lviii, where Bagley lists eighteen parallel items) and of course the *Jawāmiʿ al-Ḥikāyāt* (pp. 76–84). Where similar stories are common to *Siyar al-Mulūk* and other books but with different names (e.g. the story about Bahrām Gūr in chapter 4, which appears in *Counsel for Kings*, p. 93, with the name Gushtasb), we may suspect that it was Niẓām al-Mulk who made the changes. Here it must be remembered that for Niẓām al-Mulk the object of these stories lay in the moral to be drawn from each; they are to be entertaining too, as he says in his prologue, but not scrupulously historical. This book is addressed to an uneducated ex-nomad Turk, who would hardly have been impressed or pleased if many of the stories had been concerned with names unfamiliar to him. So sometimes the author changed the names of characters in traditional stories in order to introduce well-known names and incidentally to glorify his own idols, especially Sultan Maḥmūd of Ghazna.

Long stories. The long stories, running to ten or twenty pages are in quite a separate category; they may be called historical romances and as such they represent some of the earliest prose fiction in the Persian language. They tend to be rambling and even tedious, for they contain much repetition and padding; the author's invention is in the main limited to minute details of words and actions, and he introduces several anachronisms. One of these stories, however, is not the author's own composition; in fact it is the only item in the book which can be assigned to a definite source. This is the story about the Barmakids in chapter 41, para. 34. The whole story with scarcely a word changed is taken from the opening pages of the *Tārīkh-i Barāmika*; only the name of the principal character has been changed from Barmak to Jaʿfar. This 'History of the Barmakids', then, could well have been the model which Niẓām al-Mulk had before him in writing these long stories. It is not so much a history as a collection of anecdotes, some of which are quite humorous; like those of Niẓām al-Mulk, they contain much conversation, which though partly fictional gives the impression of being based on real life, whereas one cannot conceive that the words of Ya'qūb-i Laith or Mazdak, as detailed by Niẓām al-Mulk, are other than pure fiction. The fictional element in Niẓām al-Mulk's stories is greater; he went a stage further than his model.

The following are the long stories in this category:

Stories about contemporary events. There are only five stories in the book dealing with contemporary persons or events, most of them pertaining to the reign of Alp Arslan; these are:

1 Chapter 10, para. 18. A conversation between Sultan Alp Arslan and Abu'l-Faḍl Sigzī on the subject of intelligence agents.

2 Chapter 21, paras 3–5. A story in the first person about the author's meeting with an envoy of the khan of Samarqand.

3 Chapter 35, para. 2. A reference to Sultan Malikshāh's expedition to Samarqand and Ūzgand.

4 Chapter 38, para. 2. A story about the attempt of 'Abd ar-Raḥmān Khāl to convince Alp Arslan that a certain famous man (surely Abd-Allāh Anṣārī) was an idolator.

5 Chapter 41, paras 3–17. A story about the displeasure of Alp Arslan on hearing that Ardam was employing a Shī'ī as his secretary.

Historical narrative. The material of this class is found in chapters 45–7, where in Niẓām al-Mulk sets forth, as a warning for the present, the history of some of the past seceders and heretics who revolted against the religion and the state.

These are straightforward accounts without any obvious fictional element (except for the story of Naṣr ibn Aḥmad which we have already removed to another category), and they appear to be derived more or less directly from the books which Niẓām al-Mulk used as his sources; some of these are mentioned in the text and they are:

1 *Tārīkh-i Iṣfahān.* Although the *Maḥāsin Iṣfahān* of Māfarrūkhī in this original Arabic version could have been available to Niẓām al-Mulk, Browne's survey of the contents of the Persian translation ('Account of a rare manuscript history of Isfahan') shows that it could not have been the major source that Niẓām al-Mulk claims it to have been in chapter 43, para. 6 (p. 189); he names it again in chapter 47, para. 13 (p.237). Other histories of Isfahan are known to have existed which are now lost.

2 *Tārīkh-i Ṭabarī*; named in chapter 47, para. 13 (p. 237).

3 *Tārīkh-i Khulafā-yi Banī 'Abbās*, named in chapter 47, para. 13 (p. 237); this was probably the *Kitāb al-Aurāq* of aṣ-Ṣūlī.

4 *Makhāriq al-Anbiyā (Ḥiyal al-Mutanabbiyīn)* of Muḥammad ibn Zakariyyā Rāzī, mentioned in chapter 46, para. 2 (p. 209).

Comments and remarks. Stories long or short are water-tight units and reflections or comments on the part of the author are not admitted in the body of a story, unless they are expressed by means of speeches put into the mouths of the characters. Only at the end of a story or chapter are there often three or four lines of brief comment on what has gone before.

Doctrines

In the first two chapters of the book, and again at the beginning of Part Two, Niẓām al-Mulk, like other writers of mirrors for princes, sets forth the traditional Persian theory of kingship, handed down from the Sasanian period, which holds that kings are selected by God for the good of mankind and endowed by Him with wisdom and justice, and that they are accountable to Him on the resurrection day for the rule they have exercised. Indeed the picture in the first chapter of an evil and godless age being ended by a divinely appointed saviour king is strikingly similar to a passage in the 'Oracles of Hystaspes', king of the Medes, a document which is ascribed to the third or second century B.C. and recorded by the Christian writer Lactantius. When

xviii

the author makes another allusion to the doctrine in chapter 6, para. 3, he expressly puts it into a Sasanian context. The parallel teaching that 'religion and kingship are two brothers', given in chapter 8, para. 3, is also Zoroastrian in origin. On the subject of vazirs, Niẓām al-Mulk says in chapter 41, para. 34 that vazirship, like kingship, should be hereditary as it was in the Sasanian period. In this book he does not actually say that vazirs are appointed by God; when he did say that, it cost him his job. For according to *Rāḥat aṣ-Sudūr*, pp. 133-4, shortly before their departure from Iṣfahān for Baghdad in 485/1092 relations between Malikshāh and Niẓām al-Mulk became strained to the limit; Tarkan Khatun, who favoured her own protégé Tāj al-Mulk against Niẓām al-Mulk and also wanted her own son Maḥmūd to be declared heir-apparent rather than the elder Berk-yaruq, the child of another wife, had been filling the ears of the sultan with stories of Niẓām al-Mulk's failings; Malikshāh sent a message of rebuke to Niẓām al-Mulk, charging him with doing what he liked without consulting him and giving important posts to his own sons, and threatened to remove the turban from his head, that is dismiss him. Niẓām al-Mulk sent back the answer, 'He who gave you the crown put the turban on my head; the two are interconnected and interdependent'. The people who carried the answer added their own embroidery, making matters worse. Malikshāh was furious and dismissed Niẓām al-Mulk, putting Tāj al-Mulk in his place.

All the subsequent chapters of Part One deal with the practical aspects of rulership; advice is given on what the sultan should do and what his officers should do, in order to run the state efficiently and peacefully, and keep the people contented and under control. The army, of course, is the basis of his power and it must be maintained in a high state of preparedness. Civil officials, especially those concerned with discipline such as judges, censors and prosecutors, are to have wide powers and great prestige; but the people must be dealt with fairly and there must be no oppression otherwise they will become discontented. The orthodox faith must be sustained and promoted, but there is no vehement condemnation of Shī'ism in this part, while 'Alī and his family are mentioned with respect; the only reference to Ismā'īlism is the rather unlikely suggestion that Ya'qūb-i Laith was a convert. It can now be seen that Niẓām al-Mulk made a distinction between the Shī'īs/Rāfiḍīs and the much more formidable Ismā'īlīs/

Bāṭinīs; if formerly he appeared to lump them together, this was partly due to the fact that where our MS has Seveners (Sabʿiyān), inferior MSS read Shīʿīs (Shīʿiyān); both words have the same shape in Arabic script and are easily confused. The author warns that nobody can be trusted to be either loyal or honest, so, to ensure that duties are performed and orders carried out, an elaborate intelligence system ought to be organized to obtain secret reports about the conduct of officials, high and low. Meanwhile, the king may sport with his boon-companions, giving parties, maintaining a huge household, and surrounding himself with all kinds of pomp and magnificence; his court is to be thronged with retainers and troops of slaves; his hospitality and generosity are to be on a lavish scale; the Saljuqs are blamed for not giving enough importance to ceremony and protocol. But the king should not issue too many written (chapter 11) or verbal (chapter 15) orders; thus he is tactfully steered away from interfering in routine administration, the preserve of the vazir; his only public function is to give audiences and hold court for listening to complaints and redressing wrongs. Although not everything is perfect in the state in the author's view, the defects are not serious or fundamental; there is criticism of the sultan, but it is gentle and polite.

In Part Two all is different; the times are sick, the evil eye is at work; things are going seriously wrong and disaster is feared. In fact in the opening paragraph of chapter 40 all the ills are specified, but by a masterly piece of dissimulation the whole diagnosis is expressed as a hypothetical case. Evil practices and wrong procedures are threatening the safety of the state; noble families are being weakened and the proletariat are becoming uppish; experienced men are being left idle and unemployed, and economy in the army is jeopardizing security; women are meddling in affairs of state and underlings are overstepping their bounds. Criticism of the sultan becomes more outspoken in chapter 40, para. 18, in chapter 41, paras 1, 2 and 43, and in chapter 42, para. 1; while in chapter 41, paras 18–20, the author is clearly attacking his rival, Tāj al-Mulk. His concern about the misapplication of titles in chapter 40, para. 1 and paras 19–34 may seem trivial, but it is his discreet way of expressing his apprehension at the growth of Turkish military control over the Persian civil service; he seeks to preserve 'the prestige of the administration' (raunaq-i dīvān).

His worst fears arise from the spread of Isma'ilism; the immediate cause for alarm was that in 483/1090 Hasan-i Ṣabbāḥ returned to Iran from Egypt, was appointed chief propagandist in Dailamān and occupied the fortress of Alamūt, from which he directed the revolt against the Saljuqs and the deployment of the assassins. Chapters 43–7 are devoted to the history of several heretical sects; at the beginning and end of this part we find the two most poignant passages in the book (chapter 43, para. 3 and chapter 47, para. 15), in which we cannot fail to hear, as Barthold says, 'the voice of a man of deep convictions going to death for their sake'. Niẓām al-Mulk leads up to his long chapter (46) on the origin of Isma'ilism and the revolts of the Qarmaṭīs, as the early adherents to the sect were called, with two chapters about former heretics, Mazdak (44) and Sinbad (45), and he follows it with an account of Bābak and the Khurrama-dīns. In the last three chapters (48–50) he introduces some more administrative topics in the style of Part One, as if they are afterthoughts; and in the final paragraph of the book he takes leave of his master with the advice that he should pursue the middle course in affairs and practice moderation in all things.

Transliteration, etc.

Diacritical marks have been omitted throughout the text, and have not been rigorously applied in the notes. In the bibliography and index all names are fully pointed. The transliteration system is generally that approved by the Royal Asiatic Society; however, in the notes, where it is important to indicate the exact reading of the MS, the system is modified to avoid digraphs; thus ' = alif, θ = th, c = ch, x = kh, δ = dh, $\check{\zeta}$ = zh, $\acute{s}$ = sh, γ = gh; while * indicates a letter of the shape of b, p, t, θ, n, y, with no distinguishing dots.

Words in round brackets are in the original Persian, but are in some measure superfluous to the English.

Words in square brackets are not in the Persian, but are added by way of amplification or explanation.

Where Persian words are quoted in the notes without comment, the purpose is sometimes to correct the 1968 edition of the Persian text.

Bibliography

Persian and Arabic texts

Asrār at-Tauḥīd fī maqāmāt ash-Shaikh Abī Saʿīd of Muḥammad ibn Munavvar, ed. Dhabīḥ-Allāh Ṣafā, Tehran, 1332/1953.

Farhang-i Jughrāfiyā-yi Īrān, ed. General Razmārā, 10 vols, Tehran, 1328/1950–1332/1954.

Kimiyā-yi Saʿādat of Ghazzālī, ed. Aḥmad Ārām, 2 vols, Tehran, 1319/1940 and reprints.

Lughat-i Furs of Asadī, ed. P. Horn, Berlin, 1897. Ed. ʿAbbās Iqbāl, Tehran, 1319/1940.

Mafātīḥ al-ʿUlūm of Muḥammad ibn Yūsuf Khwārazmi, ed. G. van Vloten, Leiden, 1885.

Maḥāsin Iṣfahān of Mufaḍḍal ibn Saʿd ibn Ḥusain al-Māfarrūkhī al-Iṣfahānī (written 465/1072–485/1092), ed. Jalāl ad-Dīn Ḥusainī Ṭihrānī, Tehran, 1312/1933. Persian translation (729/1029) by Ḥusain ibn Muḥammad ibn Abī Riḍā Āvī, ed. ʿAbbās Iqbāl, Tehran, 1328/1949.

Mujmal-i Faṣīḥī of Faṣīḥ Aḥmad ibn Jalāl ad-Dīn Muḥammad Khwāfī, ed. Maḥmūd Farrukh, 3 vols, Mashhad, 1339/1960–1341/1962.

Mujmal at-Tawārīkh waʾl-Qiṣaṣ, ed. Malik ash-Shuʿarā Bahār, Tehran 1318/1939.

Rāḥat aṣ-Ṣidūr of Rāvandī, ed. Muḥammad Iqbāl (Gibb Memorial, New Series II), London, 1921.

[Ṭabarī's 'Commentary'] *Tarjuma-yi Tafsīr-i Ṭabarī*, Persian translation made in the time of Manṣūr ibn Nūḥ, the Samanid (350/961–365/976), ed. Ḥabīb Yaghmāʾī, 7 vols, Tehran, 1339/1960–1344/1965 (Tehran University Publications 589 etc.).

Tārīkh-i Baihaq of Abu ʾl-Ḥasan ʿAlī ibn Zaid Baihaqī known as Ibn Funduq, ed. Aḥmad Bahmanyār, Tehran, 1317/1938. Ed. Kalīm-Allāh Ḥusainī, Hyderabad-Deccan, 1968.

Tārīkh-i Baihaqī of Abu ʾl-Faḍl Muḥammad ibn Ḥusain Baihaqī, ed. Dr Ghanī and Dr Fayyāḍ, Tehran, 1324/1945.

Tārīkh-i Barāmika, ed. ʿAbd al-ʿAẓīm Garakānī, Tehran, 1313/1934.

Tārīkh-i Sīstān, ed. Malik ash-Shuʿarā Bahār, Tehran 1314/1935.

Zain al-Akhbār of Gardīzī, ed. Muḥammad Nāẓim, Berlin, 1928. Ed. ʿAbd al-Ḥayy Ḥabībī, Tehran 1347/1968.

Persian and Arabic texts available in translation

Alberuni's India (*Kitāb al-Bīrūnī fī taḥqīq mā liʾl-Hind*), translated by E. Sachau, 2 vols, London, 1910.

Chahār Maqāla of Niẓāmī ʿArūḍī Samarqandī, translated by E. G. Browne (Gibb Memorial, Old Series, XI.2), London, 1921.

The Chronology of Ancient Nations (*al-Athār al-bāqiya* of Bīrūnī), translated by E. Sachau, London, 1879.

Counsel for Kings (*Naṣīḥat al-Mulūk* of Ghazzālī), translated by F. R. C. Bagley, London, 1964.

The Fihrist of al-Nadim, translated by B. Dodge, 2 vols, New York, 1970.

The History of the World-Conqueror of Juvainī, translated by J. A. Boyle, 2 vols, Manchester, 1958.

The History of Bukhara of Narshakhī, translated by R. N. Frye, Cambridge, Mass., 1954.

Ḥudūd al-'Ālam, translated by V. Minorsky (Gibb Memorial, New Series, XI), London, 1937.

Introduction to the Jawāmi' al-Ḥikāyāt of 'Aufī by M. Nizamu'd-din (Gibb Memorial, New Series, VIII), London, 1929.

Kashf al-Maḥjūb of Hujvīrī, translated by R. A. Nicholson (Gibb Memorial, Old Series, XVII), London, 1911.

Le Livre de la couronne (*Kitāb at-Tāj fī akhlāq al-mulūk*, attributed to al-Jāḥiz) translated by C. Pellat, Paris, 1954.

Ma'ālim al-Qurba of Ibn al-Ukhuwwa, Arabic text and abridged translation by Reuben Levy (Gibb Memorial, New Series, XII), London, 1938.

A Mirror for Princes (*Qābūs-nāma* of Kai Kā'ūs ibn Iskandar) translated by Reuben Levy, London, 1951.

Nuzhat al-Qulūb of Ḥamd-Allāh Mustaufī, translated by G. Le Strange (Gibb Memorial, Old Series, XXIII, 2), London, 1919.

[Qur'ān] *The Koran Interpreted* by A. J. Arberry, 2 vols, London, 1955. *The meaning of the Glorious Qur'an*, text and explanatory translation by Marmaduke Pickthall, 2 vols, Hyderabad-Deccan, 1938.

[Ṭabari's 'History'] *The Reign of al-Mu'taṣim* from Ṭabari's History, translated and annotated by Elma Marin (American Oriental Series), New Haven, Conn., 1951.

Tārīkh-i Guzīda of Hamd-Allāh Mustaufī, abridged translation and indices by Browne and Nicholson (Gibb Memorial, Old Series, XIV.2), London, 1914.

Tārīkh-i Ṭabaristān of Ibn Isfandyār, abridged translation by E. G. Browne (Gibb Memorial, Old Series, II), London, 1905.

Modern studies and works of reference

Arberry, A. J., *Classical Persian Literature*, London, 1958.

Barthold, W., *Turkestan down to the Mongol Invasion* (Gibb Memorial, New Series, V), 3rd edition, London, 1968.

Bosworth, C. E., 'The Banū Ilyās of Kirmān' in C. E. Bosworth (ed.), *Iran and Islam; in memory of the late Vladimir Minorsky*, Edinburgh, 1971, pp. 107–24.

Bosworth, C. E., *The Ghaznavids,* Edinburgh, 1963.

Bosworth, C. E., *The Islamic Dynasties*, Edinburgh, 1967.

Browne, E. G., 'Account of a rare manuscript History of Isfahan', *Journal of the Royal Asiatic Society*, 1901, pp. 411–46, 661–704.

Browne, E. G., *A Literary History of Persia*, vols I and II. Cambridge, 1928.

Bulliet, R. W., *The Patricians of Nishapur*, Cambridge, Mass., 1972 (Harvard Middle Eastern Studies 16).

The Cambridge History of Iran, vols III, IV and V [*CHI*].

Christensen, A., *Le règne du roi Kawādh I et le communisme Mazdakite*, Copenhagen, 1925.

Christensen, A., 'Two versions of the history of Mazdak', in *Dr. Modi Memorial Volume*, Bombay, 1930, pp. 321–30.

Encyclopedia of Islam, 1st edition, 4 vols, Leiden, 1913–38; 2nd edition, in progress, Leiden, 1960–.

Grignaschi, M., 'Quelques spécimens de la littérature sassanide', *Journal Asiatique*, 1966, pp. 1–42.

Klausner, C. L., *The Seljuk Vizierate: a study of civil administration*, Cambridge, Mass., 1973 (Harvard Middle Eastern Monographs Series).

Lambtnn, A. K. S., 'Islamic Mirrors for Princes' in *La Persia nel Medioevo*, Rome (Accademia Nazionale dei Lincei), 1971, pp. 419–42.

Lambton, A. K. S., *Landlord and Peasant in Persia*, Oxford, 1953.

Lane-Poole, S., *The Mohammadan Dynasties*, London, 1893 (reprints Paris, 1925 etc.).

Le Strange, G., *The Lands of the Eastern Caliphate*, Cambridge, 1905, reprinted 1930.

Lewis, B., *The Origins of Isma'ilism*, Cambridge, 1940.

Nāzim, Muhammad, *Sultān Mahmūd of Ghazna*, Cambridge, 1931.

Stern, S. M., 'The early Isma'ili missionaries in north-west Persia and in Khurasan and Transoxiana', *Bulletin of the School of Oriental and African Studies*, XXIII, 1960, pp. 56–90.

For quick reference the biographical indices in *Counsel for Kings* and *The Fihrist of al-Nadim* will be found particularly useful.

THIS IS THE BOOK OF RULES FOR KINGS COMPOSED BY THE VAZIR, THE WISE, THE JUST, THE SUCCESSFUL, THE VICTORIOUS, NIZAM AL-MULK HASAN[1] OF TUS

In the name of Allah, The Merciful, The Clement
O my Lord, make easy and do not make difficult

[*Prologue*]

1 Thanks and praise be to God (to Him be power and glory) who is the Creator of heaven and earth, the Provider of daily food for His servants, the Knower of the hidden and the open, the Pardoner of sins; and blessings upon the best of mortals, The Chosen One (the prayers of Allah and His peace be upon him), who is the greatest of prophets, the elect of the God of the world, the vehicle of the Qur'an, and the advocate of his people on the day of judgment; blessings too upon his Companions and the people of his house.

2 Thus says Hasan[2] of Tus that in the year 479 [of the Hijra/ 1086 A.D.] Abu'l-Fath Malikshah ibn Muhammad, Glorifier of the World and the Faith, Right Hand of the Commander of the Faithful (may Allah strengthen his helpers and double his power), issued a sublime, imperial command to his servant and to several others, instructing each one of them to give thought to the condition of the country, and to consider – 'whether there is in our age and time anything out of order either in the divan, the court, the royal palace or the audience-hall – anything whose principles are not being observed by us or are unknown to us; whether there are any functions which kings before us have performed and we are not fulfilling: consider further what have been the laws and customs of kings and kingship, followed in past time by the Saljuq sultans, make a digest of them and present them for our judgment; we shall then reflect upon them and give orders that hereafter affairs religious and worldly should proceed in accordance with their proper rules; what is remediable we shall remedy;

we shall see that every duty is discharged correctly and according to God's commands, and that all wrong practices are discontinued; for since God (be He exalted) has given us His consummate grace and bestowed the world and the kingship of the world upon us and subdued all our enemies, henceforward nothing in our empire must exist or happen that is deficient or disordered or contrary to the religious law.' I then, drawing upon what I have found out, seen, experienced and learned from masters, have described what I know of this subject and composed this book in fifty chapters; the following list shews the contents of each chapter; moreover at various points in every chapter I have introduced suitable quotations from the traditions of the Prophet and stories about great men, so that the book may be interesting and not wearisome to read. There is much of profit in this book; if it is read and acted upon, it will yield reward in both worlds. I have written this manuscript for the magnificent Royal Library (may Allah prosper it) and I offer it in service; if Allah wills, it may be approved and accepted.

3 No king or emperor can afford not to possess and know this book, especially in these days, for the more he reads it, the more he will be enlightened upon spiritual and temporal matters, the better he will appreciate the qualities of friends and foes; the way of right conduct and the path of good government will be open to him; the rules for the management of the court, the audience-hall, the divan, the royal palace and the parade ground, and the methods of administering taxes, transacting business and settling the affairs of the people and the army will be clear to him; and nothing in the whole realm whether great or small, far or near, will remain concealed (if Allah wills—be He exalted).

4 This book is composed of fifty chapters in the following order:

[*Part One*]

[*Part Two*]

[Librarian's Note].

5 First of all Nizam al-Mulk composed this book ex tempore in thirty-nine chapters and delivered it [to Sultan Malikshah]. Then he revised it, and because of the constant anxiety that was in his mind on account of the enemies of this dynasty he added another eleven chapters, and in each chapter he set forth what was relevant to it. At the time of his departure he gave the book to me. Then

after the calamity that happened to him on the road to Baghdad [in the year 485/1092], when the Batinis revolted and people suffered harm, I did not dare to publish the book until the present time, when justice and Islam have gained strength from the ever-lasting reign of The Master of the World[3] (may God Almighty preserve this dynasty in perpetuity until the resurrection).

[*Part One*]

Chapter I

On the turn of Fortune's wheel and in praise of The Master of the World—may Allah confirm his Sovereignty

1 In every age and time God (be He exalted) chooses one member of the human race and, having endowed him with goodly and kingly virtues, entrusts him with the interests of the world and the well-being of His servants; He charges that person to close the doors of corruption, confusion and discord, and He imparts to him such dignity and majesty in the eyes and hearts of men, that under his just rule they may live their lives in constant security and ever wish for his reign to continue.

2 Whenever – Allah be our refuge! – there occurs any disobedience or disregard of divine laws on the part of His servants, or any failure in devotion and attention to the commands of The Truth (be He exalted), and He wishes to chasten them and make them taste the retribution for their deeds – may God not deal us such a fate, and keep us far from such a calamity! – verily the wrath of The Truth overtakes those people and He forsakes them for the vileness of their disobedience; kingship disappears altogether, opposing swords are drawn, blood is shed, and whoever has the stronger hand does whatever he wishes, until those sinners are all destroyed in tumults and bloodshed, and the world becomes free and clear of them; and through the wickedness of such sinners many innocent persons too perish in the tumults; just as, by analogy, when a reed-bed catches fire every dry particle is consumed and much wet stuff is burnt also, because it is near to that which is dry.

3 Then by divine decree one human being acquires some prosperity and power, and according to his deserts The Truth bestows good fortune upon him and gives him wit and wisdom, wherewith he may employ his subordinates every one according to his merits and confer upon each a dignity and a station proportionate to his powers. He selects ministers and their functionaries from among the people, and giving a rank and post to each, he relies upon them for the efficient conduct of affairs spiritual and temporal. If his subjects tread the path of obedience and busy them-

selves with their tasks he will keep them untroubled by hardships, so that they may duly pass their time in the shadow of his justice. If one of his officers or ministers commits any impropriety or oppression, he will only keep him at his post provided that he responds to correction, advice or punishment, and wakes up from the sleep of negligence; if he fails to mend his ways, he will retain him no longer, but change him for someone who is deserving; and when his subjects are ungrateful for benefits and do not appreciate security and ease, but ponder treachery in their hearts, shewing unruliness and overstepping their bounds, he will admonish them for their misdeeds, and punish them in proportion to their crimes. Having done that he will cover their sins with the skirt of pardon and oblivion. Further, he will bring to pass that which concerns the advance of civilization, such as constructing underground channels, digging main canals, building bridges across great waters, rehabilitating villages and farms, raising fortifications, building new towns, and erecting lofty buildings and magnificent dwellings; he will have inns built on the highways and schools for those who seek knowledge; for which things he will be renowned for ever; he will gather the fruit of his good works in the next world and blessings will be showered upon him.

4 Since the decree of God was such that this should be the era by which bygone ages are dated and the standard by which the deeds of former kings are judged, whereby He might bestow on His creatures a felicity granted to none before them, He caused The Master of the World, the mightiest king of kings, to come forth from two noble lines whose houses were cradles of royalty and nobility, and had been so from generation to generation as far back as the great Afrasiyab;[1] He furnished him with powers and merits such as had been lacking in the princes of the world before him, and endowed him with all that is needful for a king – such as a comely appearance, a kindly disposition, integrity, manliness, bravery, horsemanship, knowledge, [skill in] the use of various kinds of arms and accomplishment in several arts, pity and mercy upon the creatures of God, [strictness in] the performance of vows and promises, sound faith and true belief, devotion to the worship of God and the practice of such virtuous deeds as praying in the night,[2] supererogatory fasting, respect for religious authorities, honouring devout and pious men, patronizing men of learning

and wisdom, giving regular alms, doing good to the poor, being kind to subordinates and servants, and relieving the people of oppressors. Following all this God gave him power and dominion as befitted his worthiness and good faith, and made all the world subject to him, causing his dignity and authority to reach all climes; all the dwellers on earth are his tributaries, and as long as they seek his favour they are safe from his sword.

5 Now in the days of some of the caliphs, if ever their empire became extended it was never free from unrest and the insurrections of rebels; but in this blessed age (praise and thanks be to Allah) there is nobody in all the world who in his heart meditates opposition to our lord and master, or ventures his head outside the collar of obedience to him – may God perpetuate this empire until the resurrection and keep the evil eye far from the perfectness of this kingdom, so that His creatures may pass their days under the equity and authority of The Master of the World and be ever intent on blessing him.

6 Such is the happy state of this great empire; and in proportion to its greatness it is blessed with an abundance of wise and good institutions. The wisdom of The Master of the World is like a taper from which many lamps have been lighted; by its light men find their way and emerge from the darkness. He has no need of any counsellor or guide; nevertheless he is not without cares, and perhaps he wishes to test his servants, and assess their intelligence and wisdom. So when he commanded his humble servant to write down some of those good qualities that are indispensable to a king, and make note of every principle which kings have followed in the past but now do not observe, indicating what is good and what is bad, whatever came to the mind of his humble servant that he had seen, learnt, read or heard, was written down, and The Sublime Command was fulfilled; these few chapters were composed in the manner of an epitome, and what was proper to each chapter was mentioned in that chapter in a clear style.

Chapter II

On recognizing the extent of God's grace towards kings

1 It is for kings to observe His pleasure (His name be glorified) and the pleasure of The Truth is in the charity which is done to His creatures and in the justice which is spread among them. A kingdom which is blessed by its people will endure and increase from day to day, while its king will enjoy power and prosperity; in this world he will acquire good fame, in the next world salvation, and his reckoning will be the easier. Great men have said [in Arabic], 'A kingdom may last while there is irreligion, but it will not endure when there is oppression.' (The meaning is . . .[1])

2 Tradition tells that when Joseph the prophet (the prayers of Allah and His peace be upon him) went out from this world, they were carrying him to Abraham's tomb (upon him be peace) to bury him near his forefathers, when Gabriel (upon him be peace) came and said, 'Stop where you are; this is not his place; for at the resurrection he will have to answer for the sovereignty which he has exercised.' Now if the case of Joseph the prophet was such, consider what the position of others will be.

3 It has come down in a tradition from The Prophet (may Allah bless him and save him) that on the day of the resurrection, when anyone is brought forward who [in his life] wielded power and command over God's creatures, his hands will be bound; if he has been just, his justice will loose his hands and send him to paradise; but if he has been unjust, his injustice will cast him into hell as he is, with his hands bound in chains.

4 There is also a tradition that on resurrection day whoever had any command in this world over God's creatures, even[2] over the inhabitants of his own house or over his own underlings, will be questioned about it; likewise the shepherd who tended his sheep will be required to answer for that too.

5 They say that at the time of his father's leaving this world 'Abd-Allah ibn 'Umar ibn al-Khattab (may Allah be pleased with them both) asked, 'O father, where and when shall I see you again?' 'Umar said, 'In the next world.' 'Abd-Allah said, 'I would

it were sooner.' He said, 'You will see me in a dream tonight, tomorrow night, or the next night.' Twelve years passed by without his appearing in a dream. Then one night he saw him in a dream and said, 'O father, did you not say that within three nights I should see you?' He said, 'O son, I was occupied, because in the country around Baghdad[3] a bridge had become dilapidated and officials had not attended to repairing it. One day a sheep's forefoot fell into a hole on that bridge and was broken. Till now I have been answering for that.'

6 Of a certainty The Master of the World (may Allah perpetuate his reign) should know that on that great day he will be asked to answer for all those of God's creatures who are under his command, and if he tries to transfer [his responsibility] to someone else he will not be listened to. Since this is so it behoves the king not to leave this important matter to anyone else, and not to disregard the state of God's creatures. To the best of his ability let him ever acquaint himself, secretly and openly, with their conditions; let him protect them from extortionate hands, and preserve them from cruel tyrants, so that the blessings resulting from those actions may come about in the time of his rule and benedictions will be pronounced upon his age until the resurrection.

Chapter III

On holding court for the redress of wrongs and practising justice and virtue

1 It is absolutely necessary that on two days in the week the king should sit for the redress of wrongs, to extract recompense from the oppressor, to give justice and to listen to the words of his subjects with his own ears, without any intermediary. It is fitting that some written petitions should also be submitted if they are comparatively important, and he should give a ruling on each one. For when the report spreads throughout the kingdom that

on two days in the week The Master of the World summons complainants and petitioners before him and listens to their words, all oppressors will be afraid and curb their activities, and no one will dare to practise injustice or extortion for fear of punishment.

2 I have read in the books of the ancients that most of the Persian [Sasanian] kings used to put up a high platform and sit up there on horseback so that they could see all the complainants gathered round about, and they would redress the grievances of every one. The reason for this was that when the king sits in a place protected by doors, gates, locks, vestibules, screens and chamberlains, self-interested and oppressive persons can keep people back and not let them go before the king.

3 I have heard that a certain king was rather hard of hearing. He was anxious lest the chamberlains and persons who acted as interpreters might not report the words of the complainants correctly, and that he, not knowing the true facts, might give an order quite unsuitable to the case. So he commanded that all complainants were to wear red clothes, so that he could recognize them; no one else at all was to wear red. This king used to appear on the plain seated upon an elephant, and wherever he saw people in red clothes, he ordered them to be collected in a group. Then he would sit in a place apart and they were brought before him; they stated their cases in a loud voice and he gave them justice.

Men have taken all this care so that they may not be found ignorant when they have to give their answer in the next world.

The story of The Just Amir and the Saffarids

4 One of the kings of the Samanid line was called Isma'il ibn Ahmad. He was extremely just, and his good qualities were many. He had a pure faith in God (to Him be power and glory) and he was generous to the poor – to name only one of his notable virtues. His seat was at Bukhara. Khurasan, 'Iraq[1] and Transoxiana all belonged to his ancestors.

5 Ya'qub ibn Laith emerged in revolt from the City of Sistan [Zaranj] and took the whole of Sistan; then he went to Khurasan, and captured that province; from Khurasan he went to 'Iraq, and seized the whole of 'Iraq. Propagandists deceived him and he secretly swore allegiance to the Isma'ilis; he hardened his heart

against the caliph of Baghdad. Then he mustered the armies of Khurasan and 'Iraq and prepared to march to Baghdad to kill the caliph and overthrow the house of the 'Abbasids.

6 The caliph received information that Ya'qub was marching upon Baghdad. He sent a messenger to say, 'You have no business at Baghdad; it were better that you should attend to Kuhistan of 'Iraq and Khurasan, and administer them so that no disorder or anxiety may arise. Turn back.' He did not obey the command, but said 'It is my desire that without fail I should come to the court, and carry out the rites of homage and renew my obligations; until I have done this, I will not turn back.' However many messengers the caliph sent, he gave this same answer. Then he moved his army towards Baghdad. The caliph became suspicious of him; he summoned the nobles of the state and said, 'I see that Ya'qub ibn Laith has withdrawn his head from the collar of obedience to us, and is coming here with treacherous intent, for we have not commanded him to come and yet he is coming; we command him to turn back; he turns not. At all events he has some evil design in his heart and I think he has sworn allegiance to the Batinis;[2] he will not reveal it until he arrives here. We must not neglect to take precautions against him; what is the best way to deal with this matter?'

They settled on the following plan: that the caliph would not stay in the city, but go into the open country and pitch camp, and the courtiers and nobles of Baghdad and all of his retinue would be with him; so that when Ya'qub arrived and saw the caliph encamped in the open country with his troops, his plan would misfire and his rebellion against The Commander of the Faithful would become manifest; thereupon men would go to and fro from one camp to the other; for if he were starting a rebellion, not all the nobles and chiefs of 'Iraq and Khurasan would agree with him and assent to his plans: if he openly shewed his rebelliousness they would contend with his troops as best they could, but if they failed and were unable to cope with him in battle, very well – the road would be open before them and they would not be caught like prisoners within four walls; they would betake themselves wherever they could. This plan was acceptable to The Commander of the Faithful. Thus they did. And this caliph was al-Mu'tamid 'ala 'llah Ahmad.

7 When Ya'qub arrived he dismounted opposite the caliph's

camp and pitched his tents; and the men of the two armies mingled together. On that very day he bid defiance to the caliph and sent a messenger to him to say, 'Give up Baghdad and go where you like.' The caliph asked for two months' grace; Ya'qub refused him. When night came on, the caliph secretly sent someone to the officers of Ya'qub's army to say, 'He has openly revolted, and made common cause with the Seveners³; he has come on purpose to overthrow our house, and set our adversary in our place. Are you too in sympathy with him in this, or not?' One party said, 'From him we have received our subsistence and by virtue of service to him we enjoy the position and prosperity which we have. Whatever he has done we have done.' The majority said, 'We are not aware of these circumstances of which The Commander of the Faithful speaks; we do not think that he will oppose The Commander of the Faithful; hereafter if he openly rebels, we shall entirely disapprove; on the day of confrontation we shall be with you, not with him, and in the hour of battle we shall come to your aid.' This party consisted of the army-commanders of Khurasan.

8 When the caliph heard the words of the chiefs of Ya'qub's army on this wise, he was glad. The next day in a bold spirit he sent a message to Ya'qub, saying, 'Now that you have openly displayed your ingratitude and have made an agreement with my adversary, the sword is betwixt me and you; I am not afraid because my forces are few and yours are many. God (to Him be power and glory) is the helper of the right, and He is on my side. Those troops which you have really belong to me.' He gave the command, and his troops armed themselves, beat the drums of war and blew the trumpets; they went forth from the camp and drew ranks upon the plain.

9 When Ya'qub heard the caliph's message in those terms, he said, 'I am now attaining my desire.' And he too gave orders for the drums to be beaten; all his troops mounted and went in formation on to the plain and drew ranks opposite the caliph's forces. On the one side the caliph came and took up his position in the centre, and on the other side Ya'qub ibn Laith. Then the caliph ordered a certain man who had a powerful voice to go between the two arrays, and proclaim aloud, 'O assembly of Muslims, know that Ya'qub is a rebel and has come on purpose to overthrow the house of 'Abbas, and to bring the caliph's adversary to replace him; he wishes to remove the *sunna* [orthodox tradition] and make

heresy rife. Whoever opposes the caliph [successor] of The Prophet of God, has opposed The Prophet himself; and if any man plucks his head out of the collar of obedience to The Prophet (upon him be peace), it is as if he has renounced obedience to God and quitted the circle of Islam; as God (be He exalted) says in His incontrovertible book [Qur'an 4. 62], "Obey Allah, and obey The Messenger and those of you who are in authority." Who is there now amongst you who will choose heaven instead of hell, and will assist the truth and turn his face from vanity? Then let him be with me, not with my enemy.'

10 When the army of Ya'qub ibn Laith heard these words the commanders of Khurasan turned with one accord and approached the caliph and said, 'We thought that he was coming to your presence in obedience to your command; now that he has declared his opposition and rebellion, we are with you, and as long as we have life, we shall wield the sword on your behalf.'

11 When the caliph had thus acquired strength he ordered his total forces to make an assault. Ya'qub ibn Laith was defeated in the first charge, and took to flight in the direction of Khuzistan. His treasury, stores and camp were all plundered, and the caliph's troops became rich with the spoil. When he reached Khuzistan he sent persons in all directions to call up troops; he began to summon his officers and gave orders that they should bring stores and money from the treasuries of 'Iraq and Khurasan.

12 When the caliph received news that Ya'qub had settled in Khuzistan, he immediately sent a messenger with a letter to him saying, 'It is known to us that you are a simple-hearted fellow; you succumbed to the deceits of our adversaries, and you had no regard for the outcome of your venture. You saw how God (be He exalted) displayed His working to you; He caused you to be defeated even by your own troops, and He preserved our family. It was merely a misunderstanding on your part. I know that now you have woken up and are sorry for your deeds. Nobody is more suitable than you to be amir of 'Iraq and Khurasan; we shall not impose a higher authority over you, for by your services you are entitled to many rewards from us. We regard those admirable services as outweighing this your single error.' [The caliph considered that] since he was prepared to forgive his unruliness and regard his action as undone, Ya'qub ought to forget the affair and go with all speed to 'Iraq and Khurasan, and devote himself to

administering those provinces: for in the track of that letter he was sending a standard and a robe of honour as authority, so that no disorder might arise.

13 When Ya'qub read the caliph's letter his heart was in no way softened, nor did he repent of his actions. He ordered some leeks, onions and fish to be brought on a wooden tray and put before him. Then he ordered them to bring in the caliph's courier and make him sit; he turned towards him and said, 'Go and tell the caliph that I was born a coppersmith; I learnt that trade from my father, and my victual used to be barley-bread, fish, onions and leeks. The sovereignty, treasure and wealth which I enjoy, I have acquired by my own bold enterprise⁴ and daring; I neither have it as an inheritance from my father, nor did I get it from you. I shall not rest until I have sent your head to Mahdiyya⁵ and destroyed your family. Either I shall do as I say or I shall go back to eating barley-bread, fish and leeks. Behold I have opened the doors of my treasuries and summoned my troops; and I am coming in the tracks of the bearer of this message.' He despatched the courier. The caliph then sent many couriers and letters but Ya'qub refused to abandon his project. He collected his army and set out from Khuzistan towards Baghdad. When he had gone three stages the colic gripped him, and his condition reached the point where he knew that he would not be delivered from the pain. He nominated his brother 'Amr ibn Laith as his heir, gave him the treasure-books, and died.

14 'Amr ibn Laith returned to Kuhistan (of 'Iraq) and stayed there a while. Then he went to Khurasan and reigned as king, keeping allegiance to the caliph. The army and the people liked 'Amr better than Ya'qub, for 'Amr was magnanimous, generous, enlightened and statesmanlike to a degree. His humanity and magnanimity went so far, that four hundred camels were required to transport his kitchen; other things can be inferred by analogy.

15 However, the caliph continued to be apprehensive, lest 'Amr too should follow the ways of his brother, and later engage in the same activities. Although 'Amr had no such beliefs, still the caliph was anxious on this score. Frequently and secretly he sent messengers to Bukhara to Isma'il ibn Ahmad to say, 'Go out against 'Amr ibn Laith; lead your army and wrest the kingdom from his grasp, for you have more right to govern Khurasan and 'Iraq, seeing that for many years this was the kingdom of your fathers,

and they [the Saffarids] have usurped it. Firstly you have the right, secondly your conduct is more acceptable, and thirdly my prayers are behind you. Considering these three points I have no doubt but that God will assist you against him. Regard not the fact that your supplies and troops are few; look at what God says [in the Qur'an 2. 250]: How many a little company has overcome a great company by Allah's leave! Allah is with the steadfast.'

16 The caliph's words had their effect on Isma'il. He firmly resolved to oppose 'Amr ibn Laith. He gathered all the forces he had, and having crossed to this [south] side of the Oxus, he counted them with the tip of his whip. They amounted to 10,000 horsemen, most of whom had only wooden stirrups; one in ten had no shield, one in twenty had no coat of mail, and one in fifty had no lance; and there were men who, for lack of a mount, were carrying their coats of mail themselves, tied on to saddle-straps. Then he moved off from Amuy [Amul] and came to the city of Balkh.

17 'Amr ibn Laith was informed that Isma'il ibn Ahmad had crossed the Oxus and come to Balkh, and the city prefects of Marv and Sarakhs had fled; Isma'il was aiming at capturing the province. 'Amir ibn Laith was at Nishapur; he paraded 70,000 cavalry, all clad in horse-armour with weapons and full equipment. He set out for Balkh. When the two armies met they joined battle. It so happened that 'Amr ibn Laith was defeated at the gates of Balkh and his 70,000 horsemen fled without one man being wounded or taken prisoner; of them all 'Amr alone was captured. When they brought him in front of Isma'il, he ordered them to hand him over to his guards. And this victory is one of the wonders of the world.

18 At the time of afternoon prayers a certain groom belonging to 'Amr ibn Laith was wandering in the camp. He happened to see 'Amr; he was sorry for him and he went up to him. 'Amr said, 'Stay with me tonight for I am left all alone': then he said, 'As long as a man is alive, there is no escaping the need for food; contrive to find something to eat, for I am hungry.' The groom procured one maund of meat and borrowed an iron frying-pan from the soldiers. Then he ran around and collected a little dry dung, and he put together two or three clods of earth, intending to make a dry fry. When he had put the meat in the frying-pan, he just went to look for some salt. The day had then come to its

close. A dog came and put its head into the frying-pan to take out a bone, so burning its mouth; it raised its head and the ring of the frying-pan fell round its neck. On feeling the heat of the fire it leapt up and carried off the frying-pan. When 'Amr ibn Laith saw that, he turned towards the soldiers and guards and said, 'Take warning: I am that man whose kitchen in the morning was transported by four hundred camels; at evening a dog has picked it up and taken it away.' Then he said [in Arabic], 'I was an *amir* in the morning: I became an *asir* [prisoner] in the evening.' (That means: In the morning I was an amir: at evening I am a prisoner.) And this event too is one of the wonders of the world.

19 In connection with the amir Isma'il and 'Amr ibn Laith, even more remarkable than these two events is the fact that when 'Amr was captured, the amir Isma'il turned to the nobles and chiefs of his army and said, 'God granted me this success, and to no one am I indebted for this favour except to God (His name be magnified).' Then he said, 'Know that this 'Amr ibn Laith was a man of lofty purposes and great generosity; he was well provided with equipment and supplies, and possessed wisdom and prudence besides. In the conduct of affairs he was vigilant, and he was abundantly hospitable and liberal in his expression of gratitude. It is my idea to see to it that he suffers no harm and is freed from his bonds.' The nobles said, 'The amir's opinion is best; let him command whatever is advisable.' He then sent someone to 'Amr ibn Laith to say, 'Do not fear, because I am planning to ask the caliph for your life to be spared. Even if it costs the whole of my treasury. I shall not mind so long as you suffer no mortal harm and can pass the rest of your life in safety.'

20 When 'Amr ibn Laith heard this, he said, 'I know that there will never be any escape for me from these bonds; I have not long to live; the caliph will not be satisfied but with my death; nevertheless, thou who art Isma'il, send me a confidant, for I have some words to say; let him report them to you just as he hears them from me.' The man came and told Isma'il what 'Amr had said. Isma'il at once sent him a confidant, and 'Amr said to him, 'Tell Isma'il: it was not you that defeated me, but it was your piety, faith and character, together with the displeasure of The Commander of the Faithful. God (to Him be power and glory) has recently taken away this realm from me and given it to you, and you are more worthy and deserving of this favour. I have surrendered

to God (to Him be power and glory), and I do not wish you anything but good. Meanwhile you have acquired a new kingdom, but you have no wealth or backing. Now I and my brother have many treasures and buried hoards, and the list of them is in my possession; I offer them all to you, so that you may gain backing and power; you should procure supplies and stores, and replenish your treasury.' Thereupon he produced the treasure list from his sleeve and sent it to Isma'il by the hand of that confidant.

21 When the confidant came and repeated what he had heard and placed the treasure-list in front of Isma'il, he turned towards the nobles and said, 'This 'Amr ibn Laith is so cunning that he thinks he can escape from our cunning hands and catch us in the traps and snares of eternal ruin.' He picked up the treasure-list and threw it in front of the confidant, saying, 'Take this treasure-list back to him and say: You with your wiles think you can escape from everything. Whence fell treasure to you and your brother, for your father was a coppersmith and taught you that trade? Through some celestial chance you seized dominion, and by reckless ventures your affairs prospered. This treasure with its dirams and dinars is all that which you have taken from the people by extortion; it comes from the price of thread spun by decrepit old women and widows, from the provisions of strangers and travellers, and from the property of weaklings and orphans. Tomorrow you will have to answer for every grain before God (to Him be power and glory) and taste divine retribution; so now you promptly want to cast these wrongs about our neck, so that on the morrow at the resurrection when creditors seize you and ask you to give back all the property which you wrongfully took, you will say, "All that we took from you, we gave to Isma'il; seek it from him." You will transfer it all to me and I shall be powerless to answer the creditors and to withstand the wrath and interrogation of God.' Such was his piety and fear of God that he did not accept the treasure-list but sent it back to 'Amr. So he was not deluded by worldly goods.

22 Is that like the amirs of these times who think nothing of making ten forbidden things lawful or nullifying ten just claims for the sake of one ill-gotten dinar? They have no regard for the consequences.

23 Now it was the custom of this Isma'il ibn Ahmad that on days when the cold was severe and snow was falling heavily, he

would mount his horse and go alone to the square [of Bukhara], remaining there on horseback until the midday prayers. He used to say, 'It may be that a complainant will come to the court with a petition, and he may not have any money for expenses or anywhere to stay. If we excused ourselves from appearing because of the snow and cold, it would be difficult for such a person to stay and gain access to us. If he knows that we are standing here, he will come and discharge his business and go away in peace.'

24 There are many stories of this kind; only a few have been repeated here. And all this care has been taken for the sake of the answer in the next world.

Chapter IV

Concerning tax-collectors and constant enquiry into the affairs of Vazirs

1 Tax-collectors,[1] when they are given a fiscal district, must be instructed to deal honourably with their fellow creatures, and to take only the due amount of revenue, and to claim that too with civility and courtesy, and not to demand any taxes from them until the time comes for them to pay; because when they demand payment before the time, trouble comes upon the peasants, and to pay the tax they are obliged to sell their crops for half [of what they would be worth when they ripen], whereby they are driven to extremities and have to emigrate. If any peasant is in distress and in need of oxen or seed, let him be given a loan to ease his burden and keep him viable, lest he be cast out from his home into exile.

2 I heard that in the time of King Qubad there was famine in the world for seven years, and blessings [rain] ceased to come down from heaven. He ordered the tax-collectors to sell all the grain which they had, and even to give some of it away as charity. All over the kingdom the poor were assisted by gifts from the central treasury and [local] treasuries, with the result that not one

person died of hunger in those seven years – all because the king chid his officers.

3 One must enquire constantly into the affairs of the tax-collector. If he comports himself in the manner just described, the fiscal district can be kept in his hands, but if not, he must be changed for someone suitable. If he has taken more than is due from the peasants, it must be recovered from him and given back to them; after that if he has any property left, it must be seized and brought into the treasury. The officer should be dismissed, and never employed again. Others will then take warning and give up practising extortion.

4 It is also necessary to enquire secretly into the affairs of vazirs and confidants, to see if they are fulfilling their function properly or not. The good or ill of king and kingdom depends on the vazir. When the vazir is of good character and sound judgment, the kingdom is prosperous, the army and peasantry are contented, peaceful and well supplied, and the king is free from anxiety. But when the vazir is bad, irreparable harm is done to the kingdom; the king is constantly perplexed and distressed and the provinces are in a state of disorder.

The story of Bahram Gur and Rast-ravishn

5 They say that Bahram Gur had a vazir whom they called Rast-ravishn [Right-Conduct]. Bahram Gur had put the whole country in his hands, and placed reliance upon him; he would not hear any word against him. He himself was occupied day and night with entertainments, hunting and drinking. This Rast-ravishn said to a certain person who was the [so-called] 'deputy' of Bahram Gur, 'The peasantry have become unruly and refractory because of our abundant justice; unless they are chastised I am afraid a catastrophe will occur. The king is busy drinking and hunting, and is heedless of the condition of his subjects. Chastise them, before a catastrophe occurs; and know at once that chastisement has two aspects – getting rid of the bad, and fleecing the good. Whomsoever I tell you to seize, seize him.' From everyone that the 'deputy' caught and held in custody Rast-ravishn extracted a bribe for himself and then ordered the 'deputy' to let him go; until eventually all the property in the country, whether houses, or pages, or beautiful girls, or estates, or farms, was seized by him.

The peasantry were impoverished, the nobility all emigrated, and nothing came into the treasury.

6 When some time had passed after these events, an enemy rose against Bahram Gur. He wanted to provide his troops with money and supplies, and send them against the enemy. He went into the treasury. Not a thing did he see. He enquired after the notables and mayors of city and village. People said, 'It is several years since so-and-so and so-and-so emigrated, and went to such-and-such a country.' He said, 'Why?' They said, 'We do not know.' Nobody dared to say anything for fear of the vazir. All day and all night Bahram Gur was in meditation; he could not think what was the cause of the trouble. The next day, worried and alone, he mounted his horse and set out into the desert. Deep in thought he went along until the day was high. He travelled a distance of six or seven farsangs without being aware of it. The sun was very hot; thirst prevailed over him, and he needed a drink of water. He surveyed the open country; he saw some smoke going up, and said, 'At all events there will be people there.' He made for the smoke. When he got near he saw a flock of sheep sleeping, a tent pitched, and a dog hanging on a gibbet. He was astonished, and went close up to the tent. A man came out and greeted him; he helped him to dismount and brought him something to eat, not knowing that he was Bahram. Bahram said, 'First of all before we eat bread, tell me about this dog; I would like to know what happened to it.'

7 The young man said, 'This dog was my custodian in charge of these sheep; I knew his virtues were such that he could contend with ten men, and no wolf would dare to roam near the sheep for fear of him. Many a time I used to go to the city for some business and come back the next day. He would take the sheep to graze and bring them back safely. One day, after some time had passed, I counted the sheep; several were missing; and every few days when I looked at them some more had disappeared; and nobody ever remembers a thief coming here. I could not understand at all why the sheep were getting fewer every day. The state of my flock reached such a point of diminution that when the collector of [compulsory] alms came and demanded from me the usual amount [assessed] upon the whole flock, [yet to be paid] out of what was left of my flock, that remnant too went to pay the alms. So now I perform the pastoral office for that collector.

8 'Now this dog had made friends with a she-wolf and they had mated; and I was ignorant and unaware of what was going on. It so happened that one day I had gone into the fields in search of fire-wood. When I returned, I came up from behind a hill, and saw the flock of sheep grazing and a wolf running around looking at them. I sat down behind some thorn bushes and secretly watched. When the dog saw the wolf he went to meet her and wagged his tail. The wolf quietly stood still. The dog mounted and covered her; then he went into a corner and slept. The wolf ran into the midst of the flock. She seized one sheep, tore it to pieces and ate it; and the dog never made a sound. When I saw this commerce of wolf and dog, I realized and knew that the ruin of my affairs was due to the waywardness of the dog. So I caught him and hanged him on the gibbet because of his treachery.'

9 Bahram Gur was astonished at this story. As he returned, all the way he pondered over this thing, until it crossed his thoughts that, 'Our subjects are our flock, and our vazir is our custodian. I see that the country and the people are in a very distracted and disturbed state, and when I question people, they do not tell the truth but keep it hidden. What I must do is to enquire into the relations between the people and Rast-ravishn.'

10 When he came back to his abode, firstly he called for the daily lists of prisoners. From beginning to end he saw the evil hand of Rast-ravishn, and recognized that he had maltreated and oppressed the people. He said, 'This is not *rāst ravishn* [right conduct] but dark falsehood.'[2] Then he repeated the proverb which wise men have spoken truly, that, 'He who is deceived by a name forfeits his bread; he who cheats for bread forfeits his life.'[3] 'I have strengthened the hand of this vazir; as long as people see him so dignified and august, they will not dare to speak the truth for fear of him. My plan is that tomorrow when he comes to the court I will disgrace him in front of the nobles; I will detain him and order heavy fetters to be put on his feet; then I will call the prisoners before me and ask about their cases; I will command a proclamation to be read in these terms, "We have removed Rast-ravishn from the office of vazir and ordered his imprisonment; we shall not employ him any more; if any man has suffered injury from him and has a claim, let him come and make his case known to us, so that we may give him justice." When people hear this they will let us know how things really are. If he has treated

people well and practised no unjust extortion, and if they speak well of him, we will bestow favours on him and reinstate him in his post; but if his behaviour has been otherwise, we will punish him.'

11 The next day when King Bahram Gur held his court with the nobles in attendance and the vazir sitting in his usual place, Bahram Gur turned towards him and said, 'What is this confusion which you have spread abroad in the kingdom? You have failed to keep the troops supplied and you have ruined the peasants. We commanded you to provide the people's subsistence in due time, continually to promote the prosperity of the country, and to take no more than what is due in taxes from the peasants; you were required to keep the treasury stocked with supplies; as it is I see the treasury is empty, the army lacks provisions, and the peasants are destitute. You may think that I have been occupied in drinking and hunting, and neglectful of the affairs of the kingdom and the condition of the people.' He ordered Rast-ravishn to be removed with ignominy from his place and to be taken into a certain house; heavy fetters were put on his feet, and it was proclaimed at the doors of the palace that 'The king has removed Rast-ravishn from the office of vazir and is angry with him and will not employ him any more. If any man has suffered injury from him and has a complaint, let him without any fear of danger come to the court and reveal his case, so that the king may give him justice.' Immediately he ordered them to open the doors of the prison and bring the prisoners before him; one by one he asked them, 'For what crime were you detained?'

12 One said: I had a rich brother and he owned much property and wealth. Rast-ravishn seized him, took all his property away from him and killed him under torture. People asked why he had killed this man. He said, 'He had correspondence with the king's enemies.' So he sent me to prison to prevent me from complaining before the king and to keep the case concealed.

13 Another said: I had a very flourishing and pleasant garden which was left to me as an inheritance from my father. Rast-ravishn had an estate next to it. One day he came into my garden; he was attracted by it and wanted to buy it; I would not sell it. He seized me and put me in prison, saying, 'You are in love with the daughter of such-and-such a person, and it is clear you have committed an offence. Give up possession of this garden and make out a deed certifying that you have relinquished it and have

no claim to it, and that it is the rightful property of Rast-ravishn.'
I refused to give such a certificate; and it is five years today that I
have been in prison.

14 Another said: I am a merchant, and it is my occupation to
travel on sea and land. I have only a small amount of capital, and
such choice things as I find in one city, I buy and take to the next
city to sell them; I am content with a minimum of profit. Perchance I had a pearl necklace; when I came to this city I put it up
for sale. Information reached the king's vazir; he sent someone
and summoned me; he purchased that string of pearls from me.
Without paying me for it he sent it to his treasury. For several days
I kept going to call on him. He shewed no inclination to pay the
price of the necklace, nor did he give it back to me. I could not
wait any longer; I was due to leave. One day I went to him and
said, 'If that necklace suits you, command that I be paid for it; if it
is not suitable, let it be given back, for I must leave.' He gave me
no answer. When I came back to my tent, I saw an officer with
four soldiers, who entered the tent and said, 'Come along, the
vazir is calling for you.' I rejoiced and said, 'He is going to pay
me for the pearls.' I got up and went with those guards; they took
me to the thieves' prison and said to the gaoler, 'The order is that
you keep this man in prison and put heavy fetters on his feet.' It is
now a year and a half that I have been suffering bondage and
imprisonment.

15 Another said: I am the mayor of such-and-such a district,
and my house always used to be open to guests, strangers and men
of learning; I used to give assistance to all kinds of destitute
people, and I was constantly dealing out alms and charities to the
deserving, a habit which I acquired from my forefathers. I used to
spend all the income from my inherited property and estates on
acts of charity, generosity and hospitality. The king's vazir seized
me on the pretext that I had discovered treasure; he detained me
in prison and subjected me to inquisition and torture. Every
property and farm which I owned I was obliged to sell at half
price and give to him. I have now endured imprisonment and
bondage for four years; and I have not a single diram to my name.

16 Another said: I am the son of such-and-such a chieftain.
The king's vazir mulcted my father and killed him under rod and
inquisition; he put me in prison, and for seven years I have been
undergoing the ordeal of incarceration.

17 Another said: I am a military man and for so many years I served the king's father and campaigned with him; and for so many years I have been serving Your Majesty. I have a small salary from the government; last year nothing was paid to me, and this year I applied to the vazir and said, 'I am a family man and last year my salary was not paid. Please pay it this year, so that I may use some of it for repaying creditors and spend the rest on my subsistence.' He said, 'The king has no war in view for which he will need troops, and it matters not whether you and the likes of you are in service or not; if you need bread, go and do labourer's work.' I said, 'I am entitled to so much for my services to this government; I ought not to have to do labourer's work. But you need to learn something about administration, for I am more skilled in swordsmanship than you are in penmanship; when it comes to fighting I sacrifice my life for the king and do not swerve from his command; but on pay-day you withhold my bread from me and fail to carry out the king's order. Do you not know this much, that to the king you are a servant as much as I am? He has engaged you in one capacity and me in another: the difference between me and you is that I am obedient and you are not. If the king doesn't need the likes of me, he doesn't need the likes of you any more either. If you have an order saying that the king has removed my name from the payroll, shew it to me; otherwise continue to pay what the king has ordained for me.' He said, 'Be off! It is I who look after both you and the king; if it were not for me the vultures would have eaten your brains out long ago.' Then two days passed. He sent me into confinement, and now it is four months that I have been in prison.

18 There were more than 700 prisoners. Less than twenty men turned out to be murderers, thieves and criminals. All the others were those whom the vazir had detained and imprisoned out of cupidity and cruelty. When the people of the city and the surrounding district heard about the royal proclamation, the next day so many complainants came to the court that they were beyond limit or measure.

19 When Bahram Gur heard these reports of the condition of the people and the illegal, unjust and tyrannous conduct of the vazir, he said to himself, 'The corruption which this man has wrought in the country seems to be beyond description; the defiance which he has displayed towards God and the creatures of

God (be He exalted) and against me is too great to be imagined. I must look deeper into this affair.' He ordered men to go to the house of Rast-ravishn and bring his files of papers and seal up all the doors of the house. Trusted men went and did this. They brought the files and began to look at them. Among them they found one file full of overtures sent to Rast-ravishn by a certain king who had revolted and attempted to usurp Bahram Gur's kingdom; and in Rast-ravishn's writing they found a letter which he had written to this king saying, 'Why are you so slow? The wise have said that negligence is the thief of empire. I have used every possible means to espouse and serve your cause; I have won over several officers of the army and brought them into your allegiance; I have left most of the troops without provisions or equipment, but I have sent a number to a certain station and appointed them to a certain task. I have rendered the people hungry, destitute and homeless; with all that I have acquired in the course of time I have prepared a treasury for you such as no other king today possesses; and I have made ready crown and girdle, together with a golden and jewelled tray[4] the like of which no one has ever seen before. My life is in danger from this man; the field is empty and the enemy unaware; hasten as fast as you can before he wakes up from the sleep of negligence.'

20 When Bahram Gur saw these documents, he said, 'Indeed! So it is he who has incited and inveigled the enemy who is at this moment advancing against me; now there remains no doubt about the wickedness and treachery of this man.' He commanded that all his possessions should be brought into the treasury; they took his slaves and animals, and gave back to the owners everything that he had received in bribes or seized by force; his estates and lands were sold or given back to claimants, and his house and home was razed to the ground. Then he ordered a gallows to be erected at the gate of the palace, and in front of that thirty other gibbets. First they hanged Rast-ravishn, just as that Kurd had hanged his dog; then they hanged his associates and persons who were in league with him. The king commanded a proclamation to be read for seven days, saying, 'This is the punishment for a man who plots against the king, associates with his enemies, prefers treachery to loyalty, oppresses the people, and defies his God and his sovereign.'

21 On the infliction of this punishment all malefactors became

afraid of King Bahram. He removed from office all whom Rast-ravishn had employed, and never engaged them again; he gave employment to those who Rast-ravishn had dismissed and he transferred all the secretaries and officials. When news of this reached the king who was attacking Bahram Gur's kingdom, he turned straight back from where he was and regretted his action; he sent much money and many choice gifts in homage to Bahram, making excuses and obeisances, and saying, 'I would never have thought of rebelling against Your Highness; however Your Highness's vazir persuaded me to this course through the many letters and messengers which he sent me; the suspicions of your servant were all the time testifying that he was a criminal who was seeking a refuge.' King Bahram accepted his excuse and pardoned him. He gave the vazirship to a God-fearing man of sound faith and good character. The affairs of the army and the people were all restored to order, and work proceeded again; the world set its face towards prosperity and the population were delivered from tyranny and injustice.

[To return to] the man who had hanged his dog on a gibbet – one day he was outside his tent and was about to go in again, when King Bahram Gur drew an arrow out of his quiver, shot it in front of him and said, 'I ate your bread and salt, and came to know of the troubles and losses you have suffered; so I am indebted to you. Know that I am one of the chamberlains of King Bahram, and all the nobles and chamberlains of his court are my friends and know me well. You must arise and come with this arrow to King Bahram's court; whoever sees you with this arrow will bring you to me, and I will discharge my debt to you in a way that will recompense you for some of your losses.' And Bahram departed.

22 After several days that man's wife said to him, 'Arise and go to the city, and take that arrow with you, for that rider with all his finery was undoubtedly a rich and respected man. Even if he does you but little good, that amount will be much for us in these days. Do not lose time, for such a person's word will not be false.' The man arose and came to the city. He slept that night and next day went to the court of King Bahram. Now Bahram Gur had told the chamberlains and courtiers, 'When such-and-such a man comes to the court, and you see my arrow in his hand, bring him to me.'

23 When the chamberlains saw him with that arrow, they called

him and said, 'O noble sir, where have you been? We have been expecting you for several days. Sit here and we will take you to the owner of the arrow.' A time passed. Bahram Gur came out and sat on the throne and gave audience. The chamberlains took the man's hand and led him to the audience-hall; the man's eye fell upon King Bahram and as he recognized him, he said, 'Woe! I am ruined! that rider was King Bahram, and I did not pay him homage as I ought, but I spoke to him rather rudely. May it not be that he has taken a dislike to me!'

24 When the chamberlains led him before the throne he did obeisance to the king. Bahram Gur turned towards the nobles and said, 'This man was the cause of my becoming aware of the state of the country'; – and he related the story of the dog to the nobles; – 'and I regard him as an omen.' He gave the command and they invested him with a robe of honour, and presented him with seven hundred sheep – as many ewes or rams as he desired; and he ordered that as long as he (Bahram Gur) was alive, they should demand no compulsory alms from him.

25 It is well known how Alexander killed Darius. The reason for this was that Darius's vazir had secret dealings with Alexander. When Darius was slain, Alexander said, 'The negligence of the amir and the treachery of the vazir have taken away his kingship.'

26 At no time must the king be ill-informed about his officers. He must constantly enquire about their conduct and character, and should any impropriety or treachery be found in any one of them he must not be retained; let him be removed from office and chastised according to his crime, so that others will take warning, and no one will dare to plot any mischief for fear of the king's punishment. Whenever anyone is appointed to a big post, the king must secretly (so that he does not know) put someone to supervise him and report on his actions and affairs.

27 Aristotle thus said to King Alexander, 'If you ever offend one of those who ply their pens in the public service, do not employ that person again because he will combine with your enemies and strive for your destruction.'

28 Parviz the king thus said, 'There are four groups of men whose sins a king should not overlook – firstly those who aim at his kingdom, secondly those who have designs on his harem, thirdly those who do not keep his secrets, and fourthly those who

with their tongues support the king, but in their hearts espouse the cause of his enemies and secretly follow their policies.'

29 A man's secrets may be deduced from his actions. If the king is awake to all affairs, nothing will remain concealed from him.

Chapter V

Concerning assignees of land and enquiry into their treatment of the peasantry

1 Officers who hold assignments[1] must know that they have no authority over the peasants except to take from them – and that with courtesy – the due amount of revenue which has been assigned to them to collect; and when they have taken that, the peasants are to have security for their persons, property, wives and children, and their goods and farms are to be inviolable; the assignees are to have no further claim upon them. If peasants want to come to the court to state their cases, they are not to be prevented from doing so; any assignee who does otherwise must be checked; his assignment will be taken away and he will be reprimanded as a warning to others. They must know that the country and the peasants belong to the ruling power; assignees and governors are like prefects over the peasants [on their lands], in the same relation to them as the king is to other peasants [not on assigned lands]; then everything will be correct and they will be secure from the king's punishment and from torment in the world to come.

The story of The Just King

2 They say that when Qubad the king died Nushirvan (The Just), who was his son, succeeded to the throne; he was only eighteen years old, yet he reigned as king. He was a youth whose

nature had been infused with justice right from infancy; he recognized evil things as evil and he knew what was good. He always used to say, 'My father is weak in judgment and simple hearted; he is quickly deceived. He has left the country to the hands of officials and they are doing whatever they please; so the country is being ruined and the treasury emptied; they are embezzling the revenue,[2] and the shame and guilt will be for ever upon his neck.' Qubad completely succumbed to the wiles of the wicked Mazdak; similarly he was deceived by two men – a governor and a tax-collector – who together had ruined their province and impoverished the peasantry by illegal extortions; such was his love of money that when they proffered him a purse of dinars he was seduced and satisfied; he had not sufficient discernment to question them and to say [to the one], 'You are the governor and the commander of this province. I assigned you such proportion of the provincial revenue as would suffice for the pay, rations and clothing of you and your retinue; I am sure that you will have extracted the full amount from the people. Then where did you get this surplus which you have brought to me and all the luxuries which you have recently acquired and never had before? I know that you did not inherit it from my father; it is all what you have illegally extorted from the people.' Nor did he speak likewise to the tax-collector, saying, 'The revenue of the province is so much; some of it you have used for [encashing] drafts and some you have sent to the treasury. This surplus which I see you have – where did you obtain that? Is it not part of your illegal extortions?' He never investigated such matters nor took suitable measures against the offenders so that others might have made a practice of honesty.

3 When three or four years of his reign has passed, the assignees and officials were still practising their wonted oppression, and complainants were clamouring at the king's threshold. Nushirvan The Just held court for the redress of wrongs and summoned all the nobles; he sat upon the throne and first gave thanks to God, then he said, 'You know that God (to Him be power and glory) has granted me this kingdom; furthermore I inherited it from my father; and thirdly my uncle rebelled against me and I did battle with him and regained the throne by the sword. As God has bestowed the world upon me, so have I assigned it to you, and to each one have I given authority; I did not leave without a portion

anyone who had deserved well of this dynasty; the nobles who had received high rank and command from my father were maintained in their rank and station, and I did not in any way reduce their degree or subsistence. I have constantly exhorted you to treat the people well and to gather only the due amount of taxes; I respect you but you neither respect me nor listen to my words; you have neither fear of God nor sense of shame. Wherefore I fear retribution; I do not wish that your iniquity and injustice should redound upon the days of my reign. The world is free of enemies; you have prosperity and ease; if you concentrated on thanskgiving to God for the benefits which He has bestowed upon you and upon us, it would be better than practising injustice and ingratitude, for injustice brings about the decline of empires and ingratitude causes the stoppage of benefits. Henceforth there must be no ill-treatment of God's creatures; you must keep the peasants light-burdened and never oppress the weak; respect learned men, consort with the good, avoid the bad, and do no harm to those who mind their own business. I call upon God and the angels to be my witnesses that if any man follows a path contrary to this, I will not suffer him further.' All said, 'We will do as you say and obey your command.'

4 A few days later thay all returned to their posts. They engaged in the same injustice and oppression; they looked upon Nushirvan as a mere boy and each one in his arrogance imagined that it was he who had set Nushirvan upon the throne, and that he could at his own will regard him or not regard him as king. Nushirvan held his peace and continued to put up with them. So five years passed.

5 Now there was a certain army-commander, incomparably wealthy and affluent, whom Nushirvan The Just had made governor of Adharbaygan; in all the kingdom there was no more powerful commander, and nobody could match him in arms, horses and other paraphernalia. This man was seized with the desire to build a mansion and a garden in the city where he was stationed; in the environs of the city there was a piece of land belonging to an old woman, of such an extent that the income from it sufficed for her to pay the royal quota and for the cultivator to take his share, while enough remained to provide her with four loaves of part-barley-bread for every day of the year; one loaf she exchanged for other eatables, and one for oil for her lamp; then she ate one loaf

for breakfast and one for supper; people took pity on her and gave her clothing; she never went outside her house but passed her life in retirement and poverty. Now it suited this army-commander to include that piece of land in the rest of his property; he sent someone to the wretched old woman to say, 'Sell this piece of land as I have need of it.' The poor old woman said, 'I will not sell it as I need it more; I have only this piece of land in all the world; it gives me my sustenance, and nobody sells his own sustenance.' The man said, 'I will pay you for it or else I will give you in exchange another piece of land which will provide just as much income and produce.' The old woman said, 'This land is my lawful property; I inherited it from my mother and father; the water-supply is near to it, and the neighbours are agreeable and kind to me. Any land which you may give me will not have these particular features. Kindly keep your hands off my land.' The army-commander did not listen to the old woman but he forcibly seized the land and extended his garden wall around it. The wretched old woman was helpless and reduced to indigence; she resigned herself to accepting payment for the land or else a substitute. She threw herself in front of the man and said, 'Either give me the price or a substitute.' He did not listen to her or look at her, but completely ignored her. The wretched old woman gave up hope and went away; and thereafter they did not admit her into his house. But every time the army-commander mounted and went out for recreation or hunting the old woman sat in his way; when he approached her, she called out and demanded payment for the land. He gave no answer but just rode past her. If she spoke to his retainers or companions or chamberlains, they said, 'Very well; we will speak to him about it.' But nobody ever did so. Two years passed after this.

6 The wretched old woman was reduced to extreme destitution; she found no justice and gave up hope of ever getting it from the man. She said to herself, 'I am simply hammering cold iron. Over every authority God has placed a higher authority; with all his tyranny this man is but a servant and minion of Nushirvan The Just. The best thing I can do is, no matter what hardships I may suffer, to make my way to Mada'in, throw myself in front of Nushirvan, and acquaint him of my case; maybe I shall obtain justice from him.' She told no one of her designs, but secretly set out and with great trouble and difficulty went from Adharbaygan

to Mada'in; when she saw Nushirvan's palace she said to herself, 'They will never let me go in there; they refused to let me enter the house of the governor of Adharbaygan, and he is a mere servant of this sovereign; so how should they allow me to enter the palace of him who is the lord of the world and let me see him? I had better find a lodging in this vicinity and keep myself hidden; perhaps out in the country I can throw myself at his feet and present my petition.'

7 By chance the army-commander who had seized the old woman's land came to the court, and King Nushirvan decided to go hunting. The old woman found out that the king was going to a certain hunting-ground on such-and-such a day. She set off and by constant enquiry and strenuous effort made her way to the hunting-ground; she sat down behind a straw-stack and slept the night. The next day Nushirvan arrived; the nobles and retainers all passed by and began the chase. Nushirvan stayed behind with one arms-bearer; he was just riding off to the hunt, when the old woman, seeing the king alone, got up from behind a thorn bush and ran up to him; she handed him the petition and said, 'O king, if you rule the world, give justice to this poor wretch; read her petition and learn her case.' When Nushirvan saw the old woman and heard her speak, he knew that she would not have come to the hunting-ground except out of dire necessity; he rode towards her, took her petition and read it and heard what she had to say. Tears came into his eyes and he said to her, 'Do not worry any more; up to now this has been your affair; now that we know about it, you are free; it has become our responsibility. We shall satisfy your want; then we shall send you home. Rest a few days here as you have come a long way.' He looked round and saw one of his grooms coming along mounted on a riding-mule; he said, 'Dismount and set this woman on your mule; take her to a village, hand her over to the headman and come back yourself. When we return from hunting take her from the village to the city and keep her in your own house. Allow her two maunds of bread and one maund of meat daily, and let her have five gold dinars a month from our treasury, until such time as I call for her.' The groom did so.

8 As he returned from the chase King Nushirvan spent the whole day pondering how he should contrive a means of examining this case without the knowledge of any of the courtiers. So one

afternoon at the time of the siesta, when everyone was alseep and the palace was deserted, he ordered a servant to go to such-and-such a tent and summon a certain page. The servant went and brought the page; the king said, 'O page, you know that I have many worthy pages; I have particularly chosen you to be entrusted with a certain task. You must draw some money from the treasury for your expenses, and go to Adharbaygan; you should lodge in a certain quarter of a certain city and stay for twenty days; you will pretend to the inhabitants that you have come in search of a runaway page. You should associate with all kinds of people, and as you mix with them in drunkenness and sobriety, in the course of conversation enquire about an old woman called so-and-so, who used to live in their district and seems to have disappeared; find out where she went and what she did with the piece of land which she had; listen to what each person says, remember it well and bring back a verified report. This is the true object of your mission; but at tomorrow's audience I shall call you in front of me and say to you in a loud voice for all to hear: Go, draw money for expenses from the treasury, and travel to Adharbaygan; each city and district that you reach, take note and enquire about the state of the cereals and fruits this year; see whether any celestial calamity has befallen or not, and at the same time look at the condition of the pastures and hunting-grounds. Come back without delay and report what you find without letting anyone know why I sent you.' The page said, 'I will obey your command.'

9 The next day Nushirvan did thus. The page departed and went to that city. He stayed there twenty days, enquiring about the old woman from everyone he talked to. They all said the same; 'That old woman was of good family and gentle manners; formerly we used to see her with her husband and children; but the husband and children all died and she was left alone in reduced circumstances. She had a piece of land which she had given to a peasant to cultivate and the produce from it was just enough for her to pay the royal quota and the peasant's share; the portion which remained sufficed until the next harvest to provide her with a ration of four loaves a day; she exchanged one loaf for other eatables and one for oil for her lamp; then she ate one loaf for breakfast and one for supper. Now the governor desired to make a garden with a pavilion and a fine view. He forcibly seized her plot of land and incorporated it in his estate; he neither paid for it nor

offered a substitute. For two years the old woman kept going to his house, crying out and demanding payment; nobody listened to her, and now it is some time since anyone saw her in this city; we do not know where she has gone, whether she is dead or alive.'

10 The page returned to the capital. Nushirvan The Just had begun audience; the page entered and bowed; Nushirvan said, 'Ah! tell us what you found.' He said, 'Thanks to Your Majesty the crops are good everywhere this year; no calamity has befallen; the pastures are fresh and the hunting-grounds well stocked.' The king said, 'Praise be to Allah! You have brought good news.' When the audience was over and the palace was empty of strangers, he summoned the page and questioned him; the page related what he had heard. Nushirvan was convinced that what the old woman had said was true. All that day and night he could not sleep from anxiety and distress. Next day early he called for the great chamberlain and instructed him that, when the nobles began to arrive, if a certain one came in, he was to keep him in the vestibule until he told him what to do.

11 When all the nobles and priests were present in the audience-hall, Nushirvan appeared and gave audience. After some time he turned to the nobles and priests and said, 'I wish to ask you something; answer me truthfully according to your lights and judgment.' They said, 'We will obey.' He said, 'This man (of such-and-such a name) who is the army-commander of Abhar-baygan, how great is his wealth in gold coin?' They said, 'He probably has 2,000,000 dinars which he does not need, put away unused.' He said, 'How about salvers and utensils?' They said, 'He has 500,000 dinars' worth of gold and silver articles.' He said, 'And jewels?' They said, '600,000 dinars' worth.' He said, 'Carpets and luxuries?' They said, '30,000 dinars' worth.' He said, 'What about landed property, estates and farms?' They said, 'In Khurasan, 'Iraq, Pars and Adharbaygan there is not a district or city where he does not possess seven, eight or even ten villages with caravanserais, hot-baths, mills and farms.' He said, 'How many horses and mules has he?' They said, 'Thirty thousand.' He said, 'Sheep?' They said, 'Two hundred thousand.' He said, 'Camels?' They said, 'Thirty thousand.' He said, 'Slaves and hirelings?' They said, 'He owns 1,700 Turkish, Rumi and Abyssinian pages and 400 moon-faced slave-girls.' He said, 'A man who has this amount of wealth and every day eats 20 dishes of lamb,

soups, fries, sweet and rich concoctions, while another human being, a devout servant of God (to Him be power and glory), weak and helpless, having in all the world only two loaves of dry bread to eat, one for morning and one for evening – supposing the rich man unlawfully seized the other's two dry loaves and deprived him of them, what would he deserve?' All said, 'He would deserve every punishment; whatever penalty he were made to suffer, it would be less than he deserved.' Nushirvan said, 'I require you immediately to strip the skin from his body, throw his flesh to the dogs, stuff the skin with straw and hang it upon the palace gate. Then let it be proclaimed for seven days that hereafter if any man commits oppression, taking even a bag of straw, a chicken or a handful of leeks wrongfully from somebody else, and if a complainant comes to the court, the same will happen to him as happened to this man.' They did as Nushirvan commanded.

12 He told the groom to bring the old woman. Then he said to the nobles, 'This is the injured party; and there is the oppressor who has met his reward.' To the page whom he had sent to Adharbaygan he said, 'O page, why did I send you to Adharbaygan?' He said, 'To investigate the case of this old woman and her complaint, and to bring Your Majesty a true and exact report.' Then Nushirvan said to the nobles, 'So that you may know that I have not inflicted this punishment wantonly, [I warn you that] hereafter I shall not deal with oppressors except by the sword; I shall protect the ewes and lambs from the wolves, I shall restrain grasping hands, I shall remove evil-doers from the face of the earth and fill the world with justice and security, for this is the task for which I was born. If it were right for men to do as they wished, God would not have created the king and appointed him over them. So now strive to do no act that would lead to your suffering the same fate as this impious criminal.' All those present were so awed by the king's majesty and authority that they nearly died of fear. He said to the old woman, 'I have punished him who wronged you, and his mansion and the garden which contains your piece of land are now granted to you; I am also giving you animals and money so that you can return home to your own city in safety with my warrant, and I trust that you will remember me in your prayers.' Then he addressed the company, saying, 'Why is it that the door of my palace is open for oppressors and closed to the oppressed? Soldiers and peasants are all my underlings and

labourers; nay, the peasants are the givers and the soldiers are the takers; so the door ought to be open wider for the giver than for the taker. Now one of the current irregularities, injustices and unofficial instructions[3] is that when a complainant comes in the court, he is not allowed to come before me and state his case. If the old woman had gained access to me here, she would not have needed to go to the hunting-ground.' Then the king commanded that a chain should be set up with bells attached to it, within the reach of even a child of seven years old, so that any complainant who came to the court would not need to see a chamberlain; he would pull the chain and the bells would ring; Nushirvan would hear it, summon the person, hear his case and give justice. This was done.

13 When the nobles left the palace and returned to their homes, they straightaway summoned their stewards and underlings and said, 'See how much you have unjustly extorted in the last ten years, whose blood you have drained through the nose, and whom you have harmed in drunkenness and sobriety; we and you must look into this matter and satisfy all our creditors before anyone goes to the court and complains against us.' So they all set to and politely summoned their creditors or called at their houses and satisfied every one either with apologies or indemnities; they also took signed statements to the effect that so-and-so had received satisfaction from so-and-so and had no further claim upon him. By this salutary exercise of his authority Nushirvan The Just reduced his whole kingdom to order; he eliminated oppression and all the world was so relieved that seven years passed without anyone coming to the court to complain of injustice.

14 Seven years later one afternoon when the palace was empty and everyone had gone, and the guards were asleep, the bells began to ring; Nushirvan heard them and at once sent two servants to see who had come to complain. When they entered the audience-court they saw an old donkey, lean and scabby, which had come inside the gate and was rubbing its back on the chain, causing the bells to ring. The servants went back and said, 'There is no complainant, but only a scabby donkey which has come inside the gate; it happened to scrape its back against the chain and liked it; it is rubbing itself on it to relieve the itching of the scab.' Nushirvan said, 'O fools that you are! it is not as you think; when you look at it well, even this ass has come to seek justice. I desire you both

to go, take the ass into the centre of the city; ask everyone about its history and let me know.' The servants went out, took the donkey into the bazaar and asked the people if there was anyone who recognized it. All said, 'Yes, by Allah, there is hardly anybody in the city who does not know this donkey.' They said, 'What do you know about it?' They said, 'It belongs to a certain washerman, and for about twenty years we have seen him with it; every day he used to put people's clothes on its back and take them to the washing-place, and bring them back in the evening. As long as the donkey was young and could do its work, he used to feed it; now that it has grown old and incapable of work, he has disowned it and turned it out of his house; it is now a year since it was given its freedom; night and day it wanders through the streets, bazaars and quarters of the city; people give it fodder and water or a handful of grass out of charity; it may go for two whole days and not get any water and grass, roaming in vain.'

15 Since the servants heard the same story from everyone they asked, they soon went back and informed the king. Nushirvan said, 'Did I not tell you this ass had come to seek redress? Look after it well tonight and tomorrow bring the washerman to me together with four headmen from his quarter, and I will deal with him as necessary.' The next day the servants did so; they brought the ass and the washerman together with four headmen in front of Nushirvan at the time of audience; Nushirvan said to the washerman, 'As long as this poor donkey was young and could work for you, you used to feed it and look after it; now that it has grown old and can no longer work, so that you won't have to feed it you have given it its freedom, and turned it out of your house. So where are his rights for his twenty years' service?' He ordered the man to be given forty lashes, and said, 'As long as this donkey is alive, every day to the knowledge of these four men you must give it as much straw and barley as it can eat, and if you fail and I come to know of it, I shall punish you severely, so that you may know that kings have always been concerned for the rights of the weak and watchful of the doings of officers, assignees and pages, for the sake of their reputation in this world and salvation in the next.'

16 Every two or three years tax-collectors and assignees should be changed lest they become too securely established and

entrenched, and begin to cause anxiety. In this way they will treat the peasants well and their provinces will remain prosperous.

Chapter VI

Concerning judges, preachers and censors
and the importance of their activities

1 It is necessary for full information to be available about every single judge in the country. Those that are learned, pious and un-covetous should be retained in their appointments, while any that are not so, should be dismissed, and worthy persons installed in their place. Let each one be paid a salary according to his position, so that he will have no excuse for dishonesty. This is a most important and delicate matter, because they have power over the lives and property of Muslims. If any judge gives sentence capriciously or out of avarice or malice, the other judges must carry out the sentence and inform the king about it; then that judge must be dismissed and punished.

All other officers must strengthen the hand of the judge and uphold the dignity of the court. If anyone makes excuses and fails to appear in court, however exalted he may be, he must be forcibly compelled to be present. For in the time of The Companions of The Prophet (upon him be peace and blessings) justice was dispensed by them in person and not delegated to anyone else, so that there could be no scope for injustice or evading the law. In every age from the time of Adam (peace be upon him) until now, in every transaction in a country men have practised equity, given justice and striven after righteousness, and where this has been so, dynasties have endured for generations.

2 They say that it was the custom of the Persian kings to give special audiences for the common people at the festivals of Mihrjan[1] and Nauruz,[2] and nobody was debarred. Several days beforehand proclamations were read telling the people to be ready

for a certain day; then they prepared their cases, wrote their petitions and collected their documents, and their opponents did likewise. When the day came the king's herald stood outside the palace gate and shouted, 'If any man this day impedes another from submitting his needs, the king will be innocent of his blood.' The king then received the people's petitions and laid them all before him; one by one he looked at them, and if amongst them there was one complaining against himself he rose and came down from the throne and knelt before the *mūbad-mūbadān* (this meant chief justice in their language, and he sat on the king's right hand) saying, 'Before all other cases judge between me and this man, impartially and regardlessly.' Then it was announced that all whose suit was against the king should stand on one side as their cases would be dealt with first.

3 Then the king would say to the *mūbad*, 'In the eyes of God (be He exalted) there is no sin greater than a king's sin. The right way for a king to acknowledge God's grace is by looking after his subjects, giving them justice, and preserving them from oppressors. When a king is a tyrant all his courtiers begin to practise tyranny; they become forgetful of God and ungrateful for His bounty. Verily God abandons them in His wrath, and before long the world goes to ruin and they are all destroyed because of the vileness of their sins. Then the kingship is transferred to another house. O God-fearing *mūbad*, take care that you do not favour me against your conscience, because everything which God in future will demand of me, I ask of you; so I hereby make you responsible.' Then the *mūbad* considered the case and having decided between the king and his opponent, he awarded judgment in full to the winning party; but if anyone made a false accusation against the king and had no proof, he was severely punished and it was proclaimed that this was the punishment for one who had the audacity to find fault with the king and the state. When the king had finished with these disputes he returned to the throne, put on the crown and turning to his nobles and retainers said, 'For this purpose I commenced the proceedings with myself, namely that if any one of you should have oppressive desires against another they might be suppressed. Now let all of you who have adversaries give them satisfaction.' On that day whoever was nearest to the king was furthest and he who was strongest was weakest.

4 From the time of Ardashir Papakan until Yazdijird The

43

Sinner this procedure was followed. But Yazdijird changed the customs of his fathers; he made injustice the rule in the world and introduced evil practices. The population suffered distress and their curses upon his name were unceasing. Until one day it happened that a bare-back horse suddenly entered his palace; its form was such that all the nobles who were present agreed on its excellence, and all tried to catch it. Nobody was successful until it came in front of Yazdijird and stood still at the side of the hall. Then Yazdijird said, 'All stand back, for this is a gift which God (be He exalted) has sent to me.' He got up and gently approaching the horse, caught it by the mane. He stroked the horse's head and patted its back. The horse never moved, but remained quiet. Yazdijird called for saddle and bridle; he bridled the horse and after putting on the saddle and making the girth tight, he came to the hind quarters to pass the crupper under its tail. Suddenly the horse kicked him right upon the heart and killed him on the spot. Then it bolted out of the door before anyone could stop it. Nobody knew whence it had come nor whither it went. All agreed that it was an angel sent by God to deliver them from that tyrant.

5 It is said that 'Umara ibn Hamza was sitting in the company of Abu Dawaniq[3] on the day for hearing grievances. A man got up – one of the injured parties – and complained that 'Umara had forcibly seized his farm. The Commander of the Faithful said to 'Umara, 'Rise and confront your adversary and plead your defence.' 'Umara said, 'I am not this man's adversary. If the farm is mine, I make him a present of it. I do not wish to leave the place in which the caliph has honourably seated me, nor will I throw my dignity and rank to the winds for the sake of a farm.' All the nobles were impressed by his magnanimity.

6 It must be understood that the king should give judgment in person and hear the words of opposing parties with his own ears. If the king is Turkish or Persian or one who does not know Arabic and has not learnt the precepts of the *shari'a* [Islamic law], of course he will need a deputy through whom he may perform his function. It is the judges who are the king's deputies, so it is essential for the king to strengthen their hands. Besides, their reputation and dignity must be above reproach because they are the lieutenants of the caliph and wear his badge. At the same time they are appointed by the king and are his agents.

Likewise the preachers who read the prayers in the public

mosques should be chosen by the king for their piety and knowledge of the Qur'an. For it is a crucial point about the prayer of
Muslims that it depends upon the *imām* [leader]. When the leader's
prayers are invalid the prayers of the whole congregation are
ineffectual.

In every city a censor[4] must be appointed whose duty is to check
scales and prices and to see that business is carried on in an orderly
and upright manner. He must take particular care in regard to
goods which are brought from outlying districts and sold in the
bazaars to see that there is no fraud or dishonesty, that weights are
kept true, and that moral and religious principles are observed.
His hand must be strengthened by the king and other officers, for
this is one of the foundations of the state and is itself the product of
justice. If the king neglects this matter the poor will suffer distress,
and the traders in the bazaars will buy as they like and sell as they
like, and sellers of short weight will be predominant; iniquity will
be rife and divine law set at nought. The post [of censor] always
used to be given to one of the nobility or else to a eunuch or an old
Turk, who, having no respect for anybody, would be feared by
nobles and commoners alike. Thus business was transacted with
justice and the precepts of Islam were guarded as the following
story shews.

The story of the drunkenness of 'Ali Nushtgin

7 They say that Sultan Mahmud had been drinking all night with
his nobles and boon-companions and at dawn had drunk the
morning draught. 'Ali Nushtgin and Muhammad 'Arabi, both
generals of Mahmud, were among those present and they had
drunk all night and kept awake with Mahmud. By breakfast-time
'Ali Nushtgin was in a state of giddiness and he was suffering
badly from lack of sleep and excess of wine. He asked permission
to go home. Mahmud said, 'It is not fitting for you to go out in
this state in broad daylight. Rest here indoors until the afternoon
prayer and then go when you are sober. If the censor sees you like
this in the bazaar, he will arrest you and give you the lash. You
will be put to shame, and I shall be very embarrassed and unable
to help you.' Now 'Ali Nushtgin was a general in command of
50,000 men and the hero and champion of his time, being regarded
as equal to a thousand men.[5] He never imagined that the censor

would dare to think of such a thing; he became impatient and quarrelsome, and said, 'I am going all the same.' Mahmud said, 'You know best'; [and to his henchmen] 'loose him and let him go.' 'Ali Nushtgin mounted his horse[6] and with a great crowd of retainers, pages and servants set out for his house.

8 It chanced that in the middle of the bazaar the censor appeared with a hundred men, mounted and on foot; when he saw 'Ali Nushtgin in such a drunken state he ordered his men to drag him off his horse. Then he dismounted himself and with his own hand beat 'Ali Nushtgin forty strokes with a stick, without respect or regard, so that he bit the dust, while his servants and followers looked on. Nobody was bold enough to say a word; and that censor was a Turkish eunuch, old and venerable, who had acquired many rights by his long service.

After he had gone they carried 'Ali Nushtgin home, and all the way he kept saying, 'This is what happens if you disobey the sultan's orders.' The next day when he entered the royal presence, Mahmud said, 'Well, did you escape the censor?' 'Ali Nushtgin bared his back and shewed it to Mahmud, black and blue. Mahmud laughed and said, 'Now repent and resolve never to go outdoors drunk again.'

Since the rules of administration and discipline were firmly established in the country, the workings of justice took this course that we have related.

The story of the bakers of Ghaznain

9 I have heard that one day the bakers in Ghaznain shut the doors of their shops, and bread became dear and unobtainable. Strangers and poor people were in distress and went to the court to state their grievance, and they complained about the bakers in front of Sultan Ibrahim. He ordered all of them to be brought to his presence; then he said, 'Why have you cut off the supply of bread?' They said, 'Every load of wheat and flour which is brought into the city is bought by your baker and put into his store; he says that this is the order and he does not allow us to buy a single maund.' The sultan gave orders that his private baker was to be taken and thrown under elephants' feet. When he was dead they tied him to an elephant's tusks and paraded him through the

city, proclaiming, 'This is what we will do to any baker who does not open the door of his shop.' Then they dealt out his stocks [to all the other bakers]. By evening prayer there were fifty maunds of bread left over in every shop and not enough customers to buy it all.

Chapter VII

On obtaining information about the conduct of tax-collectors, judges, prefects of police and mayors, and keeping them in check

1 Let observation be kept in every city to see who there is in it who shews interest in religious matters, fears God (be He exalted) and is not self-seeking. Let such a person be addressed thus, 'We have now made you responsible for the security of this city and its district. All that God asks of us, we shall require of you. We desire that you make constant enquiries and be always well-informed in matters small and great concerning the conduct of the tax-collector, the judge, the prefect of police and the censor towards the people. Make us acquainted with the truth whether your findings are kept secret or made public, so that we may give our orders as appropriate.' If persons who are of the right quality refuse to accept this trust, they must be coerced and however reluctantly commanded to do it.

2 They say that 'Abd-Allah ibn Tahir was a just amir. His grave is at Nishapur and I have visited it and seen it. It is constantly thronged with people praying for their needs, and God always grants their requests. He was a man who habitually appointed devout and pious men to be his officers, and persons who had no need of worldly goods and did not busy themselves with their private interests, with the result that taxes were duly

47

collected, the peasants were not troubled and he himself was not embarrassed.

3 Abu 'Ali Daqqaq¹ one day called upon the amir Abu 'Ali Ilyas.² The latter was general and governor of Khurasan, and in spite of his high rank was an extremely virtuous man. When Abu 'Ali Daqqaq knelt in front of him, Abu 'Ali Ilyas said, 'Give me good counsel.' He said, 'O amir, I will ask you a question; will you answer me frankly?' He said, 'I will.' He said, 'Tell me, which do you love more, your gold or your enemy?' He said, 'My gold.' He said, 'Then how is it that that which you love more, you will leave behind you, and your enemy whom you love not, you will take with you to the next world?' Tears came into the eyes of Abu 'Ali Ilyas and he said, 'You have counselled me well and roused me from the sleep of negligence; these words are the sum of all philosophy and they will profit me in both worlds.'

The story of Sultan Mahmud's ugliness

4 They say that Sultan Mahmud Ghāzī [The Raider] was not handsome; he had a drawn face, his skin was dry, his neck long, his nose high, and his beard was thin. Because he always ate clay, his complexion was yellow. One day after his father Sabuktigin died, and he ascended the throne and Hindustan became subject to him, in the early morning he was sitting on his prayer-mat in his private room; he had been saying his ritual prayers and in front of him was his mirror and his comb and two private pages were in waiting, when his vazir Shams al-Kufat Ahmad ibn Hasan entered the room, and bowed; Mahmud nodded to him to sit down. When he had finished his private devotions, he put on his hat and cloak and shoes, and looked at himself in the mirror; he saw his face, then smiled and said to Ahmad ibn Hasan, 'Do you know what is passing through my mind at this moment?' He said, 'My lord knows best.' He said, 'I am afraid that people don't love me because I am not handsome; they always prefer handsome kings.' Ahmad ibn Hasan said, 'Master, do just one thing, and they will love you more than their wives and children and their very selves, and at your command they will go through water and fire.' He said, 'What am I to do?' He said, 'Take gold as your enemy and men will regard you as their friend.' Mahmud was pleased at this and said, 'A thousand meanings and profits are hidden in these

words.' Then he opened his hand in generosity and charity. All the world adored him and praised him, and many noble works and great victories sprang from his hands; he went to Somnat and broke the idol and brought it back; he went as far as Samarqand and came also to 'Iraq. Then one day he said to Ahmad ibn Hasan, 'Since I renounced gold, both worlds came into my hand, and when I repudiated money, I became beloved of both worlds.'

The title of sultan did not exist before him;[3] the first ruler in Islam to call himself sultan was Mahmud. After him it became the general rule. As a king he was just, God-fearing, fond of learning, generous, alert, sound in judgment, orthodox in religion and a gallant battler for the faith. The best time is that in which a just king reigns.

5 Tradition says that The Prophet (the prayers of God be upon him) said [in Arabic], 'Justice is the glory of the faith and the power of the government; in it lies the prosperity of nobility and commons.' (The meaning is . . .) It is the measure of all good things, as God (be He exalted) said [in the Qur'an 55. 6], 'He raised up the heavens and He set the Balance' – that is, there is nothing better than justice. And in another place [Qur'an 42.16] He said, 'Allah it is who sent down the Book with truth, and the Balance.' The person most worthy for kingship is he whose heart is a repository of justice, whose house is a haven for wise and religious men, and whose boon-companions and agents are discreet and God-fearing.

6 Fudail ibn 'Iyad[4] used to say, 'If my prayers were to be granted I should pray only for a just ruler, because the ruler's virtue underlies the well-being of his subjects and the prosperity of the world.'

7 Among the traditions of The Prophet (may God pray for him and give him peace) is the following [in Arabic]: 'Those who do justice in this world for God's sake (to Him be power and glory) [will sit] upon platforms made of pearl on the resurrection day.' (He said: Those who do justice in this world for God's sake will be in paradise on platforms of pearl on the resurrection day.)

8 For the sake of justice and the welfare of the people kings have always put in charge of affairs abstemious and God-fearing men who, being without self-interest, will on every occasion report

on matters truthfully, as The Commander of the Faithful al-Mu'tasim did at Baghdad.

The story of the Turkish amir and the severity of al-Mu'tasim

9 And that was on this wise. Of the 'Abbasid caliphs none had such authority, such dignity, such profusion of wealth as al-Mu'tasim; nor did any own as many Turkish slaves as he. They say he had 70,000 Turkish pages; many of his pages he promoted and appointed to governorships. He always used to say there was none like the Turk for service.

10 One day an amir summoned his steward and said, 'Do you know any of the citizens or merchants of Baghdad who would do business with me to the extent of five hundred dinars? I need that sum urgently and would give it back at harvest time.' The steward thought; he remembered a friend of his who had a small business in the bazaar and possessed six hundred caliphal gold dinars which he had acquired in the course of time. He said to the amir, 'I have an acquaintance who has a shop in such-and-such bazaar, and from time to time I go to his shop and do business with him, he has got six hundred caliphal dinars. If you sent someone to invite him here, and if you placed him in a seat of honour, favoured him with constant attention, treated him with ceremony at dinner; and then after eating, if you were to mention the financial matter, maybe he would feel abashed at your kindness and not be able to refuse.' The amir did this; he sent someone with the following message, 'Would you trouble yourself for a few moments, as I want to see you about something?' The man got up and went to the amir's house. He was not previously acquainted with this amir. He greeted him when he went in. The amir answered him and turned to his retainers, saying, 'Is this the person?' They said, 'Yes.' The amir rose and had him ushered to a good seat. Then he said, 'Sir, I have heard so much about your nobility, honesty and piety that I have been captivated by you without ever having seen you; they say that in all the bazaars of Baghdad there is no one of finer character or fairer business principles than yourself.' He went on to say, 'Why not discard ceremony and let me do something for you; I want you to regard this house as your own and treat me as a friend and brother.' The man bowed at each thing the amir said; while the steward kept saying, 'It is

so – a hundred times so.' After some time trays of food were brought in; the amir placed the man next to himself and was assiduous in his attentions, constantly plying him with tit-bits.

11 The food was removed, they washed their hands and outsiders departed; only the amir's personal retainers remained. He turned to the man and said, 'Do you know why I troubled you to come here?' He said, 'The amir knows best.' The amir said, 'Know that in this city I have many friends who would not fail to carry out my slightest suggestion; if I were to ask them for five or ten thousand, they would give it at once without grudge, because they have profited much by doing business with me, and never suffered loss in any dealings or relations with me. At the present moment I am anxious that there should be friendship and informality between us. Although I have many creditors, in the present circumstances I would like you to assist me with a thousand dinars for four or five months. I will repay you at harvest time and present you with a suit of clothes for good measure; I know that you have this much and more, and will not refuse.' The man was abashed at the amir's attentions and said, 'It is for the amir to command; but I am not one of those merchants who have a thousand or two thousand dinars. One must speak nothing but the truth to one's superiors; my whole capital is six hundred dinars and with it I manage to scrape a living and do a little trade in the bazaar; it has taken much time and toil to accumulate this sum.' The amir said, 'I have plenty of fine [special standard] gold in my treasury, but it is unsuitable for my present purpose. My object in doing business with you is to gain your friendship. What profit do you get from your slender trade? Let me have the six hundred dinars and I will give you a receipt for seven hundred, witnessed by honourable persons, and a promise of repayment at harvest time with a handsome present in addition.' Meanwhile the steward was saying, 'You have not got to know the amir yet; of all the pillars of the state there is no one of stricter business principles than he.' The man said, 'It is for the amir to command. As much as I have I will not grudge.' So he gave the amir the gold and took a receipt.

12 Ten days after the expiry of the term the man went to call on the amir. Verbally he made no request; he said to himself, 'When the amir sees me, he will know that I have come for the

money.' He continued to visit the amir in this way until it was two months after the agreed date, and he had seen the amir ten times. The amir appeared not to understand that the man wanted anything or that he himself owed anything to the man. When the man saw that the amir kept silent, he wrote a petition and handed it to him; it said, 'I now need that paltry sum of money, and it is two months after the agreed date. If the amir sees fit could he kindly advise his steward to deliver the money to his humble servant.' The amir said, 'Do you think that I have forgotten your case? Don't worry; be patient for a few days as I am arranging about your money; I will send it to you in a sealed purse by the hand of one of my confidants.' The man waited another two months and saw no sign of his money. Once more he went to the amir's house and sent in another petition and also spoke personally. The amir put him off with a few pleasantries; and the man kept pressing his demand every two or three days, but without result. Then eight months passed from the due date.

13 The man was in distress. He persuaded people of the city to intercede for him; he went to the judge and summoned the amir to the *shari'a* court; there was not a single noble or grandee who had not spoken to the amir and interceded on the man's behalf. It had no effect. Even when he took fifty men from the judge's house, he was unable to bring the amir to court; nor did the amir listen to what the grandees said. Then a year and a half passed. The man was desperate; he resigned himself to forgoing the interest and taking back a hundred dinars less than the full sum. But even that was no use. He abandoned hope of help from the nobles; and he was tired of running hither and thither. Instead he put his trust in God; he went into the Fadlumand mosque and performed several *rak'ats*[5] of prayer. He murmured and moaned to God, saying, 'O Lord, hear my prayer and restore me to my rights; extract justice from this oppressor.' Now it chanced that a dervish was sitting in the mosque and heard his wailing and moaning. His heart was moved to sympathy; when the man had finished his supplications, he said, 'O shaikh! what affliction has befallen you that you wail so loud? Tell me what it is.' The man said, 'My distress is such that it will not avail to speak to any mortal; only God (be He exalted) can succour me.' He said, 'Yet tell me, for there must be some reason.' The man said, 'O beggar, there remains only the caliph whom I have not spoken to. I have spoken to all the amirs

and nobles, and I have been to the judge; but it has had no effect. If I tell you, what good will it do?' The dervish said, 'You should tell me; even if it does you no good to tell me, neither will it do you any harm. Have you not heard what the sages say? – "If you have a pain, you should tell everyone you meet; you may discover the remedy from the humblest of men." If you tell me your case, maybe you will find some comfort, and even if you do not, you will be no worse off than you are now.' The man said to himself, 'He is right.' Then he told him what had happened.

14 When the dervish had heard the story, he said, 'O noble sir, now that you have told me what your trouble is, a remedy has immediately presented itself. Don't worry, for if you do as I tell you, you will get back your gold this very day.' The man said, 'What am I to do?' He said, 'Go at once to a certain quarter of the city where there is a mosque with a minaret; beside the mosque is a gate, and behind the gate is a shop. There is an old man sitting there, wearing ragged clothes and sewing canvas; one or two boys are also doing some sewing with him. Go into that shop and greet the old man; sit down in front of him and tell him your story. When you have attained your object, remember me in your prayers. Do what I have told you without delay.' The man came out of the mosque; he thought to himself, 'Fancy! I appealed to all the nobles and amirs, and they earnestly pleaded on my behalf; but it was of no use. Now this beggar is directing me to a feeble old man and saying that I shall attain my object from him. This seems to me like a trick, but what am I to do? At all events I will go; even if no good comes out of it, things will not be any worse than they are at present.' So he went to the gate of the mosque, entered the shop and, saluting the old man, sat down in front of him. Some time passed as the old man was doing some sewing. After putting it down he said, 'Is there anything I can do for you?' The man told him his story from first to last.

15 After hearing all the circumstances the old tailor said, 'It is God (to Him be power and glory) who orders the affairs of His servants. We can do no more than speak; so let me also speak to your debtor on your behalf. I hope that God will put things right and you will get what you want. Sit with your back to that wall and rest a while.' Then he said to one of the two apprentices, 'Put down your needle and go to the house of such-and-such amir. Sit outside the door of his private room, and if anyone goes in or

comes out, ask them to tell the amir that a certain tailor's apprentice is waiting and has a message for him. When he calls you in,
after greeting him, say, "My master sends his compliments and says
that a man has come to him to complain against you; he has a
receipt signed by you for seven hundred dinars, and it is now
eighteen months after the due date. I request you forthwith to give
the man his money in full and satisfy him completely without fail
or delay." Bring me back his answer quickly.'

16 The boy went in haste to the amir's house, while I⁶ was
struck dumb with amazement, for no king would send his own
slave such a message as the tailor had just sent to the amir through
the medium of a boy. After some time the boy came back and said
to his master, 'I did as you said. I saw the amir and delivered the
message. The amir got up and said, "Convey my greetings and
respect to your master, and tell him that I thank him; I will do as
he says. I am coming now bringing the money with me; I shall
apologize for my fault and hand over the money in his presence."'
An hour had not passed when the amir was on his way with a
groom and two attendants. He dismounted from his horse, entered the shop and greeted the old tailor, kissing his hand. Then
he sat down in front of him, took a purse of gold from an attendant and said, 'Here is the gold. Please do not think that I was
going to misappropriate this man's money. What happened was
not my fault but my steward's.' He apologized profusely, then said
to an attendant, 'Go and fetch an assayer with a balance from the
bazaar.' He went and brought an assayer. The gold was assayed
and weighed. It came to five hundred caliphal dinars. The amir
said, 'He will have to take these five hundred dinars today, and
tomorrow when I return from the court I will summon him and
hand over the other two hundred dinars, asking pardon and trying
to satisfy him. And I will arrange for an encomiast to call on you
tomorrow before the noon prayer.' The old man said, 'Put these
five hundred dinars into his skirt, and see that you do not go back
on your word.' He said, 'Very well.' He put the money into my
skirt, kissed the old man's hand and departed; while I scarcely knew
where I was for astonishment and happiness. I put out my hand,
took hold of the balance and weighed out a hundred dinars; I laid
them before the old man. He said, 'What is this?' I said, 'I was
prepared to take back a hundred dinars less than the full amount;
now that through your good offices I am going to receive my

money in full, I freely grant you these hundred dinars as a reward for your efforts.' The old man looked cross and frowned, saying, 'I am content that as a result of what I said a Muslim found release from grief and trouble; but if I allowed myself to take one grain of your money, I should be a worse oppressor than this Turk. Arise and go in safety with the gold you have got; and if he does not send you the other two hundred dinars tomorrow, let me know. Hereafter you had better know who your associates are before you do business with them.' In spite of all my entreaties he would accept nothing; so I got up and went joyfully back to my house. That night I slept free from care.

17 The next day I was sitting in the house, and about the middle of the morning someone came from the amir to see me and said, 'The amir asks you to trouble yourself to visit him for a moment.' I went to the amir's house; when I went in he rose and put me in a seat of honour; then he began to revile his stewards, saying that they were to blame, and that he had been constantly busy in the service of the king. Then he said to his treasurer, 'Bring the purse and the balance.' He weighed out two hundred dinars and put them in my hands. I bowed and got up to go. He said, 'Sit down for a bit.' Food was brought in. When we had finished eating and washed our hands, the amir whispered something in a servant's ear. The servant went out and came back with a robe of honour. The amir said, 'Invest him.' So they invested me with a cloak of great price and put a turban of fine linen on my head. Then the amir said to me, 'Are you now genuinely satisfied?' I said, 'Yes.' He said, 'Then give me back my receipt and go this very hour to the old man and tell him that you have received your rights and obtained satisfaction from me.' I said, 'Certainly, and in any case he told me to report to him tomorrow.' I rose and went from the amir's house to the tailor's shop. I told him what had happened – how the amir had called me, and treated me well, and paid me the rest of the money, and presented me with the cloak and turban. I said, 'I know that all this has come about through your good offices. How would it be if you accepted two hundred dinars from me?' Whatever I said he would not take anything, so I got up and returned in good spirits to my own shop.

18 The next day I roasted a lamb and a few chickens, and took them with a plate of sweets and pastries to the old tailor. I said, 'O shaikh, if you will not take money, please accept these few

eatables with my best wishes; it is all from my legitimate earnings; I shall be very pleased if you will.' He said, 'I accept.' He put out his hand and ate some of the food and gave some to his apprentices. Then I said to him, 'I have one request to make, if you will permit me.' He said, 'What is it?' I said, 'All the nobles and amirs of Baghdad spoke to this amir on my behalf, and all without avail; he listened to nobody; even the judge was powerless to deal with him. Why did he listen to you and do what you said at once and give me my money? How did he come to have such respect for you? Please tell me.' He said, 'Haven't you heard what happened to me with The Commander of the Faithful?' I said, 'No.' He said, 'Listen and I will tell you.'

19 He began: Know that I have proclaimed the hours of prayer from the minaret of this mosque for thirty years. I am a tailor by trade; I have never drunk wine, never indulged in adultery and sodomy, and never approved of improper acts. Now in this street is the house of an amir. One day after the afternoon prayer I left the mosque to come back to this shop; I saw the amir coming along in a drunken state, holding on to a young woman's veil; he was dragging her by force and she was crying for help and saying, 'O Muslims, rescue me; I am not a woman of this sort; I am the daughter of such-and-such and the wife of so-and-so, and my house is in a certain quarter; everyone knows of my chastity and virtue. This Turk is presumptuously and forcibly carrying me off with mischievous intent. Moreover my husband has sworn to divorce me if I am ever away from the house at night.' She was weeping and nobody went to her assistance, for this amir was too proud and tyrannous; he had 10,000 horsemen, and nobody dared say anything to him. I shouted a bit, but it was useless, and he took the woman to his house. Thus frustrated, my religious ardour was kindled and I could not restrain myself. I went and rallied the elders of the district, and we all went to the amir's house and raised clamorous protests, shouting, 'Islam is no more, for in the city of Baghdad on the caliph's doorstep women are presumptuously and forcibly seized in the street, carried off and raped. If you send this woman outside, well and good; but if not, we shall go at once to al-Muʻtasim's court and complain.' When the Turk heard our noise he came out of his house with a party of pages who beat us well and truly and broke our resistance.

20 When this happened we all fled and dispersed. It was the

time of the evening prayer. I prayed. Later on I got into my night clothes and lay down upon the ground. I was so vexed and roused that I could not sleep. I lay awake half the night, thinking; and then it occurred to me that if any mischief was going to be done it would have happened by now and could not be helped. What made it worse was that the woman's husband had sworn to divorce her if she went out at night. I had heard that when wine-bibbers get drunk they fall asleep, and when they wake up they do not know how much of the night has passed. I decided immediately to go up the minaret and utter the call to prayer; when the Turk heard it he would think it was daybreak; he would let go of the woman and send her out of his house; inevitably she would pass the door of this mosque; having sounded the call to prayer I would quickly come down from the minaret and stand at the door of the mosque; when the woman appeared I would escort her back to her husband's house, so that at least the poor wretch would not forfeit her husband and her matronage.

21 So I did all this. I went up the minaret and uttered the call to prayer. Now The Commander of the Faithful al-Muʻtasim was awake. When he heard the call to prayer at the wrong time he was very angry, and said, 'A man who sounds the call to prayer in the middle of the night is a miscreant, for whoever hears it will think it is daytime; and as soon as he goes out into the street he will be caught by the night-watch and get into trouble.' He said to a servant, 'Go and tell the porter that I want him to go at once and bring the muezzin who has sounded the call to prayer in the middle of the night; I shall punish him so severely that no muezzin will again utter the call to prayer at the wrong time.' I was standing at the door of the mosque waiting for this woman, when I saw the porter coming with a torch. When he saw me standing there he said, 'Did you sound the call to prayer?' I said, 'Yes.' He said, 'Why did you sound it at the wrong time? The caliph has taken exteme exception to it and is very angry with you; he has sent me to find you so that he can punish you.' I said, 'It is for the caliph to command; but a certain barbarian forced me to utter the call to prayer at the wrong time.' He said, 'Who is this barbarian?' I said, 'One who fears neither God nor the caliph.' He said, 'Who could that be?' I said, 'This is a matter which I can only tell to The Commander of the Faithful. If I did this with evil intent whatever punishment the caliph gives me will be less than my deserts.' He

said, 'In the name of Allah, come, let us go to the caliph's palace.'

22 The servant was waiting for us when we reached the palace. The porter repeated to the servant what I had told him. The servant went and told al-Mu'tasim. He said, 'Go and bring the man to me.' The servant took me before the caliph. He asked me why I had sounded the call to prayer at the wrong time. I then told him the story of the Turk and the woman from start to finish. On hearing it he was very disturbed; he told the servant to instruct the porter as follows: 'Go with a hundred horsemen to the house of such-and-such amir and tell him that he is summoned by the caliph; having found him you are to rescue the woman whom he brought to the house yesterday and send her to her husband's house with this old man and two or three lackeys; call her husband to the door and say that al-Mu'tasim sends his greeting and wishes to intercede on the woman's behalf and says that she was not at all at fault in what happened; he ought to look after his wife better in future; then bring the amir to me at once.' To me he said, 'Remain here for a while.' An hour later they brought the amir to al-Mu'tasim; al-Mu'tasim looked at him and said, 'Wherefore do you suppose that I lack zeal for the Islamic faith? Have you seen me oppress my people? Or is there something wrong with the religion in my time? Am I not the same man who, to save a Muslim who had been taken prisoner by the Rumis [Byzantines], marched from Baghdad, defeated the Rumi army, and put the Caesar to flight, remaining to ravage the lands of Rum for six years and not returning until I had sacked and burned Qustantiniyya [Constantinople], built the Cathedral Mosque and delivered that man from captivity?[7] Today through awe of me and my justice, wolf and sheep can drink together at one place, so how can you dare, here in Baghdad upon my very threshold, to seize a woman by force, take her to your house for a wicked purpose, and then when people protest, to beat them?' He ordered a sack to be brought, the amir to be put into it, and the sack done up tightly. This was done. Then at his behest two clubs were procured, of the kind used for pounding plaster, and he told two men to stand one on each side and beat the amir to pieces. Straightaway the men laid on with the clubs and smashed him to smithereens. They said, 'O Commander of the Faithful, all his bones are minced. What is your command?' He ordered them to take the closed sack as it was and throw it into the Tigris.

23 Then he said to me, 'O shaikh, know that a man who does not fear God (to Him be power and glory) will not be afraid of me, while the man who does fear God will of course not do an act for which he would be brought to book in both worlds. Since this man committed a crime, he has met his just reward. So I command you that in future if anyone wrongs another or unjustly hurts another or holds the religious law in contempt and you become aware of it, you are to sound the call to prayer like this at the wrong time, so that I shall hear it and summon you and ask what is the matter, and deal with any malefactor as I did with this dog, even if it should be my own son or brother.' Then he gave me a present and dismissed me. Now all the nobles and courtiers are aware of this story, so it was not out of respect for me that the amir gave back your money but rather for fear of that sack and the plaster-pounders and the river. For if he had failed, I would immediately have gone up the minaret and sounded the call to prayer and the same would have happened to him as happened to that Turk.

24 There are many stories of this kind. I have related this much in order that The Master of the World may know how caliphs and kings have always guarded the sheep from the wolves, how they have kept their officials in check, what precautions they have taken against evil-doers, and how they have strengthened, upheld and cherished the Islamic faith.

Chapter VIII

On enquiry and investigation into matters of religion, religious law and suchlike

1 It is incumbent upon the king to enquire into religious matters, to be acquainted with the divine precepts and prohibitions and put them into practice, and to obey the commands of God (be He exalted); it is his duty to respect doctors of religion and pay their

salaries out of the treasury, and he should honour pious and abstemious men. Furthermore it is fitting that once or twice a week
he should invite religious elders to his presence and hear from
them the commands of The Truth; he should listen to interpreta-
tions of the Qur'an and traditions of The Prophet (may Allah
pray for him and give him peace); and he should hear stories about
just kings and tales of the prophets (upon them be peace). During
that time he should free his mind from worldly cares and give his
ears and attention [wholly] to them. Let him bid them take sides
and hold a debate, and let him ask questions about what he does
not understand; when he has learnt the answers let him commit
them to memory. After this has gone on for some time it will
become a habit, and it will not be long before he has learnt and
memorized most of the precepts of divine law, the meanings of
the Qur'an and the traditions of The Prophet (upon him be peace).
Then the way of prudence and rectitude in both spiritual and
temporal affairs will be open to him; no heretic or innovator will
be able to turn him from that path. His judgment will be strengthened and he will increase in justice and equity; vanity and heresy
will vanish from his kingdom and great works will spring from his
hands. The roots of wickedness, corruption and discord will be
cut out in the time of his empire. The hand of the righteous shall
become strong and the wicked shall be no more. In this world he
shall have fame, and in the next world he shall find salvation, high
degree and inestimable reward. In his age men will more than ever
delight in gaining knowledge.

2 ['Abd-Allah] ibn 'Umar (may Allah be pleased with him)[1]
says that The Prophet (peace be upon him) said, 'The righteous
shall dwell in paradise in palaces [full] of the light of their justice
towards their underlings.'

3 The most important thing which a king needs is sound faith,
because kingship and religion are like two brothers; whenever
disturbance breaks out in the country religion suffers too; heretics
and evil-doers appear; and whenever religious affairs are in disorder, there is confusion in the country; evil-doers gain power and
render the king impotent and despondent; heresy grows rife and
rebels make themselves felt.

4 Sufyan Thauri[2] says, 'The best of rulers is he who keeps
company with men of learning, and the worst of learned men is he
who seeks the society of the king.'

5 Ardashir says, 'Any ruler who has not the power to check his courtiers must know that he will never be able to control his commoners and peasants.' There is a passage in the Qur'an [26. 214] to this effect, 'And warn thy relatives of near kin.'

6 The Commander of the Faithful 'Umar (may Allah be pleased with him) says, 'There is nothing more detrimental to the country and more ruinous to the peasantry than difficulty of access to the king: conversely there is nothing more profitable to the people than ease of access to the king – or more impressive, especially to officers and tax-collectors, for when they know that the king is accessible they will not dare to practise oppression and extortion on the peasants.'

7 Luqman The Wise said, 'Man has no better friend in this world than knowledge, and knowledge is better than wealth, because you must take care of wealth but knowledge takes care of you.'

8 Hasan of Basra[3] (Allah's mercy upon him) says, 'The wise man is not he who knows more Arabic and is more competent in its grammar and vocabulary; the wise man is he who knows what he ought to know. If he knows languages in addition that is well. If anyone knows the precepts of religious law and meanings of the Qur'an in Turkish or Persian or Greek, and knows no Arabic whatever, he is still a learned man. If he knows Arabic as well, that is all to the good; for God (be He exalted) sent down the Qur'an in the Arabic tongue and Muhammad The Elect (the prayers of Allah and His peace be upon him) spoke in Arabic.'

9 But when a king possesses divine grace[4] and sovereignty, and knowledge withal is wedded to these, he finds happiness in both worlds, because everything he does is informed with knowledge and he does not allow himself to be ignorant. Consider how great is the fame of kings who were wise, and what great works they did; names such as these will be blessed until the resurrection – Afridun, Alexander, Ardashir, Nushirvan The Just, The Commander of the Faithful 'Umar (may Allah be pleased with him), 'Umar ibn 'Abd al-'Aziz (may Allah illumine his resting place), Harun, al-Ma'mun, al-Mu'tasim, Isma'il ibn Ahmad the Samanid, and Sultan Mahmud (Allah's mercy be upon them all). The deeds and ways of them all are well known for they are recorded in histories and other books; men never cease reading about them and singing their praises and blessings.

The story of 'Umar ibn 'Abd al-'Aziz and the famine

10 They say that in the days of 'Umar ibn 'Abd al-'Aziz (Allah's mercy be upon him) there was a famine and the people were in distress. A party of Arabs approached him and complained saying, 'O Commander of the Faithful, we have consumed our own flesh and blood in the famine (that is, we have become thin), and our cheeks have turned yellow because we have not enough to eat. We need what is in your treasury; and as for that treasure, it belongs either to you or to God or to the servants of God. If it belongs to God's servants it is ours; if it belongs to God, He has no need of it; if it is yours, then [as the Qur'an 12. 88 says] "be charitable unto us, for Allah will requite the charitable" (the interpretation is . . .); and if it is ours let us have it that we may escape from these straits, for the skin is withered on our bodies.' 'Umar ibn 'Abd al-'Aziz was moved to sympathy for them, and tears came into his eyes; he said, 'I will do as you have said', and in the same hour he gave orders for their requests to be attended to and their wants to be supplied. When they were about to get up and go, 'Umar ibn 'Abd al-'Aziz (Allah's mercy be upon him) said, 'O men where are you going? As you presented your case and that of the rest of God's servants to me, so do you present my case to God' (meaning: remember me in your prayers). Then those Arab tribesmen lifted their eyes to heaven and said, 'O Lord, by Thy glory [we pray] that Thou wilt do unto 'Umar ibn 'Abd al-'Aziz as he did unto Thy servants.'

11 When they had done praying, immediately a cloud came up and it began to rain heavily; a hailstone fell upon the bricks of 'Umar's palace; it broke in two and a piece of paper fell from inside it. They looked at it and there was written upon it [in Arabic], 'This is a grace from Allah The Mighty to 'Umar ibn 'Abd al-'Aziz [exempting him] from the fire.' (The Persian translation . . .)

12 There are many stories on this subject; but what has been related in this chapter will suffice.

Chapter IX

Concerning overlords and their emoluments

1 Persons who are completely reliable are to be made overlords with the task of keeping themselves informed of all that goes on at the court and making reports as called for and whenever necessary. They will on their own responsibility send lieutenants, who must be upright and honest, to every district and city to supervise the collection of taxes and revenue, and to get to know every event, great or small. Their monthly salaries are not to be a burden upon the peasants and a fresh source of distress, but their requirements must be met from the treasury so that they will have no excuse for corruption and bribery. If they do their work honestly the benefit of them will ultimately prove to be ten or a hundred times what it costs to keep them.

Chapter X

Concerning intelligence agents and reporters and [their importance in] administering the affairs of the country

1 It is the king's duty to enquire into the condition of his peasantry and army, both far and near, and to know everything that goes on. If he does not do this he is at fault and people will charge him with negligence, laziness and tyranny, saying, 'Either the king knows about the oppression and extortion going on in the country, or he does not know. If he knows and does nothing to prevent it and remedy it, that is because he is an oppressor like the rest and acquiesces in their oppression; and if he knows not he is very negligent and ignorant.' Neither of these imputations is

desirable.[1] Inevitably therefore he must have postmasters; and in every age in the time of ignorance and of Islam, kings have had postmasters, through whom they have learnt everthing that goes on, good and bad. For instance if anybody wrongly took so much as a chicken or a bag of straw from another – and that five hundred farsangs away – the king would know about it and have the offender punished, so that others knew that the king was vigilant and had put informers everywhere. The activities of oppressors were checked so that men enjoyed security and justice for the pursuit of trade and cultivation. But this is a delicate business involving some unpleasantness; it must be entrusted to the hands and tongues and pens of men who are completely above suspicion and without self-interest, for the weal or woe of the country depends on them. They must be directly responsible to the king and not to anyone else; and they must receive their monthly salaries regularly from the treasury so that they may do their work without any worries, and nobody but the king should know what they report. In this way the king will know of every event that takes place and will be able to give his orders as appropriate, meting out unexpected reward, punishment or commendation to the persons concerned. When a king is like this, men are always eager to be obedient, fearing the king's displeasure, and nobody can possibly have the audacity to disobey the king or plot any mischief. Thus the employment of intelligence agents and reporters contributes to the justice, vigilance and prudence of the king, and to the prosperity of the country.

The story of the robbers of Kuch Baluch

2 At the time of Sultan Mahmud's conquest of 'Iraq it happened that at Dair Gachin[2] robbers stole the chattels of a woman who was travelling by caravan. These robbers came from Kuch Baluch,[3] a district which joins the province of Kirman. The woman went before Sultan Mahmud to complain, saying, 'Robbers stole my chattels at Dair Gachin. Get back my things from them, or else give me compensation for them.' Mahmud said, 'And where might Dair Gachin be?' The woman said, 'Take no more territory than what you can know the extent of, and be responsible for, and look after properly.' He said, 'You are right; but do you know of what kind these robbers were and whence

they came?' She said, 'They were of the Kuch Baluch and had come from the neighbourhood of Kirman.' He said, 'That place is far distant and outside my territory; I cannot do anything to them.' The woman said, 'What sort of administrator of the world are you who cannot administer your own possessions? And what kind of a shepherd are you if you cannot protect the sheep from the wolves? Look at me in my weakness and loneliness and you with all your army and power.' Tears came into Mahmud's eyes and he said, 'You are right; I will give you compensation for your chattels and deal with these people as best I can.'

3 Then he had some money given to the woman out of the treasury, and he wrote a letter to Abu 'Ali Ilyas,[4] amir of Kirman and Tiz,[5] saying, 'The purpose of my coming to 'Iraq was not conquest, for I was at that time fully engaged in war in Hindustan; but I came because of frequent letters which I received from the Muslims complaining that the Dailamites had spread corruption, oppression and heresy in 'Iraq; that they had set up ambushes on the highways and were pouncing on every beautiful woman or boy that came along and taking them inside and committing immoral acts; they were painting and dyeing with henna the arms and legs of young boys, keeping them as long as they liked and releasing them at their pleasure; they were openly cursing The Companions of The Prophet (upon him be peace) and were calling 'Ayisha The Honest, who is Mother of Believers (may Allah be pleased with her), an adulteress; the assignees were doing whatever they wished and were taking tribute from the peasants two or three times a year; their king, called Majd ad-Daula,[6] had nine wives, all in wedlock, and was pleased to be styled King of Kings; moreover the peasants were spreading atheistic and Batini doctrines; they were abusing God and The Prophet; they were denying The Creator in public, and repudiating prayer, fasting, pilgrimage and alms; the assignees were unable to restrain them from uttering these blasphemies, nor could they say anything about the impiety, tyranny and wickedness of the assignees; both parties were equally steeped in iniquity.

4 'When I came to know about this state of affairs in 'Iraq, I decided to attend to the matter and give it priority over the war in Hindustan. I detailed Turkish forces, who were all pure Muslims of the Hanafi rite, to oppose the Dailamites and the atheists and the Batinis, and they were all exterminated; some fell by the sword,

some were taken into bondage, and others were driven into exile. I gave all the fiscal and governmental posts to civil servants and administrators from Khurasan, who were of the Hanafi or Shafi'i schools; both these groups are orthodox like the Turks, and hostile to the Rafidis,[7] Batinis and other rebels. I did not permit a single 'Iraqi secretary to put pen to paper, because I knew that most of the scribes of 'Iraq belonged to heretical sects and would wreck Turkish interests. Thus in a short time by this process I cleared the country of heretics by the grace of Allah (to Him be power and glory); for God (be He exalted) created me and appointed me over the heads of His creatures for this purpose, that I should remove unbelievers from the face of the earth, protect the people of righteousness, and bring prosperity to the world through generosity and liberality.

5 'Meanwhile I have been informed that a party of unbelievers from Kuch Baluch have committed highway robbery at Dair Gachin, and carried off some property. I wish you to apprehend them immediately and recover the property; then you may hang them all or send them manacled to the city of Rayy along with the stolen goods; that will teach them not to have the audacity to come from Kirman into my province for highway robbery. Failing this, Kirman is not as far as Somnat; I will send my armies and wreak vengeance upon Kirman.'

6 When the messenger delivered this letter to Abu 'Ali Ilyas he was very much afraid; he entertained the messenger well and sent back some gifts in deference to Mahmud – consisting of jewels of various kinds, choice objects out of the sea and purses of gold and silver – saying, 'I am your obedient servant; but perhaps the king is not acquainted with the affairs of his servant and the province of Kirman; otherwise [he would know that] his servant has never acquiesced in any disorder, and that the men of Kirman are all Sunnis and righteous men who mind their own business; the mountains of Kuch Baluch are cut off from Kirman; they are inaccessible and the roads are difficult; I am exasperated by these people as most of them are robbers and criminals, and they render two hundred farsangs of road unsafe by their activities; moreover they are very numerous and I cannot cope with them. The Sultan of the World is more powerful; in all the world no one but he can deal with them; my loins are girt for any service he may require of me.'

7 When Mahmud received this reply from Abu 'Ali, he knew that what he said was true. He sent the messenger back again, with a robe of honour and told him to say to Abu 'Ali, 'Concentrate the troops of Kirman and make a circuit of the province; at the beginning of such-and-such month come to the frontier which faces towards Kuch Baluch and wait there. When a messenger comes from me with a certain sign, you should march immediately and attack the province of Kuch Baluch; kill every young man of them that you can find and give no quarter; seize the possessions of their women and old men and send them here so that I may distribute them among those who claim to have lost their property; make a firm agreement and settlement with them and then come back.'

8 Having sent the messenger to Abu 'Ali he made a proclamation that all merchants bound for Tiz and the Kirman road should settle their affairs and pack their loads; he would provide them with an escort and guarantee that if the robbers of Kuch Baluch carried off anyone's goods he would give compensation from the treasury.

9 When this news spread abroad an enormous number of merchants from surrounding parts gathered in the city of Rayy. Then at a definite time Mahmud despatched them with an amir and a hundred and fifty horsemen as escort, and reassured them by saying, 'Do not be anxious, for I am sending some troops in your tracks.' As he dismissed the escort, he summoned the amir in charge by himself and gave him a phial of deadly poison saying, 'When you reach Isfahan stay there, so that the merchants of that place may settle their affairs and travel in your company; during your stay you should buy ten ass-loads of Isfahan apples of the best quality and load them upon ten camels; when you depart you should disperse these among the merchants' camels and keep going until you arrive at the stage after which, on the following day, you will reach the robbers; that night bring the loads of apples into your tent and strew them on the ground; plunge a packing-needle into each apple, pare down a stick thicker than a needle, dip it into the poison and put it into the hole in the apple; carry on until all the apples are poisoned; then arrange them back in the baskets with their cotton packing; next day disperse these camels among the others and set out. When the robbers come out and attack the caravan, do not attempt to fight with them as they

will be many and you few; retreat immediately taking with you any men that have arms, both mounted and on foot; go about half a farsang away and wait for a good hour; then set upon the robbers and I doubt not but that most of them will have perished from eating the apples; draw your swords and kill the remainder; pursue any that flee and kill as many as you can. Having finished with them, send ten good riders with two horses apiece to Abu 'Ali Ilyas, taking my ring; inform him what you have done to the robbers of Kuch Baluch and instruct him to attack the province with his own troops in accordance with orders which he has already received, for by then it will be empty of brigands and trouble makers; take the caravan into the city of Kirman, and then join up with Abu 'Ali if you can.'

10 The amir said, 'I will do this, and my heart testifies that by Your Majesty's help the action will be successful, and that road will remain open to Muslim travellers until the resurrection'; and he left Mahmud's presence. He moved off with the caravan and brought it to Isfahan; there he got ten camel-loads of apples and set out for Kirman. The robbers had sent out spies to Isfahan and found out that the caravan was coming with so many thousand animals, bearing such a quantity of luxuries and valuables that God alone knew how much there was; such a caravan had not been seen before in a thousand years and they had an escort of a hundred and fifty Turkish horsemen. The robbers were delighted; they had informed and summoned all the youths and brigands from the whole of Kuch Baluch; four thousand fully armed men had gathered on the roadside, waiting for the caravan.

11 When the amir arrived with the caravan at a certain stage, the residents of the place said, 'So many thousand robbers have blocked your road and have been waiting for you for a number of days.' The amir asked how many farsangs it was from there to the place where they were. They said it was five farsangs. When the people in the caravan heard this they were very anxious. They dismounted there. In the afternoon the amir called all the caravan leaders and men in charge of the freight and reassured them, saying, 'Tell me, which is better, life or wealth?' They all said, 'Life.' He said, 'You are rich men; we are ready to risk our lives for your sakes but we are not worried; so why do you worry about riches which can be replaced? After all, Mahmud has sent us here for a purpose; he is not angry with any of us that he should deliver us to

destruction; his plan is to get back from these robbers some property which they stole at Dair Gachin belonging to an old woman; do you think then that he would let them have yours? Be of good cheer! Mahmud is not neglecting you; in fact he told me what he is doing; tomorrow when the sun comes up help will reach us from him, and all will be well, if Allah wills; however, you must do everything that I tell you for your welfare lies in that.'

12 When the people heard these words they were pleased and encouraged; they said, 'We will do whatever you tell us.' He said, 'All those of you who have weapons and can fight, let them come to me.' They came and he counted them; with his own troops they came to three hundred and seventy men, both mounted and on foot. He addressed them, 'Tonight we march; those of you who are mounted will be with me at the front of the caravan, and those on foot will be at the rear, for it is the custom of these robbers only to take goods and not to kill anyone except a man who resists them and is killed fighting. Tomorrow by the time the sun reaches the height of two arrows,[8] we shall reach them; when they attack the caravan, I shall take to my heels in flight; when you see me turn my back, you all do the same, and I will make some show of fighting until you gain a distance of about a farsang; then I will gallop away and join you; after waiting for an hour we will return all together and fall upon the robbers, whereupon you will behold marvellous things; for thus I have been instructed and furthermore I know something about this which you do not; tomorrow you will see for yourselves; you will come to realize the greatness of Mahmud and understand that what I say is true.' They all undertook to obey and departed.

13 When night came on, the amir undid the loads of apples, poisoned them all and put them back in their baskets; he appointed five of his own men to look after these ten camel-loads of apples and said, 'When we run away and the robbers fall upon the caravan and begin to break open the merchandise, cut the fastenings of the loads of apples, take off the tops of the baskets and turn them upside down; then get yourselves gone.'

14 At midnight he ordered them to move off and they travelled in the same formation until it was day and the sun was up. The robbers rose up on three sides and ran towards the caravan with drawn swords. The amir made two or three counter-attacks and shot a few arrows; then he turned to flight. When the men on foot

saw the robbers they fled; the amir picked them up about half a farsang away and kept them there. When the robbers saw that the escort were few and that they and the travellers in the caravan had fled, they were delighted and began breaking open the loads at their ease and getting busy with the merchandise. When they came to the apples they fell to and plundered the lot, eating them with relish; those who failed to get any were given some by the others and there were hardly any who ate no apples at all. After an hour they were falling down one by one and dying.

15 Two hours after daybreak the amir went alone to the top of a hill and looked down upon the caravan and the robbers; he saw men lying all over the plain as if they were asleep; he ran down the hill in joy and said, 'Congratulations to you all! Help has come from Sultan Mahmud, the robbers have been killed and scarcely one is left alive. Come on, my hearties, make haste; let us destroy the remnant!' He rode with his men towards the caravan and those on foot ran behind him. When they reached the caravan they saw the plain strewn with corpses, shields, swords, clubs, bows and arrows; a few of them who were still alive fled when they saw the soldiers. The amir rode after them and the men on foot also joined in the chase; they pursued them for two farsangs and did not turn back until they had killed them all; not a soul remained alive to carry the news of the event back to their own country. The amir ordered all their weapons to be collected and they amounted to several ass-loads. Then he took the caravan on to the next stopping place; nobody lost the slightest thing and they could not contain themselves for joy. It was twelve farsangs from there to the place where Abu 'Ali Ilyas was. The amir sent two pages to him post-haste with Mahmud's ring and informed him what had happened.

16 When Abu 'Ali received the ring he immediately attacked the province of Kuch Baluch with troops who were ready and rested. The amir joined forces with him and together they killed more than ten thousand of the inhabitants, seized several thousand dinars and collected a vast amount of goods, luxuries, arms and animals. Abu 'Ali sent all this booty with the amir to Mahmud. Mahmud issued a proclamation saying, 'Since I came to 'Iraq whoever has had anything stolen by the robbers of Kuch Baluch, let them come and take compensation from me.' Those who had claims came forward and went back satisfied. And for fifty

years after that there was no report of any mischief from the Kuchis.

17 Thereafter Mahmud appointed reporters and intelligence agents in every place, so that if anyone in Ghaznain wrongfully took a chicken from another or struck another man with his fist, Mahmud knew about it at Rayy and ordered amends to be made. From ancient times onwards kings have preserved this system, except for the house of Saljuq who have shown no interest in the matter.[9]

18 Abu 'l-Fadl Sigzi[10] once asked The Martyr Sultan Alp Arslan (may Allah illumine his proof) why he had no intelligence agents. He answered, 'Do you want me to cast my kingdom to the winds and alienate all my supporters?' He said, 'Why so?' The Sultan said, 'If I institute intelligence agents, my especial favour-ites, trusting in their special position as favourites, will pay no attention to them nor offer them bribes; while my opponents and enemies will curry favour with them and give them money. Thus obviously the intelligence agents will always bring to our ears bad reports about our favourites and good reports about our enemies. Now, reports good and bad are like arrows: if you shoot enough of them, at least one will hit the target. In this way we shall become more displeased with our favourites every day and even-tually banish them, while admitting our enemies further into our intimacy. In a short time you will find that all our favourites are estranged and their places taken by our enemies. By that time irreparable harm will have been done.'

19 All the same it is better that there should be intelligencers, because having intelligencers is one of the rules of state-craft; and when they can be relied upon sufficiently to perform the function we have described, there is no anxiety.

Chapter XI

On honouring the sublime commands and edicts which are issued from the court

1 Letters are constantly being written from the court; and anything that becomes too common commands less respect. Unless there is something important, letters should not be sent from The Lofty Throne. When a letter is despatched it should carry such weight that the recipient will not dare to put it out of his hand until he has complied with the order; and if it is known that anyone has not regarded such an order with due respect or has neglected to present himself with instant obedience, that person must be severely punished, even if he is one of the king's intimates. The difference between the king and other men, such as assignees, is that his writ runs.

The story of Sultan Mahmud and the disobedient tax-collector

2 It is related that a woman having a grievance went from Nishapur to Ghaznain. She approached Sultan Mahmud and made her complaint, saying, 'The tax-collector of Nishapur has seized a farm of mine and occupied it.' A letter was sent telling him to give back the farm. As it happened the tax-collector possessed the title-deeds to that farm; he said, 'The farm is mine, and I have the deeds; I can explain the situation at the court.' The woman went to Ghaznain a second time and stated her grievance. A page was sent to bring the tax-collector from Nishapur to Ghaznain and he was given a thousand strokes at the palace gate. Before they beat him, the tax-collector, hoping for an intercessor, tried to buy off the thousand strokes with 20,000 dinars of Nishapur; but they refused to sell; they rebuked him saying, 'Even if the farm was rightfully yours, why did you not obey the order first and afterwards explain your case? We would then have ordered what was appropriate.'

3 The purpose of this was so that when others heard such cases, no one would dare to disobey or violate the king's command.

4 Whatever concerns the king and falls to him to do or to order, such as castigation, decapitation, mutilation, castration or any other kind of punishment—if anyone does such a thing without the king's permission or command, even[1] to his own servant or slave, the king must not agree to it but have the man punished, so that others may take warning and know their places.

A story about King Parviz and Bahram Chubin

5 They say that King Parviz treated Bahram Chubin very well in the beginning; he was never without him for a moment. Whether in his cups, in the chase or in the seclusion of his chamber he never dismissed him from his presence. Now Bahram Chubin was un-equalled as a horseman and unrivalled in single combat. One day they brought from the fiscal districts of Herat and Sarakhs three hundred red-haired camels for King Parviz, each carrying an ass-load of necessaries and various commodities. He ordered them to take the whole lot as it was to Bahram's palace for the supply of his household and kitchen.

6 The next day Parviz received information that that night Bahram Chubin had struck down his page and beaten him twenty strokes. King Parviz was angry and summoned Bahram. When he came he ordered five hundred swords to be brought from the armoury, and said, 'O Bahram, pick out the best of these swords.' Bahram selected a certain number. Then the king said, 'Now find the choicest of these you have chosen.' Bahram picked out ten swords. King Parviz said, 'Out of these ten swords choose two.' He did so. Then he said, 'Now tell them to put these two swords into one scabbard.' Bahram said, 'O king, two swords will not go into one scabbard.' Parviz said, 'And how will two commanders be contained in one city?' Bahram immediately understood what he meant and knew that he had done wrong; he kissed the ground and asked for pardon. King Parviz said, 'Were it not that you have served me well and I do not wish to cast down one whom I have myself raised up, I would not have forgiven you. God (to Him be power and glory) has appointed us judge over the earth, not you. Whoever has a dispute let him bring the case to us so that we may give the necessary commands with due fairness. After this if one of your underlings or slaves commits any crime, you will first inform us and we will order such punishment as may be

73

suitable, so that nobody suffers unjustly. We pardon you this once.'

Such was the rebuke which was administered to Bahram Chubin who was his general and his favourite.

Chapter XII

On sending pages from the court upon important business

1 Pages[1] are frequently sent out from the court, some at the king's behest, mostly not. They are apt to cause trouble to the people and extort money from them. [Supposing there is] a case involving a sum of two hundred dinars, a page goes out and takes five hundred as a perquisite; this causes extreme embarrassment and poverty to the people. Pages should not be sent unless there is an urgent matter, and if they are sent it should be only at The Sublime Command; and they must be given to understand the exact amount due, and they are not to take any more than this by way of perquisite. Then everything will be in order.

Chapter XIII

On sending spies and using them for the good of the country and the people

1 Spies must constantly go out to the limits of the kingdom in the guise of merchants, travellers, sufis, pedlars, and mendicants, and

bring back reports of everything they hear, so that no matters of any kind remain concealed, and if anything [untoward] happens it can in due course be remedied. In the past it has often happened that governors, assignees, officers and army-commanders have planned rebellion and resistance, and plotted mischief against the king; but spies forestalled them and informed the king, who was thus enabled to set out immediately with all speed and, coming upon them unawares, to strike them down and frustrate their plans; and if any foreign king or army was preparing to attack the country, the spies informed the king, and he took action and repelled them. Likewise they brought news, whether good or bad, about the condition of the peasants, and the king gave the matter his attention, as did 'Adud ad-Daula on one occasion.

The story of 'Adud ad-Daula and the unjust judge

2 None of the Dailamite kings was more vigilant, clever and far-sighted than 'Adud ad-Daula; he was a great builder and had lofty aspirations and strong authority. One day a reporter wrote to him as follows: On my way to perform the task for which Your Majesty sent me, I had passed through the city gate and gone about two hundred paces, when I saw a youth standing by the roadside with pale cheeks and wounds on his face and neck. He saw me and greeted me; I answered him and said, 'Why are you standing there?' He said, 'I am looking for a companion with whom I may travel to a city where the king is righteous and the judge is just.' I said, 'Do you know what you are saying? Do you want a more righteous king than 'Adud ad-Daula, or a more learned judge than the qadi of the city?' He said, 'If the king were righteous and awake to affairs, the judge would be honest: since the judge is not honest the king must be negligent.' I said, 'What negligence have you seen on the part of the king, or dishonesty on the part of the judge?' He said, 'My story was a long one, but now that I have left this city it is cut short.' I said, 'You must certainly tell me it.' He said, 'Come then; let us shorten our road with the tale.'

3 We set off together and he began, 'Know that I am the son of such-and-such a merchant, and my father's house is in such-and-such district of this city; everyone knows what sort of man my father was and how much money and wealth he had. When he died

I spent several years indulging in drinking and debauchery; then I fell seriously ill and gave up hope of recovery. During that illness I vowed to God that if I got better I would go on pilgrimage and holy war; God sent me healing and I got up from my bed safe and sound.

4 'When I had gained strength I decided to go on the pilgrimage, and later to go to the war. I freed all the slave girls and pages which I had, gave them gold and houses and farms, and betrothed them to one another. Then I sold the remainder of my property, estates and farms, realizing 50,000 dinars in cash. I reflected that the two journeys I had before me were full of danger, and that it would be unwise to take all this gold with me. So I resolved to take 30,000 dinars and leave 20,000. I went and bought two copper ewers and put 10,000 dinars in each one. I wondered with whom I should deposit them. Of all the people in the city I chose the chief judge; I said to myself, "He is a learned man and a judge; and the king relies upon him and entrusts the lives and property of Muslims to him; he would never cheat me." I went and broached the matter to him. He accepted, and I was glad. I got up in the night, took the two ewers of gold to his house and deposited them with him. Then I set off upon the road and performed the Muslim pilgrimage. From Mecca and Medina I journeyed towards the land of Rum. I joined up with the warriors and spent several years in holy war; in one battle I was caught in the midst of the infidels and was wounded in several places on face, neck, arm and thigh; I was taken prisoner by the Rumis and remained four years in bondage, until at length the Caesar of Rum fell ill and he set all prisoners free.[1] On gaining my freedom I once more fell in with the bowmen[2] and served with them long enough to save up my travelling expenses. All the time I was fortified by the knowledge that I had 20,000 dinars deposited with the judge in Baghdad. In expectation of that I set out on the return journey.

5 'Ten years later I reached Baghdad, destitute; my clothes were worn out and my body was weak from all the hardships and pains I had suffered. I went to the judge, greeted him and sat before him; two days I called on him like this and he did not speak a word to me. On the third day I called again and sat longer; when the room cleared I approached him and gently said to him, "I am so-and-so, son of so-and-so; I have returned from the pilgrimage and holy war; I have borne many hardships and everything that I took

with me has gone. I am just as you see me and I have not a single grain left. So I am in need of those two ewers of gold which I deposited with you against such a day." The judge gave not the slightest answer; he did not even go as far as to say, "What on earth are you talking about?" He simply got up and went into his room. Disappointed I went away, and in my wretched and naked state I was too ashamed to go to my own house or to any of my relations or friends. By night I used to sleep in a mosque, and in the daytime I hid in a corner. To cut my story short, I spoke to the chief judge several times in these terms, but he never answered me. On the seventh day I spoke more strongly. He said to me, "You are suffering from the melancholy; your brain has been desiccated by the dust and toil of travel and your speech is delirious. I do not recognize you nor do I know what you are talking about. As for the man whose name you mention, he was a handsome youth, prosperous and well dressed." I said, "O judge, I am that person but I have become pale and thin from hardship, and my face is ugly with wounds." He said, "Be off! don't give me a headache! go away in peace." I said, "O judge, beware! fear God! for after this world there is another world, and every action has its reward or punishment." He said, "Away with you! don't annoy me!" I said, "Out of my 20,000 dinars 2,000 or 5,000 are yours." He made no reply. I said, "O judge, I will give you one of the ewers for yourself, freely and willingly, but please give me back the other one, for I am in sore distress. Furthermore I am ready to sign a disclaimer, witnessed by honourable persons, to say that I have no claim upon you." The judge said, "You are mentally deranged, verging on the point where I shall have to certify you as insane and send you to a lunatic asylum, where you will be put in fetters and never let out for the rest of your life." At this I was afraid, realizing that he intended to keep all my gold and that whatever order he issued would be carried out. I got up quietly and left him, repeating to myself the proverb, "If meat stinks you put salt on it: but what are you to do if the salt is stinking?" All justice is administered by means of the judge; if the judge is unjust who is to bring him to justice? If 'Adud ad-Daula were a righteous ruler 20,000 gold dinars of mine would not be in the hands of the judge, nor would I be two days starving as I am, nor would I have abandoned my wealth, my property and my city.'

6 When the reporter heard the man's tale of his experiences and

circumstances, he was sorry for him and said, 'My noble friend, all hopes follow after hopelessness; trust in God, for it is God (to Him be power and glory) who sets right the affairs of His servants.' Then he said to him, 'I have a friend in this village, a generous and hospitable man, and I am going to visit him. I am very happy to have you with me, so please accompany me; we will stay with my friend today and tonight, and see what happens tomorrow.' So he took him to the friend's house; they had something to eat, then the reporter went into a room and wrote an account of the man's case and gave it to a villager, saying, 'Go to the gate of 'Adud ad-Daula's palace, call such-and-such servant and give him this letter; tell him that so-and-so has sent it and that he should deliver it immediately to 'Adud ad-Daula and bring back an answer.' The messenger went and gave the letter to the servant; the servant straightaway delivered it to 'Adud ad-Daula.

7 When 'Adud ad-Daula read the letter, he bit his fingers [in vexation]; he sent someone at once to the reporter with the command that he should bring the man to him at the hour of bedtime prayer. The reporter said to the man, 'Come, we must go to the city; 'Adud ad-Daula is calling for both of us; this messenger has come from him.' The man said, 'Is that a good thing?' He said, 'It is sure to be a good thing; maybe the walls heard what you were telling me on the road and brought it to the hearing of 'Adud ad-Daula. I am hopeful that you will soon get what you want, and find release from your troubles.' He set out and took the man to 'Adud ad-Daula. The king received him in private and asked him about his troubles. He told him every thing from first to last. 'Adud ad-Daula felt pity for him; he said, 'Do not worry; this is now my responsibility, not yours. The judge is one of my officers, so it is my duty to deal with the matter, for God has given me the guardianship of this country to the end that I should not allow anyone to suffer trouble or loss, least of all from the judge. I have made him responsible for the lives and property of Muslims; I give him a monthly salary so that he should administer the affairs of the people with rectitude, acting in accordance with the religious law without fear or favour and not taking bribes. If this is the conduct of a venerable and learned man in my own capital, imagine what perfidy may be expected of younger, more reckless judges in other places. In the beginning this judge was a humble man with a large family, and the monthly

payment which he receives consists of his salary and nothing more; today he owns such-and-such amount of landed property in the city of Baghdad; while there is no limit to the sumptuous furnishings which he has. All this wealth could not have been saved from that salary; so it is clear that he has gathered it from the Muslim people.' Then he turned to the man and said, 'I shall not eat happily nor sleep well until I restore you to your rights. Go, draw expenses from the treasury and proceed to Isfahan; remain there with a certain person and I will write and ask him to look after you well until I send for you again.' He then gave him two hundred gold dinars and five suits of clothes, and sent him to Isfahan that very night. The whole night 'Adud ad-Daula wondered how he might contrive to extract this money from the judge. He said to himself, 'If I were to exercise my sovereign power to arrest the judge summarily and torment him, he would never confess and expose his own villainy; and then the money would be lost; moreover people would begin to wag their tongues and say that 'Adud ad-Daula had seized a venerable and learned man like the judge and was tormenting him on some cunning pretext; and the ill repute would spread to the farthest borders of the kingdom. I must devise some method of exposing the judge's villainy so that this man will get back his money.'

8 A month or two passed after this and the judge saw no more sign of the owner of the gold. He said to himself, 'I have won 20,000 dinars; but I will wait for another year; maybe I shall hear news of his death, for judging from his condition when I last saw him, I am sure he will soon be dead.'

9 Two months later 'Adud ad-Daula sent someone in the hottest part of the day and called the judge; he gave him a private audience and said, 'O judge, do you know why I have troubled you to come here?' He said, 'The king knows best.' The king said, 'Know that I have become anxious about the future and because of my melancholy meditations sleep is scared away from my eyes; I have lost faith in the world and my kingdom, and I cannot depend upon further extension of life. There are two alternatives: either some upstart will arise from obscurity and snatch the kingdom from our hands as we snatched it from another – and consider what labours we endured before we could sit securely on this throne – or else The Truth's Command [i.e. death] will overtake us and suddenly cut us off, our desires

unattained, from throne and kingdom. Nobody can avoid death; and if during this span of life which is allotted to us, we are good and do good to God's creatures, people will speak well of us as long as the world exists and men are living, and on resurrection day we shall attain salvation and go to paradise; but if we are bad, and do ill to God's servants, people will speak ill of us until the end of time, and whenever they mention us they will curse and swear; at the resurrection we shall be entangled and hell will be our place. Therefore as far as possible we strive after righteousness, we judge the people fairly and we practise charity. However, the reason for this conversation with you is that in the palace I have a group of wives and children; now the matter of the boys is easy because they take wing like birds and can go from clime to clime; but the lot of the veiled ones is worse for they are weak and helpless; so I am taking thought in their regard now while I can, lest tomorrow death should befall me or the dynasty should change, and then if I wanted to do something for them I could not. Now I can think of nobody in all the kingdom more chaste, more God-fearing, more moderate and honest than you; therefore I wish to hand over a sum of 2,000,000 dinars in gold currency and jewels to you for safe keeping, so that nobody knows but you and I and God. Then tomorrow if something were to happen to me and my womenfolk were reduced to poverty and privation you would call them secretly, divide the money amongst them and espouse them to suitable husbands, lest they should suffer the disgrace and distress of begging for their daily sustenance. To this end I propose that you should select a room in the inner apartments of your house and there construct a cellar of baked brick and make it secure; you should inform me when it is ready and one night I will arrange for twenty murderers who are due for execution to be brought out of prison; they will carry this money to your house, place it in the cellar, block up the door, and come back; then I will have them all beheaded so that the matter remains hidden.' The judge said, 'I obey, I will do my utmost to perform this service.' Then the king whispered to a servant, telling him to go to the treasury, put 200 *maghribī* [western] dinars in a purse and bring it to him.

10 When the servant brought the gold 'Adud ad-Daula took it and laid it before the judge saying, 'Use these 200 dinars for making the cellar; if it is not enough, I will send this much again.'

The judge said, 'For Allah's sake, O king! If I use my own gold for this service, it is no matter at all.' 'Adud ad-Daula said, 'I cannot agree to your spending your own gold on my affairs; your gold is your lawful property and is not suitable for this purpose. If you strive to carry out the task entrusted to you, you will have performed all the service required of you.' The judge said, 'It is for the king to command'; he put the 200 dinars in his sleeve and took leave of the king, congratulating himself and thinking, 'Fortune has befriended me in my old age; my household is going to be full of gold and it will all be mine. If anything happens to the king, nobody will have a receipt or any other document and all the money will be left for me and my children. The owner of the two ewers was not able to get a tithe of his 20,000 dinars out of me, and he is alive; when the king is dead or killed, who will be able to take anything from me?' He went and busied himself in building the cellar; within a month he completed a very secure underground chamber. One night about the hour of bedtime prayer he arose and went to 'Adud ad-Daula's palace. 'Adud ad-Daula gave him a private audience and said, 'What brings you here at this hour?' He said, 'I wanted to inform Your Majesty that a cellar as you commanded has been finished.' 'Adud ad-Daula said, 'I am glad to hear it; I knew you were zealous in all things; praise be to Allah that my opinion of you was not mistaken; you have saved me a lot of trouble in this matter. I have been constantly worrying about that affair which I mentioned to you. Of the sum which I specified I have got together 1,500,000 dinars in gold and jewels, and I need 500,000 more; so I have set aside a quantity of robes, incense, ambergris, musk, camphor and other things and I am arranging for dealers to dispose of it bit by bit and bring me the money; in a week's time it will be complete; then I will bring it in one lot to your house. But tomorrow night I wish to come incognito to see the cellar – just to cast an eye over it and see how it has turned out; I do not want you to put yourself out at all as I shall return immediately.' He dismissed the judge and straight away sent a messenger to Isfahan to bring the owner of the gold. The next day he went to the judge's house in the middle of the night to see the cellar; he approved of it and said to the judge, 'You had better come and see me next Tuesday and have a look at what is ready.' He said, 'I will do so.' Having returned from the judge's house the king ordered his treasurer to put a hundred and forty ewers full of gold into one room and on top of these to place three flasks of pearls, a golden cup full of sapphires, a cup full of rubies and a cup full of turquoises.

11 Tuesday came and the treasurer had carried out this order and the owner of the two ewers arrived. 'Adud ad-Daula called the judge, took him by the hand and led him into the room where the valuables were laid out. The judge was amazed when he saw the ewers and jewels. 'Adud ad-Daula said, 'You can expect all this treasure to be brought during this week.' Then they came out of the room and the judge returned to his house in such a state of excitement that his heart was fluttering in his breast. The next day 'Adud ad-Daula said to the owner of the two ewers, 'I want you to go and see the judge straightaway and tell him that you have waited for some time and respected his authority, but you cannot forbear any longer; the whole city knows what wealth and substance you and your father had, and everyone can vouch for your claim; if he gives back your money, well and good, but if not, you will go straight to 'Adud ad-Daula to lodge a complaint against him, and you will bring such a disgrace upon his head as will serve as a warning to the whole world. See what answer he gives; if he gives the gold back, bring it to me as it is; if not, let me know what happens.'

12 The man went to the judge, sat with him and spoke in these terms. The judge thought, 'If this man plays a filthy trick on me and goes to 'Adud ad-Daula, it may arouse his suspicions about me and he may not send the treasure to my house. The best thing is to give him back his money; after all, a hundred and fifty ewers of gold with all those jewels are better than two ewers.' So he said to the young man, 'Wait a few moments; I have been looking for you everywhere.' After a time he got up and went into a room; he called the man in, embraced him and said, 'You are my friend and my friend's son; you are like a son to me. It was for precaution's sake that I said all that to you and I have been searching for you ever since. Praise be to Allah that I have been able to see you again and discharge my responsibility. Your gold is still there.' He went and brought the two ewers, and said, 'Is this your gold?' The young man said, 'Yes.' He said, 'Receive it now and take it wherever you wish.' The man went out and fetched two porters; he put the ewers on their backs and took them as they were to 'Adud ad-Daula's palace.

13 'Adud ad-Daula was holding audience and all the nobles of the state were present, when this young man came in with the two ewers, bowed and placed them in front of 'Adud ad-Daula. The king laughed and said, 'Praise be to Allah that you have regained your rightful property and the judge's treachery has been exposed; you little know what thoughts and schemes occupied me ere you recovered this gold.' The nobles asked to be enlightened. 'Adud ad-Daula told them what had happened to the youth and what measures he had taken to help him; they were all astonished. Then he ordered the great chamberlain to go and bring the judge of the city bareheaded before him, with his turban round his neck.

14 When the judge was brought in this fashion before 'Adud ad-Daula he saw the youth standing there with those two ewers; he said, 'Woe! I am ruined!' and he realized that all that 'Adud ad-Daula had said and done was aimed only at the recovery of those two ewers. 'Adud ad-Daula then bellowed forth at him, saying, 'You are an old man, a scholar and a judge, on the brink of the grave, and you dare to commit such treachery and cheat a man out of his deposit. What then are we to expect of other men? It is now clear that all the wealth which you possess has come from other Muslims' property and from bribes. As far as this world is concerned you will be punished by me; in the next world you will surely meet with due retribution. Considering that you are an old man and a scholar I am sparing your life, but all your wealth and property is for the treasury.' He confiscated all his wealth and estates and debarred him from ever holding office again: and he gave the two ewers to the noble youth and let him depart in peace.

The story of Sultan Mahmud and the unjust judge

15 Sultan Mahmud son of Sabuktigin had a similar experience. One day when Sultan Mahmud was travelling a man gave him a petition couched in the following terms: I entrusted to the judge of the city for safe keeping the sum of 2,000 dinars in a green brocade purse, closed and sealed; and I went on a journey. On the road to Hindustan robbers seized all that I had taken with me. On my return I went to the judge, recovered my deposit and took it home. When I opened the purse I found it full of copper coins. I went back to the judge and said, 'I deposited a purse full of gold with you; now I find it full of copper; how is that?' The judge

83

said, 'When you handed it over, did you shew me any gold or weigh it or count it out? You brought me a closed and sealed purse and took it back intact. When I gave it back I asked you if it was your purse and your seal; you said it was yours and accepted it. Now you have come with this tall story.' And he drove me away. For the sake of Allah, O sultan, come to my aid for I have not a single piece of bread to eat.

Sultan Mahmud took pity on him and said, 'Do not worry; I will do something about your gold. Go and bring the purse to me.' The man went and brought the purse to the sultan. However closely he examined the purse all over he saw no sign of it having been opened. He said to the man, 'Leave this purse with me, and take three maunds of bread and one of meat daily and ten dinars every month from my steward, so that you will not be without provision while I see about your gold.' Then one day about the time of the siesta Sultan Mahmud laid the purse in front of him and began to ponder how it could have happened. At last he came to the conclusion that it was possible for the purse to have been cut open, the gold taken out, and the purse mended again. He had a very fine coverlet of Tavvazi[3] gilded cloth spread over a mattress. In the middle of the night he got up and came down from the roof; he got out a knife, slit about half a yard of the coverlet and went back to bed. Early next morning he went out hunting for three days.

16 There was a certain palace cleaner who looked after this room. In the morning he went in there to sweep it, and he saw the coverlet, with about half a yard of it torn right in the middle; he was frightened and began to weep. In the cleaners' room one of them saw him weeping thus, and said, 'What is the matter?' He said, 'Someone has a grudge against me, and has gone into the sultan's summer-house, and torn about half a yard of his coverlet. If the sultan sees that he will kill me.' The other said, 'Has anyone else seen this besides you?' He said, 'No.' He said, 'Then don't worry; I know what to do and I will teach you. Firstly the sultan has gone hunting; secondly there is in this city a mender called Ahmad, a man of middle age, and his shop is in such-and-such quarter; he is a most expert mender and all the other menders in the city are his pupils. Take the coverlet to him, give whatever fee he asks, and he will do it so that not even the finest experts will know where it has been mended.' The cleaner straightaway

wrapped the coverlet in a cloth and took it to the shop of Ahmad the mender, and said, 'O teacher, how much would you want for repairing this so that no one will know it was ever torn?' He said, 'I want half a dinar.' The cleaner said, 'I will give you a whole dinar on condition that you apply all the skill at your command.' He said, 'Thank you. Don't worry.' The cleaner gave him a dinar and said, 'I need it quickly.' He said, 'Come and take it tomorrow afternoon.' Next day the cleaner went at the appointed time; the mender gave him back the coverlet; he looked at it and he could not tell at all where it had been torn; in good spirits he took it back to the palace and spread it over the mattress.

17 When the sultan returned from hunting he went into the summer-house at midday to sleep; he looked and saw the coverlet intact. He said, 'Call the cleaner.' The cleaner came. The sultan said, 'This coverlet was torn; who has repaired it?' He said, 'O master, it was never torn; they are telling a lie.' He said, 'O fool, have no fear, for it was I who tore it; I did it for a purpose. Tell me truly; who mended it? It is very well done.' The cleaner said, 'O master, such-and-such mender did it.' The sultan said, 'I want you to bring the man here immediately; don't tell him[4] the sultan summons him or he will be afraid; tell him they have a job for him in the palace; would he mind coming. When he arrives bring him to me.' The cleaner ran out and called the mender and brought him to the sultan's presence. When he saw the sultan sitting alone he was frightened; the sultan said to him, 'Have no fear, O teacher; tell me, did you repair this coverlet?' He said, 'Yes.' He said, 'You did it extremely skilfully.' He said, 'By the grace of Your Majesty it was done satisfactorily.' He said, 'Is there anyone in this city more expert than you?' He said, 'No.' He said, 'I have something to ask you; answer me the truth.' He said, 'To speak the truth to the king is always the best thing to do.' The sultan said, 'In the last six or seven years have you mended a green brocade purse at any gentleman's house?' He said, 'I have.' He said, 'Where?' He said, 'At the house of the judge of the city, and he gave me two dinars for my fee.' He said, 'If you saw that purse again would you recognize it?' He said, 'I would.' The sultan put his hand under the mattress, withdrew the purse and gave it to the mender, saying, 'Is this the purse?' He said, 'Yes.' He said, 'Shew me where you repaired it.' The mender laid his finger on the spot. The sultan was amazed at the skill with which it had been done,

and said, 'If the need arises could you give evidence against the judge?' He said, 'Why not?' The sultan sent a man at once to call the judge, and he ordered the owner of the purse to be brought in.

18 When the judge appeared he greeted the sultan and sat down in his place as usual. Mahmud turned to him and said, 'You are an old man and a scholar; I have given you jurisdiction over Muslim citizens and committed their lives and property to your judgment; I have trusted you [and preferred you] – are there not in cities and provinces two thousand men who are more learned than you but unemployed? – is it fair then, that you should deal falsely and disregard the duties of a trustee, by unjustly appropriating a Muslim's property and depriving him of it?' The judge said, 'O master, what words are these and who is saying them? Have I done such a thing?' He said, 'Thou hypocrite dog, these deeds are thine, and these words are mine': and he shewed him the purse and said, 'This is the purse which was deposited with you for safe keeping, and you cut it open, and took out the gold, and put copper in its place, and had the purse mended again; after that you told the owner that he had brought it closed with his own seal and taken it back intact; he had never shewn you any money or weighed it. Do you call this right conduct and honest dealing?' The judge said, 'I have never seen this purse before nor am I aware of the purport of Your Majesty's discourse.' Sultan Mahmud said, 'Bring in those two men.' A servant went and brought the owner of the purse and the mender. The sultan said, 'Thou liar, this is the owner of the gold, and that is the mender who mended this purse.' The judge was put to shame; his face turned pale and he began to tremble so much that he was unable to utter another word. The sultan said, 'Lay hands on him and hold him in custody; I require him to give back this man's gold immediately; if not, I shall order him to be executed; after that I shall say what is to be done.' They dragged the judge from the sultan's presence and put him in the guard-house saying, 'Now where is the gold?' He called his steward and gave him a sign; the steward went and brought 2,000 Nishapuri dinars, and gave them to the owner of the purse.

19 Next day Sultan Mahmud held court for the redress of wrongs and publicly declared the perfidy of the judge. Then at his command the judge was brought and suspended head downwards from a pinnacle of the palace. The nobles actively interceded for

him pleading his age and learning. At length he offered to redeem himself for 50,000 dinars; then they brought him down, and the ransom was exacted from him, but never again was he allowed to practise his profession.

20 There are many stories of this kind. These few have been related so that The Master of the World may know how zealous different kings have been in the pursuit of justice and equity; what care they have taken that the oppressed should receive their rights; and what measures they have adopted to remove evil-doers from the face of the earth. Sound judgment is a better thing for a king to have than a powerful army; praise be to Allah that The Master of the World possesses both these things. This chapter has dealt with spies; and this work must be in the hands of trustworthy people. Let such men continually be procured and sent to various parts for various tasks.

Chapter XIV

Concerning constant employment of couriers and flyers[1]

1 Couriers must be posted along the principal highways, and they must be paid monthly salaries and allowances. When this is done, everything that happens throughout the twenty-four hours within a radius of fifty farsangs will come [to their knowledge]. In accordance with established custom they must have sergeants to see that they do not fail in their duties.

Chapter XV

On being careful about messages in drunkenness and sobriety

1 Messages[1] [from the king] reach the divan and the treasury concerning matters of state, fiefs or gifts. It may be that some of these commands are [given] in a state of merriment. Now this is a delicate matter and it needs the utmost caution. Or possibly the spokesmen may not agree, or have not heard correctly. Such a mission must be entrusted to one person only, and he must deliver the message personally, not through a deputy. And it must be the rule that, in spite of the fact that an order has been delivered, it must not be executed or acted upon until its substance has been referred by the divan back to The Sublime Intellect [for confirmation].

Chapter XVI

Concerning the steward of the household and the importance of his post

1 The office of steward of the household has fallen into disuse nowadays. This work always used to be entrusted to someone well known and respected, for a person whose duties concern the royal palace, the kitchen, cellars and stables, the king's children and his retainers, must have monthly, nay daily access to The Lofty Throne for discourse with the sovereign: indeed he should present himself at any hour of the day to offer reports, to ask advice and to render account of all his arrangements and transactions. So he needs to command complete respect in order to be able to do his work and discharge his duties successfully.

Chapter XVII

Concerning boon-companions and intimates of
the king and the conduct of their affairs

1 A king cannot do without suitable boon-companions with
whom he can enjoy complete freedom and intimacy. The constant
society of nobles such as margraves and generals tends to diminish
the king's majesty and dignity because they become too arrogant.
As a general rule people who are employed in any official capacity
should not be admitted as boon-companions nor should those who
are accepted for companionship be appointed to any public office,
because by virtue of the liberty they enjoy in the king's company
they will indulge in high-handed practices and oppress the people.
Officers should always be in a state of fear of the king, while boon-
companions need to be familiar; if a boon-companion is not
familiar the king will not find any pleasure in his company. With
boon-companions the king can relax; they should have a fixed
time for their appearance; after the king has given audience and
the nobles have retired, then comes the time for their turn.

2 There are several advantages in having boon-companions:
firstly they are company for the king; secondly since they are with
him day and night, they are in the position of bodyguards, and if
any danger (we take refuge with Allah!) should appear, they will
not hesitate to shield the king from it with their own bodies; and
thirdly the king can say thousands of different things, serious and
frivolous, to his boon-companions which would not be suitable
for the ears of his vazir or other nobles, for they are his officials
and functionaries; and fourthly all sorts of sundry tidings can be
heard from boon-companions, for through their freedom they can
report on matters, good and bad, whether drunk or sober; and in
this there is advantage and benefit.

3 A boon-companion should be well bred, accomplished and of
cheerful face. He should have pure faith, be able to keep secrets
and wear good clothes. He must possess an ample fund of stories
and strange tales both amusing and serious, and be able to tell
them well. He must always be a good talker and a pleasant partner; he should know how to play backgammon and chess, and if

he can play a harp and other musical instruments, so much the better. He must always agree with the king, and whatever the king says or does, he must exclaim, 'Bravo!' and 'Well done!' He should not be didactic with 'Do this' and 'Don't do that' and 'Why did you do that?' and 'You shouldn't do that', for it will displease the king and lead to dislike. Where pleasure and entertainment are concerned, as in feasting, drinking, hunting, polo and gaming – in all matters like these it is right that the king should consult with his boon-companions, for they are there for this purpose. On the other hand in everything to do with the country and its cultivation, the military and the peasantry, warfare, raids, punishments, stores, matrimonial alliances and travels, it is better that he should take counsel with the ministers and nobles of the state and with experienced elders, for they are more skilled in these subjects. In this way matters will take their proper course.

4 Some kings have in the past made or called their physicians and astrologers boon-companions, so that whatever the king eats the physician tells him the beneficial and harmful effects of each item, what suits him and what does not; he looks after the king's health and temper, while the astrologer keeps watch on the time and the hour; he gives warning of good and bad auguries and chooses the right moment for every enterprise. Other kings have neglected[1] them and said, 'The physician is always forbidding us to eat pleasant and pure foods when we are not ill; he gives us medicine when we have no symptoms and bleeds us when we have no pain; likewise the astrologer prevents us from doing what we want to do and hinders us from important business; and when you consider, both of them do nothing but keep us back from the pleasures, appetites and desires of this world, and make our life miserable; so it is better that we should call for them only when we need them.'

5 A boon-companion is more highly esteemed if he is a man of experience and has travelled widely and served great people. When people want to know the character and habits of the sovereign they judge by his boon-companions; if they are good-natured, affable, tolerant, liberal and gracious, they will know that the king has a kindly nature, a pleasant disposition, good morals and acceptable manners; but if his boon-companions are sour-faced, conceited, disdainful, haughty, miserly, foolish and wanton, people will judge that the king is of unpleasant disposition, evil

nature, bad temper and bad morals, close-fisted and light-headed.

6 And further, every one of the boon-companions should have a rank and degree; some have sitting status, others standing status. From ancient times this has been the custom at the courts of kings and caliphs; and it is a custom that is still observed in the ancient family; the present caliph has as many boon-companions as his fathers had before him; and the sultans of Ghaznain have always had twenty companions, ten standing and ten sitting; they took the custom and procedure from the Samanids. The king's boon-companions must be given salaries, and treated with the highest respect among the retinue; they must know how to control themselves, be polite and shew affection for the king.

Chapter XVIII

On having consultation with learned and experienced men

1 Holding consultations on affairs is a sign of sound judgment, high intelligence and foresight. Every person has some knowledge and in every branch of knowledge one knows more and another less. One may have knowledge and never have put it into practice or tested it; another possesses the knowledge, and has also used it and tried it. For example one may have read in medical books the cure of a certain pain or sickness and know by heart the names of all the specific medicines, but no more; while another knows all the medicines and has used them in the treatment of that condition and tried them many times. Never will the first be on a level with the second. Likewise a man who has travelled widely and seen the world and experienced heat and cold and been in the midst of affairs is not to be compared with one who has never made journeys, seen countries, participated in events, or only to a limited extent. Thus it has been said that one ought to take counsel with

the wise, the old and the experienced. Further, some people have sharper wits and quicker perception of affairs; others have duller intellects. The wise have said, 'The counsel of one man is like the strength of one man, the counsel of two persons is as the strength of two, and the counsel of ten is as the strength of ten.' Of course ten men are physically stronger than one; likewise ten men in counsel are stronger than two or three or five. Everybody in the world agrees that there has never been any mortal wiser than The Prophet (upon him be prayers and greeting); and with all the wisdom that he had – for he could see behind him as well as in front; and the skies and the earth, the tablet and the pen, the throne and seat [of God], paradise and hell and all things in between were revealed to him, and Gabriel (upon him be peace) often used to visit him, bringing inspiration and giving news of things past and things to come – in spite of all this perfection, in spite of all his miracles, God (be He exalted) said to him [in the Qur'an 3. 153], 'Consult them in affairs.' ('O Muhammad, when you are going to do any work or when you are confronted with an important matter, confer with your companions.') Since God commanded him to seek advice and even he needed counsel, it is obvious that nobody can do without it.

2 Thus when the king does any work or is confronted with urgent business, it is his duty to take counsel with wise elders, loyal supporters and ministers of state. Each person will say what comes to his mind and the king's opinions will be compared with what everyone else says. When they all hear one another's words and opinions and discuss them, the right course will stand out clearly, and the right course is that which all intellects agree to be imperative.

A man who does not take counsel in affairs shews weak judgment; a man of this kind is called self-willed. No task can be accomplished without men of the proper skill; no more can any enterprise succeed without deliberation. Praise be to Allah that The Master of the World (may Allah perpetuate his reign) is endowed with sound judgment and served by men of prudence as well as skill. [I could say more] but I have set down here what comes within the scope of this book.

Chapter XIX

Concerning solitaries and their equipment and administration

1 There should be kept at the court two hundred men called solitaries, men chosen for good appearance and stature as well as for great manliness and bravery. A hundred of them should be Khurasani and a hundred from Dailam and their duty is to be in constant attendance upon the king both at home and abroad. They are permanently attached to the court and must be finely attired. Two hundred sets of weapons are to be kept ready for them and issued to them when duty commences and withdrawn when they are dismissed. Of those weapons twenty sword-belts and twenty shields should be [decorated] with gold, and a hundred and eighty belts and shields with silver, together with pikestaffs.[1] They should be paid suitably high clothing allowances in addition to their regular pay. There should be a sergeant to every fifty men and his job is to know all about his men and to give them their orders. They must all be good horsemen and be provided with the necessary trappings, so that upon all important occasions they will not fail to perform their special functions.

2 The names of four thousand unmounted men of all races should always be kept on the rolls. One thousand picked men are exclusively for the king and the three thousand are to be attached to the retinues of governors and army-commanders so as to be ready for any emergency.

Chapter XX

On the provision and use of jewelled weapons

1 Twenty special sets of arms, studded with gold, jewels and other ornaments, must always be kept ready and stored at the treasury, so that on feast days and whenever ambassadors arrive from distant parts of the world, twenty pages finely attired can take these weapons and stand round the throne. And although our sovereign (praise be to Allah The Mighty) has attained such a lofty state that he can do without such ceremonies, nevertheless the pomp and circumstance of the kingdom and kingship must be maintained, for every king's elegance and finery must accord with his exalted position and lofty ambition. Today there is no king on earth greater than The Master of the World (may Allah perpetuate his reign) and there is no kingdom more vast than his. So it is fitting that wherever other kings possess one of a thing, our sovereign should have ten; where they have ten he should have a hundred, for he has at his command all spiritual and material resources, coupled with a sound judgment. In fact he lacks nothing of majesty and dominion.

Chapter XXI

Concerning ambassadors and their treatment

1 When ambassadors come from foreign countries nobody is aware of their movements until they actually arrive at the city gates; and nobody makes any preparation for them or gives them anything; and they will surely attribute this to our negligence and indifference. So officers at the frontiers must be told that whenever

anyone approaches their stations they should at once despatch a rider [to the capital] and report who it is who is coming, how many men there are with him, mounted and unmounted, how much baggage and equipment he has, and what is his business. A trustworthy person must be appointed to accompany them and conduct them to the nearest big city; there he will hand them over to another agent who will likewise go with them to the next city or district, and so on until they reach the court. Whenever they arrive at a place where there is cultivation, it must be a standing order that officers, tax-collectors and assignees should give them hospitality at every stopping place and entertain them well so that they depart satisfied. When they return, the same procedure is to be followed. Whatever treatment is given to an ambassador, whether good or bad, it is as if it were done to the very king who sent him; and kings have always shewn the greatest respect to one another and treated envoys well, for by this their own dignity has been enhanced not diminished. And if at any time there has been disagreement or estrangement between kings, ambassadors have still come and gone as occasion requires, and discharged their missions according to their instructions; never have they been molested or treated with less than usual courtesy. Such a thing would be disgraceful, as God (to Him be power and glory) says in His incontrovertible book [Qur'an 24. 53], 'The messenger has only to deliver the message plainly.' (This means that the messenger has only to convey the outward purport.)

2 It should also be realized that when kings send ambassadors to one another their purpose is not merely the message or the letter which they communicate openly, but secretly they have a hundred other points and objects in view. In fact they want to know about the state of roads, mountain-passes and rivers, to see whether an army can pass or not; where fodder is available and where not; who are the officers in every place; what is the size of that king's army and how well it is armed and equipped; what is the standard of his table and his company; what is the organization and etiquette of his court and audience-hall; does he play polo and hunt; what are his qualities and manners, his designs and intentions, his appearance and bearing; is he cruel or just, old or young; is his country flourishing or decaying; are his troops contented or complaining; are the peasants rich or poor; is he avaricious or generous; is he negligent in affairs; is his vazir competent,

religious and righteous or the reverse; are his generals experienced and battle-tried or not; are his boon-companions polite and worthy; what are his likes and dislikes; in his cups is he jovial and good-natured or not; is he strict in religious matters and does he shew magnanimity and mercy or is he careless and slack; does he incline more to jesting or to gravity; and does he prefer boys or women. So that, if at any time they want to win over that king, or oppose his designs or criticize his faults, being informed of all his affairs they can think out their plan of campaign, and knowing what to do in all circumstances, they can take effective action, as happened to your humble servant in the time of The Martyr Sultan Alp Arslan (may Allah sanctify his soul).

3 In all the world there are only two doctrines which are good and on the right path; one is that of Abu Hanifa and the other that of ash-Shafi'i (Allah's mercy be upon them both) and all the rest are vanity and heresy. Now The Martyr Sultan (Allah's mercy upon him) was so strict and exact in his religious observances that he was often heard to say, 'What a pity! if only my vazir[1] were not of the Shafi'i persuasion.' He was exceedingly imperious and awe-inspiring and because he was so earnest and fanatical in his beliefs and disapproved of the Shafi'i rite I lived in constant fear of him.

4 Now it chanced that the sultan decided on an expedition to Transoxiana[2] because the khan of Samarqand, Shams al-Mulk Nasr ibn Ibrahim,[3] was being refractory. He called his troops and sent an envoy to Shams al-Mulk; and I sent Danishmand Ashtar on my own behalf with the sultan's envoy to let me know what happened. The envoy went there and delivered his message. The khan sent his own envoy back here together with our sultan's envoy. The khan's envoy was given audience in the usual way; he delivered his message and was given lodging next to the sultan's envoy. Now it is customary for ambassadors to have access to the vazir at any time, and to make requests and say things to him which perhaps they cannot say to the sultan to his face, and the vazir passes them on to the sultan. About the time of their departure [back to Samarqand] I happened to be sitting in my tent in the company of some of my friends, playing chess, and I had just beaten one of them and taken his ring as a forfeit. The ring was too big for the [ring-] finger of my left hand so I had put it on (the finger of) my right hand. It was announced that the envoy

of the khan of Samarqand was at the door. I said, 'Bring him in', and ordered the chess to be taken away.

5. The ambassador came in and sat down, and said what he had to say to me. I was all the time fidgeting with this ring and turning it on my finger, and the ambassador noticed both finger and ring. When he had finished his business he rose and went. The sultan gave orders that the envoy of the khan was to be dismissed, and himself appointed another ambassador to convey his reply. I again sent Danishmand Ashtar with the sultan's envoy as he was a staunch fellow. When the envoys reached Samarqand they presented themselves in front of Shams al-Mulk, and in the course of the interview he asked his own envoy, 'How did you find Sultan Alp Arslan as regards judgment, appearance and conduct? What is the size of his army? how are they equipped? what is the organization of his court, audience-hall and divan, and on what principles is the country ruled?' The envoy said, 'O master, the sultan lacks nothing in appearance, bearing, manliness, power, dignity and command. As for his forces, God knows their number; and their arms and acoutrements are of an incomparable magnificence. The organization of his court, audience-hall, divan and household is excellent. Nothing is wanting in their country; but they have one fault; if it were not for that, there would be no other.' Shams al-Mulk said, 'What is that fault?' He said, 'The sultan's vazir is a Rafidi.'[4] He said, 'How do you know?' He said, 'Because one day, at the time of noon prayer I went to his tent to speak to him. There I saw him with a ring on his right hand[5] and he was turning it on his finger as he spoke to me.' Danishmand Ashtar wrote to me immediately saying, 'Such-and-such was said about you in front of Shams al-Mulk by his ambassador; I thought you had better know.' I was very much disturbed through fear of the sultan, and said [to myself], 'He disapproves of the Shafi'i rite and he is always reproaching me for it; if by any means he should hear that the Jikilis[6] have branded me as a Rafidi and said as much in front of the khan of Samarqand, he will not let me off with my life.' In spite of my innocence I spent 30,000 dinars of my patrimony undemanded and unsolicited, and gave several presents and pensions to prevent this report from reaching the ears of the sultan.

6 Your humble servant has related this story because ambassadors are generally censorious and always on the look out to see

what faults there are in kingdom and kingship, and what virtues; then next time they will convey censure and criticism of those things from their kings. With this in mind past kings, when they have been intelligent and alert, have always refined their manners, and adopted good customs, and employed worthy men of pure faith, lest anyone should find fault with them.

7 For an embassy a man is required who has served kings, who is bold in speaking, who has travelled widely, who has a portion of every branch of learning, who is retentive of memory and far-seeing, who is tall and handsome, and if he is old and wise, that is better. If a boon-companion is sent as an envoy he will be more reliable; and if a man is sent who is brave and manly, skilled in arms and horsemanship, and renowned as a duellist, it will be extremely good, for he will shew the world that our men are like him; and if an ambassador be a man of noble family that will be good too, for they will have respect for his ancestry and not do him any mischief; and he should not be a wine-bibber, a buffoon, a gambler, a babbler or a simpleton. Very often kings have sent envoys bearing gifts of money and valuables and sued for peace and shewn themselves weak and submissive; after giving this illusion they have followed up by sending prepared troops and picked men in to the attack and defeating the enemy. The conduct and good sense of an ambassador are a guide to the conduct, wisdom, judgment and greatness of his king.

Chapter XXII

On keeping fodder ready at posting-houses and stopping places

1 When The Exalted Stirrup proceeds on a journey, there may not be fodder and provisions ready at every station where he halts, and so the rations for the day will have to be procured at great trouble and inconvenience, or even seized from the peasants by

shares. This is bad procedure. On all the roads by which the king is going to pass, at every village which is a stopping place, if it and its environs are held in fief, supplies should be requisitioned; but in places where there is no village and no wayside inn, [before requisitioning supplies] they must wait at the nearest village in the district while the harvest is being gathered; then if the provisions are required, they will be used; and if the king does not travel in that direction [after all], the produce should be sold and the money brought to the treasury like other revenues. In this way the peasants will suffer no distress, there will be no breakdown in the supply of fodder, and the king will not fail in the important task which he has undertaken.

Chapter XXIII

On settling the dues of all the army

1 The troops must receive their pay regularly. Those who are assignees of course have their salaries to hand independently as assigned; but in the case of pages who are not fit for holding assignments, their pay must be made available. When the amount required has been worked out according to the number of troops, the money should be put into a special fund until the whole sum is in hand, and it must always be paid to them at the proper time. Alternatively the king may summon the men before him twice a year, and command that they be paid, not in such a way that the task be delegated to the treasury and they receive their money from there without seeing the king; rather the king should with his own hands put it into their hands (and skirts), for this increases their feelings of affection and attachment, so that they will strive more eagerly and steadfastly to perform their duties in war and peace.

2 The system of the kings of old was that they did not give assignments: every soldier was paid by the treasury four times a

year in cash according to his rank, and they were always well supplied and provisioned, and whatever the emergency 2,000 or 20,000
horsemen instantly mounted and set out to meet it. The tax-
collectors collected the money and sent it to the king's treasury,
and once every three months it was paid out to the pages and
troops; and they called this *bīstgānī*.[1] This system and custom is
still followed by the house of Mahmud.

3 Assignees of land must be told that whenever a man becomes
absent from their troops through death or any other cause, [the
troop-leaders] should at once report the fact and not keep it concealed; and the troop-leaders should be instructed that once they
have received their pay they are to keep all their men ready for
such exigencies as may arise; and if any man takes leave of absence,
they are to report it immediately, so that the vacancy may be filled.
If they do otherwise they are to be reprimanded and to suffer
stoppage of pay.

Chapter XXIV

On having troops of various races

1 When troops are all of one race dangers arise; they lack zeal
and they are apt to be disorderly. It is necessary that they should
be of different races. Two thousand Dailamites and Khurasanis
should be stationed at the court. Those that exist at present should
be retained and the remainder be levied; and if some of these are
from Gurjistan [Georgia] and Shabankara (in Pars), it will be
suitable because men of these races are also good.

2 It was the custom of Sultan Mahmud to have troops of various races such as Turks, Khurasanis, Arabs, Hindus, men of
Ghur and Dailam. When he was on an expedition, every night
he used to detail several men of each group to go on guard and
allotted each group their station; and for fear of one another no
group dared to move from their places; they kept watch until

daybreak in competition with one another and did not go to sleep. And when it was the day of battle, each race strove to preserve their name and honour, and fought all the more zealously lest anyone should say that such-and-such race showed slackness in battle. Thus all races endeavoured to surpass one another.

3 Since the fighting men were organized on this basis they were all valiant and intrepid. Consequently once they had taken up their arms they did not retreat one pace until they had defeated the enemy.

4 When once or twice an army has waxed valiant and gained victory over the enemy, thereafter a mere hundred of their horsemen will be a match for a thousand of the enemy and no force will ever again be able to oppose that triumphant army and all the armies of neighbouring countries will fear that king and submit to him.

Chapter XXV

On taking hostages and keeping them at the court

1 The rulers of the Arabs, Kurds, Dailamites, Rumis and others who have only recently come to terms of submission must be told that each of them should keep a son or a brother resident at the court; there should be, if not a thousand, never less than five hundred of them. At the end of a year they can send replacements and the first ones can go back home, but they are not to start back until their replacements arrive here. In this way no one will be able to rebel against the king because of the hostages. In the case of the Dailamites and the people of Kuhistan, Tabaristan, Shabankara and suchlike who hold assignments and grants, similarly five hundred of them should reside at the court, and then if any need arises the court will never be lacking in useful men.

Chapter XXVI

On keeping Turkmans in service like pages

1 Although the Turkmans[1] have given rise to a certain amount of vexation, and they are very numerous, still they have a long-standing claim upon this dynasty, because at its inception they served well and suffered much, and also they are attached by ties of kinship. So it is fitting that about a thousand of their sons should be enrolled and maintained in the same way as pages of the palace. When they are in continuous employment they will learn the use of arms and become trained in service. Then they will settle down with other people and with growing devotion serve as pages, and cease to feel that aversion [to settled life] with which they are naturally imbued; and whenever the need arises 5,000 or 10,000 of them, organized and equipped like pages, will mount to perform the task for which they are detailed. In this way the empire will not leave them portionless, the king will acquire glory, and they will be contented.

Chapter XXVII

On organizing the work of slaves and not letting them crowd together while serving

1 Slaves[1] who stand in attendance are apt to crowd together,[2] so that it is constantly necessary to hurl abuse[3] at them; and when they promptly disperse [to perform a task], they just as promptly come back [in a crowd]. But when orders are given in decisive terms and they are told once or twice how they are to behave, then they will act accordingly and there will be no need for this inconvenience. Alternatively [pages should be employed and]

clear orders should be given how many water-bearers, arms-bearers, wine-bearers, robe-bearers and the like should report for duty every day, and how many of those pages who have reached the rank of amir-chamberlain and great amir should attend; then every day they will come for service from each tent by turns in the required numbers; likewise with the private [servants of the king], so that there is no crowding. Moreover in all former times, from the day they were bought until their advancement in years and promotion [to high office] pages have been efficiently organized as to their education and grading, but in these days irregularities have come into the system. Your humble servant will mention a little of what is needed to fulfil the purpose of the book, in the hope that it meets with the approval of The Sublime Intellect.

Concerning the training of pages of the palace[4]

2 This is the system which was still in force in the time of the Samanids. Pages were given gradual advancement in rank according to their length of service and general merit. Thus after a page was bought, for one year he was commanded to serve on foot at a rider's stirrup, wearing a Zandaniji[5] cloak and boots; and this page was not allowed during his first year to ride a horse in private or in public, and if it was found out [that he had ridden] he was punished. When he had done one year's service with boots, the tent-leader spoke to the chamberlain and he informed the king; then they gave him a small Turkish horse, with a saddle covered in untanned leather and a bridle of plain leather strap. After serving for a year with a horse and whip, in his third year he was given a belt to gird on his waist. In the fourth year they gave him a quiver and bow-case which he fastened on when he mounted. In his fifth year he got a better saddle and a bridle with stars on it, together with a cloak and a club which he hung on the club-ring. In the sixth year he was made a cup-bearer or water-bearer and he hung a goblet from his waist. In the seventh year he was a robe-bearer. In the eighth year they gave him a single-apex, sixteen-peg tent and put three newly bought pages in his troop; they gave him the title of tent-leader and dressed him in a black felt hat decorated with silver wire and a cloak made at Ganja. Every year they improved his uniform and embellishments and increased his rank and responsibility until he became a troop-leader, and so on until

he became a chamberlain. When his suitability, skill and bravery became generally recognized and when he had performed some outstanding actions and been found to be considerate to his fellows and loyal to his master, then and only then, when he was thirty-five or forty years of age, did they make him an amir and appoint him to a province.

3 Alptigin who was the slave and nursling of the Samanids reached the rank of army-commander of Khurasan at the age of thirty-five. He was outstandingly trustworthy, faithful and courageous. He was a Turk, prudent, skilful, popular, devoted to his troops, liberal, hospitable and God-fearing; he had all the good qualities of the Samanids. He controlled the revenues of Khurasan and 'Iraq and he had 1,700 Turkish pages and slaves. One day he had bought thirty Turkish pages; Sabuktigin, the father of Sultan Mahmud, was among them. The first piece of good fortune which happened to Sabuktigin was that he was bought by Alptigin; the second thing was that three days later he was standing among the pages in front of Alptigin, when the chamberlain came up and said to Alptigin, 'Such-and-such a page who was a tent-leader has died; to which page do you desire to hand over his tent and outfit and troop and rank?' Alptigin's eye fell upon Sabuktigin and he uttered the words, 'I grant it to this page.' The chamberlain said, 'O master, it is yet but three days since you bought this slave; he must do seven years' service before he reaches this rank; how is he fit to receive it now?' Alptigin said, 'I have spoken'; – and the page heard this and bowed – 'I give him this as an exceptional case; hereafter you must follow the usual rule.' So they gave him the tent, and the fruit of seven or eight years' service was his. Then Alptigin wondered how he could justify giving the rank of seven years' service to a newly bought little page; he thought to himself, 'It is possible that this page is of high birth, of a noble family in Turkistan; maybe he will be favoured by fortune and will have a great career.' Then he began to test him, sending him with messages for all and sundry, and saying, 'Now repeat what I have told you.' Sabuktigin would repeat it all without mistake. Then Alptigin would say, 'Go and bring back the answer.' He would go and bring back the answer even more efficiently than he had carried the message. When Alptigin found him every day increasing in aptitude he began to feel affection for him in his heart. He made him a water-bearer and ordered him to serve him

personally. He gave him a troop of ten pages and continually promoted him further.

4 When Sabuktigin was eighteen years old he had two hundred manly pages in his troop. He had assimilated all the ways of Alptigin, in such matters as etiquette and conversation, his habits in eating, drinking and entertaining, in hunting, polo and archery, in shewing kindness to people and treating the members of his troop as brothers. In fact, if ever he had an apple in his hand, he wanted to share it with ten of his fellows; and because of his pleasant disposition and good qualities everyone loved him.

The story of Alptigin and Sabuktigin

5 One day Alptigin detailed two hundred pages to proceed to the Khalaj Turks[6] and the Turkmans to collect some money which was due from them; Sabuktigin was a member of the party. When they arrived the Khalaj Turks and Turkmans refused to pay the dues in full. The pages were enraged and put their hands to their weapons, intending to fight with them and take the money by force. Sabuktigin said, 'I am certainly not going to fight and I dissociate myself from such action.' His comrades asked why. He said, 'Our master did not send us here to fight; rather he told us to go and collect some money and animals. If we fight now and they beat us, it will be extremely humiliating for us and detrimental to the prestige of our master; furthermore our master will blame us for fighting without his order; we shall have no defence or excuse and as long as we live we shall never be absolved from this blame and reproach.' When Sabuktigin said this, most of the pages agreed that it was right; there was some argument amongst them, but in the end they gave up the idea of fighting and returned home. When they reported to Alptigin and told him that they had not taken the money by force although the people had resisted and refused to pay, Alptigin said, 'Why did you not take up arms and seize the money somehow or other?' The pages said, 'We put on our weapons and were going to fight, but Sabuktigin would not let us; there was a difference of opinion amongst us, so in the circumstances we returned home.' Alptigin said to Sabuktigin, 'Why did you not fight and not allow the pages to fight?' Sabuktigin said, 'Because The Master had not commanded us to fight; if we had fought without The Master's orders, then each one of us

would have been a master not a slave, for the mark of a slave is that he does only what his master tells him. If we had been beaten, The Master would inevitably have asked who gave us the order to fight, and what defence should we have had against your wrath? and if we had beaten them, some people would undoubtedly have been killed, and not only should we have received no sympathy or thanks, but we should also have been censured. If you command us to fight, we shall go, and either we shall obtain the money or die in the attempt.' Alptigin was pleased and said, 'He is right.' So Alptigin continued to promote Sabuktigin until he reached a position where he had three hundred pages in his troop.

6 Now when the amir of Khurasan, Nuh ibn Nasr,[7] died at Bukhara, Alptigin was at Nishapur; the courtiers wrote to Alptigin from the capital to inform him of the situation and said, 'The amir of Khurasan has passed away, leaving a brother thirty years old and a son sixteen years old; which of them do you command us to put on the throne, for you are the mainstay of the kingdom?' Alptigin quickly sent his own messenger with a letter, saying, 'Both are worthy of the throne and kingdom; both are princes of my master's family; of the two the king's brother is a man of ripe experience who has known the ups and downs of life; he knows people well and he recognizes and respects everyone's merit, rank and dignity; on the other hand the king's son is an inexperienced boy; I fear he could not control the people nor could he give effective commands on every subject. Perhaps it would be better to put the brother on the throne.' The next day he sent another letter in the same terms. Five days later a messenger arrived bearing the news that the king's son had been enthroned. Alptigin then felt uneasy about the two letters which he had sent; he said, 'Ignoble stupid wretches! when all along they were going to do something on their own responsibility, why did they consult me? As far as I am concerned both the princes are as the light of my eyes; however, it worries me that I indicated a preference for the brother, because when my letters reach the capital, the king's son will be displeased; he will think that I favoured his uncle; he will be offended with me and harbour anger and resentment in his heart; then interested persons will try to influence the young prince and estrange him from me.' He straightaway sent off five dromedaries and ordered the riders to try to overtake the two messengers and turn them back before they crossed the Oxus. The

riders made haste and caught one of them in the desert near Amuy [Amul], but the other one had crossed the Oxus.

7 When Alptigin's letter reached Bukhara, the young prince and his supporters were affronted and said, 'Alptigin was wrong to choose the king's brother; does he not know that a man's heir is his son not his brother?' They continued to talk in this vein with the result that every day the prince became more displeased with Alptigin, while Alptigin sent a multitude of apologies and presents, but these in no way removed the cloud of vexation from the prince's heart; interested parties carried on their mischief and the prince's resentment and bitterness grew. Now Alptigin had originally been bought [as a slave] by Ahmad ibn Isma'il towards the end of his life; then he served Nasr ibn Ahmad for a number of years; when Nasr passed away, he served Nuh ibn Nasr, and it was during Nuh's reign that he became army-commander of Khurasan. When Nuh died, this young prince Mansur, his son, succeeded his father. Six years after the accession of Mansur to the kingship, when Alptigin had spent a large amount of money and tried every possible device, he was still unable to win his heart because of the malicious utterances of the time-servers. Meanwhile Alptigin's agents[8] wrote and told him of all that went on in the capital.

8 Then the mischief-makers said to Mansur ibn Nuh, 'Until you kill Alptigin you will not become the real ruler of this kingdom; for fifty-three years he has exercised sovereignty in Khurasan and amassed great wealth and treasure; all the troops are obedient to his word; when you capture him you will have peace of mind and your treasuries will be filled with his riches. The best plan is to summon him to the court on the pretext that since your accession to the throne he has not appeared at the court to renew his allegiance; moreover you are eager to see him because he is like a father to you; although the foundations of the dynasty rest on him and he is the mainstay of government in Khurasan and Transoxiana, nevertheless the matters which are still being discussed all arise from the fact that he never comes to see you; he should come to the court as soon as possible and rectify any faults in the organization of the court and the audience-hall; thus will your confidence in him be increased and the tongues of the self-seekers be silenced. When he comes here, summon him privately and have him decapitated.'

9 Mansur did accordingly and called Alptigin to the court. Alptigin's agents wrote and warned him of the purpose of the summons. He announced that he was going to Bukhara, and ordered his men to get ready. He set out from Nishapur and came to Sarakhs, accompanied by about 30,000 horsemen. After three days' rest there he summoned the army-commanders and said, 'I have something to say to you; tell me what you think is right and best for us and you.' They said, 'We obey.' He said, 'Do you know the reason why Mansur has summoned me?' They said, 'He wishes to see you and enter into a new agreement with you, for you are like a father to him and his forebears.' He said, 'It is not as you imagine. The king is calling me for the purpose of cutting off my head; he is a boy and knows nothing of men's worth. You know full well that for years I have been sustaining the Samanid dynasty; I defeated several of the khans of Turkistan who attacked their territory; I subdued rebels wherever they arose; and I have never been insubordinate in the slightest degree; it is I who have kept him and his father and grandfather on the throne as I still do. Now at last this is to be my reward – he wants to cut off my head!– he does not even know this much, that his kingdom is like a body and I am its head; when the head has gone how will the body survive? What then do you see fit to do? By what means can we deal with this threat?' All the amirs said, 'There is no means but the sword. If he esteems you thus and if this is to be your reward, what can we expect of him? If anyone else had been in your position he would have snatched the kingship from their hands fifty years ago. We all recognize you, not him nor his father, because we, and everyone who has acquired some standing in the Samanid empire, have all obtained our livelihood, rank, dignity, suzerainty and prosperity from you; to you we owe our positions, and with you remain; Khurasan, Khwarazm and Nimruz are yours beyond dispute. Say farewell to Mansur ibn Nuh and occupy the throne yourself. If you wish, let him keep Bukhara and Samarqand; if not, take possession of them as well.' On hearing the amirs speak thus, Alptigin said with the utmost fervour, 'Allah have mercy on you! I know that these words of yours have been spoken out of honesty and sincerity; this is indeed what I would expect of you. May God (to Him be power and glory) reward you with all blessings. Now return to your quarters for today, and we will see what tomorrow brings forth.'

10 At this time there were 30,000 horsemen with Alptigin; had he wanted he could have raised 100,000. The next day all the amirs came for audience with Alptigin; he came out and sat down. After a time he faced them and said, 'When I spoke to you yesterday I wanted to test you, to see whether you are sincerely with me or not; and whether you will stand by me and support me in the event of certain circumstances arising. In fact, the things which I heard you say were all in keeping with your nobility and loyalty; you have fulfilled the duty of gratitude and I am well satisfied with you. However, you must know and be aware that from now on I cannot guard against mischief from this boy except with the sword; he is a mere child, and knows nothing of his obligations; he listens to the words of some baseborn villains and does not know what is good for him and what is bad; he is hostile to a man like me who has all along been the mainstay of his family; and he takes a handful of rogues who only want to turn the country upside down and could not correct even the slightest disorder in the country's affairs, and regards them as his friends; while he tries to do away with me. What I could do is to depose him and put his uncle on the throne, or even take the kingship myself; but I think people would say that for sixty years Alptigin protected the house of the Samanids who were his original masters, and in the end when he was eighty years old he revolted against them and snatched the kingship from their hands by the sword, putting himself in place of his masters and scorning the duty of gratitude. I have done good works all my life and earned a good name; now that I am on the brink of the grave it is not fitting that I should do something that would bring disgrace upon me; however much it is evident to us that the fault is on the amir Mansur's side, nevertheless everyone does not know this; some would blame the amir Mansur and some would surely say that it was all Alptigin's fault. Although I do not covet their throne and wish them no harm, as long as I remain in Khurasan this kind of talk will go on and they will antagonize this boy against me more and more; but if I leave Khurasan and go out of his kingdom, the slanderers will have nothing left to say; and moreover, if hereafter I must needs fight to get my daily bread and pass the remainder of my life, very well then, let me draw my sword against the infidels and so gain the spiritual reward. Now you know, O officers and men of the army of Khurasan, Khwarazm and Nimruz, that the amir Mansur is king

of Khurasan and Transoxiana, and you are all his troops whom I have been commanding on his behalf. Arise and go to the capital; see the king, renew your commissions and place yourselves at his service; for I intend to go to Hindustan and engage in holy war against the infidels; if I am killed I shall be a martyr, and if I am given grace to succeed I shall turn the house of idolatry into the house of Islam, for the glory of The Faith and in the hope of attaining paradise and pleasing God and The Prophet. Whether my past actions have been good or bad, the amir Mansur will no longer be troubled by me, and the tongues of the talkers will be silenced. Hereafter Khurasan, its army and people are his concern.'

11 After making his speech Alptigin got up and said to the amirs, 'Come before me one by one so that I may bid you farewell.' The amirs expostulated, but without result, and they began to weep; with tears in their eyes each one came forward, embraced him and withdrew; when he had said goodbye to them all he retired into his pavilion. In spite of all this nobody believed that Alptigin would leave Khurasan and go to Hindustan, because in Khurasan and Transoxiana he possessed estates amounting to 500 villages, nor was there a city in the Samanid kingdom where he did not own houses, gardens, inns, bath-houses and farms; in addition he had 1,000,000 sheep and more than 100,000 horses, mules and camels. The next day the sound of drums was heard and Alptigin was seen to depart with his pages and followers and proceed in the direction of Balkh, leaving behind him all this wealth. The amirs of Khurasan then all went to Bukhara.

12 On arrival at Balkh, Alptigin resolved to stay there for one or two months to allow all intending holy-warriors to come together from Transoxiana, Khuttalan, Tukharistan and the neighbourhood of Balkh; he would then set out for Hindustan. The slanderers and trouble-makers persuaded the amir Mansur that Alptigin was an old wolf and that he would not be secure until he had destroyed him; he should send troops after him to capture him and bring him to the capital. So they sent an amir[9] with 16,000 horsemen from Bukhara to Balkh, but by the time they reached Tirmidh and began to cross the Oxus, Alptigin had set out from Balkh and gone towards Khulm. Between Balkh and Khulm there is a gorge four farsangs long which is called the Khulm pass, and along this gorge to the left and right there are

valleys and villages. Alptigin encamped in the gorge and set two hundred horsemen at the head of the gorge to keep watch. At this time he had 2,200 Turkish slave pages of his own, all good fighters, and 800 horsemen who had joined him for holy war.

13 When the amir Mansur's troops reached the gorge, they encamped on the plain outside because they could not enter the gorge. They sat like this for two months. Then one day Sabuktigin happened to be in charge of the watch; when he came to the head of the gorge he saw the plain full of troops, with advance guards posted. He thought, 'Our master has left Khurasan and all his riches with the amir Mansur and gone forth to holy war. Now they have designs upon his life and ours, but such is his characteristic loyalty, charity and courtesy towards them that I am afraid he will lead himself and us to destruction. This matter can only be settled by the sword, and as long as we remain quiet, they will not desist from following us. God Almighty helps those who suffer oppression; they are the oppressors and we are the oppressed.' He turned to the pages who were in his troop and said, 'Now our turn has come for action; if they win, they will not leave one of us alive. Let me try my hand today and see what happens, no matter whether our master approves or not.' So saying, he and his 300 pages attacked the enemy advance guard, overpowered them at once and fell upon their camp. By the time they had put on their weapons and mounted their horses Sabuktigin had struck down more than 1,000 of them and retreated smartly to the head of the gorge.

14 News was brought to Alptigin that Sabuktigin had engaged in battle and killed a number of the enemy. Alptigin summoned him and said, 'Why were you so hasty? You should have waited.' He said, 'O master, how could we wait any longer? Our patience is exhausted. Now is the time for us to fight for our lives. This affair cannot be settled by waiting, only by the sword. As long as we have breath we will fight for our master, come what may.' Alptigin said, 'Now that you have roused the enemy, a better plan will have to be made. Tell the men to strike camp and pack up the baggage; after the bedtime prayer they should decamp and take all the impedimenta outside the gorge; Taghan should move with 1,000 armed pages into a certain ravine on the right-hand side and you are to take 1,000 pages into another ravine on the left-hand side; I shall move out of the gorge with 1,000 horsemen and

the baggage, and stop on the plain. Next day, when they see nobody at the head of the gorge, they will think I have fled; they will mount and gallop after us, making their way into the gorge; when more than half of them have emerged from the gorge they will see me standing on the plain; you will then rush out from your ambushes on both sides, brandishing your swords; when the battle-cry goes up, some of the enemy troops who have emerged from the gorge face to face with me, will run back to see what the commotion is, while those in the gorge will all take to flight and some will fall a prey to your swords; I will then attack them from the front, and you will assault them from the gorge; we shall intercept those who have come out of the gorge and lay about them with our swords; as long as they resist we will continue to belabour them; when they turn tail, we will leave the way of flight open to them, and then retire ourselves; we will come out of the gorge, fall upon their camp and seize the booty.'

15 They followed this plan and went out of the gorge. The next day at dawn Mansur's troops put on their weapons and went to the head of the gorge, ready for battle. They saw nobody there, so they went into the gorge for a distance of about one farsang. There was no sign of Alptigin's camp; they were convinced that Alptigin had fled. The troops were told, 'Make haste! Let us pursue him. When we get out of the gorge on to the plain, we shall overtake them in an hour and capture Alptigin.' So they rode on at speed with all their best men to the fore. As they began to emerge from the gorge they saw Alptigin with a force of 1,000 horse and a few foot arrayed on the plain. As soon as half of them came out of the gorge, Taghan rushed out of the ravine on the left-hand side[10] and attacked with his 1,000 pages; he forced the advancing troops to retreat and put them to flight, killing a number of them; and on the right[10] Sabuktigin also sallied forth with 1,000 pages and attacked. Taghan and Sabuktigin then joined forces to the rear of the enemy troops who had emerged from the gorge, while Alptigin assaulted them from the front; together they engaged the enemy and soon struck a great number of them to the ground; the enemy commander was speared in the back and the lance came out through his chest, so that he fell. At this the enemy were routed and they fled in all directions wherever they could find a way of escape. Then Alptigin's pages came out of the gorge

and fell upon the enemy camp; they seized all the horses, mules, gold and silver articles, silk and slaves that they could find and departed, leaving the tents, carpets and suchlike; and for the next month the people of the villages of Balkh were carrying off goods from that camp. They counted the slain, and they came to 4,750 men, not counting the wounded.

16 Then Alptigin set out from Khulm and went to Bamiyan. The amir of Bamiyan took up arms against Alptigin and was captured. Alptigin pardoned him, gave him a robe of honour and adopted him as a son. This amir of Bamiyan was the one known as Shir Barik.[11] Alptigin proceeded from there to Kabul and defeated the amir of Kabul, capturing his son whom he subsequently favoured and sent back to his father. Then Alptigin attacked Ghaznain.[12] Now the amir of Kabul's son was the son-in-law of Lavik, the amir of Ghaznain; he flew to the aid of his father-in-law.[13] When Alptigin arrived at the gates of Ghaznain, Lavik came out and did battle with him. The amir of Kabul's son was taken prisoner a second time. The amir of Ghaznain was defeated and retired within the city. Alptigin then encamped at the gates and lay siege to the city. He issued a proclamation [to his own troops] forbidding them to take anything from the people without payment in gold and threatening to punish anyone who was found to have done so. He thus gained the respect of the population of Zavulistan.

17 Now one day Alptigin caught sight of one of his Turkish pages coming along with a nose-bag of hay and a chicken tied to his saddle-straps. He said, 'Bring that page to me.' The page was brought. Alptigin asked him, 'Where did you get this hay and this chicken?' The page said, 'I took it from a peasant.' Alptigin said, 'Do you not receive *bistgāni* and wages every month?' He said, 'I do.' Alptigin said, 'Then why did you not pay for these things? This is why I give you *bistgāni* and wages, in order that you should not harass the poor with extortions; furthermore I made a proclamation to this effect.' He then ordered that the page was to be cut in two and hung up by the side of the road at that very spot together with the nose-bag of hay; and he had it proclaimed for three days that if anybody was found to have purloined private property he would suffer the same punishment as this personal page. The soldiers were afraid and the peasants were safe. Thereafter enormous amounts of provender were brought into the camp

every day from the villages of the district; but Alptigin did not allow a single apple to be taken into the city.

18 When the citizens of Ghaznain saw such security and justice and prosperity, they said, 'We want a king who will be just and give us security for our lives, property, women and children, no matter whether he be Turk or Persian.' They opened all the gates of the city and came to Alptigin. On seeing this Lavik shut himself up in the city's fort. After twenty days he came out and went before Alptigin. Alptigin gave him a pension and made Ghaznain his permanent seat; he did no harm to anyone at all.

After that Alptigin began raiding Hindustan and brought back plunder. From Ghaznain to the land of the infidels was two days' march. The report spread in Khurasan, Transoxiana and Nimruz that Alptigin had broken open the gates of Hindustan and was making raids and finding God knows how much wealth there, in gold and silver, animals, slaves and precious things. From right and left men came to join Alptigin so that the number of his followers rose to 6,000 horsemen. He captured several provinces and subdued the country as far as Peshawar. The king of Hindustan put into the field a force of 100,000 horse and 50,000 foot and 1,500 elephants, with the object of expelling Alptigin from Indian territory. From the west Mansur, still smarting from the defeat and slaughter of his troops outside Balkh in the Khulm pass, sent a man called Abu Ja'far with 25,000 horsemen to contend with Alptigin. Alptigin let Abu Ja'far approach to one stage away from Ghaznain and charged out with his 6,000 horse; he assailed the Khurasani forces and in less than an hour he defeated their 25,000 horse a thousand times more thoroughly than he had defeated them at Khulm. Abu Ja'far fled and it happened that he became separated from his men and found himself alone. Peasants caught him without knowing who he was and after seizing his horse and all that he had, let him go. He returned to Balkh on foot and in disguise, and all the Khurasani army's animals, equipment and stores fell into Alptigin's hands. They were never able to oppose Alptigin again, for the alienation and separation of Alptigin severely weakened the position of the Samanids and left them open to attack from the khans of Turkistan.

19 Having thus dealt with Abu Ja'far, Alptigin turned his attention to the king of Hindustan. He wrote letters to Khurasan and elsewhere seeking support. So many men joined him, being

attracted by the prospect of booty, that when mustered they totalled 11,500 horse and foot, all young men, fully armed. He advanced to meet the king of Hindustan and made a surprise attack on his advance guard, killing more than 10,000 men. He did not stop to gather booty but withdrew in haste. The king's army in a great chase failed to catch up with him. There were some high mountains in the midst of which was a pass; and the Indian king's road lay through that pass. Alptigin seized the head of the pass so that when the king arrived he could not go through it; so he encamped there and remained for two months. Every now and again by night or by day Alptigin would sally forth and kill a number of the Hindus. Sabuktigin exerted himself greatly in this war and performed several valiant deeds. The king of Hindustan was in a hopeless position; he could not go forward and it was impossible for him to go back without accomplishing his purpose or reaching a settlement. Eventually the king of Hindustan made a proposal in these words: 'You have come here from Khurasan to find bread; let me give you grants of land and include you in my army; you will be secure and have enough to eat.' Alptigin's troops agreed to this. So the king granted them several towns and districts and five fortresses. However, he had secretly instructed the fortress-commanders not to hand over the fortresses when he withdrew. The king withdrew and the fortresses were not handed over. Alptigin said, 'It is they who have broken the agreement, not I.' Again he resumed his attacks, capturing towns and laying siege to those fortresses. During these operations Alptigin died. His soldiers and pages were left dumbfounded and bewildered, while on all sides they were surrounded by Hindus and infidels.

20 So they sat down and deliberated, saying, 'Alptigin has left no son whom we could put in his father's place and make our leader. Now we have gained the utmost prestige and respect in Hindustan and the Hindus stand in awe of us. If we occupy ourselves with arguments as to who is superior or who is senior, and if each man tries to go his own way, then our prestige will be shattered and the enemy will gain the upper hand over us; and if we disagree amongst outselves, instead of wielding the sword against the infidels we shall have to use it against one another, and we shall lose the territory which we have acquired. The best plan is for us to choose the most suitable man among us, make him our commander, accept whatever he commands and treat him as if he were

Alptigin.' They all said, 'We have no other remedy but this.' Then they enumerated the names of the senior pages; each one was found to have some objection or shortcoming, until they came to Sabuktigin; when his name was mentioned, they all became silent. Then one of them said, 'The only thing wrong with Sabuktigin is that there are some pages who were bought before him and have seen longer service than him; otherwise as regards intelligence, gallantry, courage, manliness, generosity, hospitality, charity, good nature, piety and fidelity Sabuktigin lacks nothing; moreover he was brought up by our master, and our master was always pleased with his work; in fact he has all the virtues, in character and conduct, of Alptigin, and he well knows the virtues and defects of each one of us. I have said what I know. You do what you think best.' For some time they discussed the pros and cons; at last they agreed to make Sabuktigin their commander. Sabuktigin would not raise his head until they pressed him; then he said, 'If it is inevitable, I accept this duty on condition that if anyone opposes me, or disobeys me, or neglects to carry out my command, you will all support me and put him to death.' All swore their acceptance and vowed their inviolable allegiance. Then they took Sabuktigin and seated him upon Alptigin's cushion, saluting him as amir and scattering gold and silver in celebration.

21 Every enterprise and every expedition that Sabuktigin undertook was successful. He married the daughter of the mayor of Zavulistan and she gave birth to Mahmud. This is why he was called Mahmud Zavuli. When he grew up he went on many expeditions and journeys with his father. After Sabuktigin had performed many great exploits and won many battles in the land of India, he received from the caliph of Baghdad the title of Nasir ad-Din [Helper of the Faith]. When Sabuktigin died, Sultan Mahmud took his father's place. He had learnt all the procedure of government from his father; he could read and write and he always loved to listen to the history of kings; so all the principles which he adopted were laudable. He went and conquered the province of Nimruz, he subjugated Khurasan, and he advanced far enough into Hindustan to capture Somnat[14] and bring back the idol; he defeated the kings of India, and finally attained that peak of eminence which he did attain.

22 My humble purpose in relating this story is that The Master of the World (may Allah perpetuate his reign) may know how to recognize a good slave and not try to wound the feelings of one who has done creditable service, who has never committed any act of treason or perfidy, but has strengthened the throne and blessed the empire; nor should he listen to the words of those who seek to incriminate him; rather he should trust him more, for dynasties, kingdoms and cities may at any time be dependent upon one man,[15] and when that man is removed from his place, the dynasty crumbles, or the city is destroyed, or the country is thrown into confusion. For instance Alptigin was a good slave and he was a pillar of the Samanid kingdom; but they did not realize his worth and sought to destroy him. When he left Khurasan, fortune deserted the Samanids and favoured the house of one of their slaves. A slave whom one has brought up and promoted, must be looked after, for it needs a whole lifetime and good luck to find a worthy and experienced slave. Wise men have said that a worthy and experienced servant or slave is better than a son. On this subject the poet says:

> One obedient slave is better
> than three hundred sons;
> for the latter desire their father's death,
> the former his master's glory.

Chapter XXVIII

Concerning the conduct of private and public audiences

1 It is necessary to have some system for giving audiences. First of all the relatives [of the king] come in, after them distinguished members of his train, then other classes of people. If they all come in at once, [the correct] distinction between humble and noble is not observed. Raising of the curtain is the sign that an audience is in progress; when the curtain is lowered it indicates that there

ON THE RULES FOR DRINKING PARTIES

is no admittance, except for persons who are summoned. Thus nobles and army officers, by sending a servant to the court, can find out whether there is an audience on that day or not; then if [there is an audience and] they need to present themselves, they come; otherwise they do not come. For there is nothing more annoying for nobles and officers than to come to the court and have to return without seeing the king. If they come several times and fail to gain audience, they form a bad opinion of the king and begin to plot mischief. When the king is difficult of access the affairs of the people are put into suspense, evil-doers are encouraged, facts remain concealed, the army suffers harm and the peasants fall into trouble. There is no better rule for a king than to hold frequent audiences. When he gives audience, margraves, amirs, sayyids and imams should bow as they come in; and the procedure is that when they have seen the king they and all their followers retire, so that only the select courtiers remain; and the pages who come in with them must retire also, so that none are left but courtiers and some skilled pages such as arms-bearers, water-bearers, food-tasters and the like, who are of course required to be present. When this system has been in force for some time, it will become habitual and remain established. Then all crowding will be avoided, and there will be no need for hurling abuse[1] and closing the door. Any arrangements other than these should not be permitted.

Chapter XXIX

Concerning the rules and arrangements for drinking parties

1 A week is occasionally given over to convivial pleasures and when this is done public audiences should be held on one or two days, so that those whose custom it is to appear, may come forward and nobody will be debarred. People will have been informed

which is the day for them to come, and on days reserved for the elite, commoners will know that there is no place for them and of their own accord will stay away, so that there will not be the necessity of admitting one person and refusing another. Those who are admitted to royal parties must be limited in number and scrutinized to see who they are and it should be a condition of their admission that they do not come with more than one page each. It is intolerable that anyone should bring his own flagon and cup-bearer; such a custom has never existed before and is extremely reprehensible; for in all ages people have taken away eatables, sweetmeats and wines from kings' palaces to their homes, not from their own homes to royal parties, because the sultan is the paterfamilias of the world, and all the human race are his children and slaves. It is not right that those who are his family and his dependants should take their own wine and food to his parties, for his housekeeping ought to be better, more lavish and cleaner than that of any of the nobles; and if the reason why they bring their own wine is that the king's wine-bearer gives them bad wine, he should be punished, because he is issued with nothing but good wine; there is no reason why he should give bad. Then this excuse will be removed and the presumption of people bringing wine to royal parties will be ended.

2 Suitable boon-companions are indispensable to the king, for if he spends too much time with slaves they become arrogant and it lessens his majesty and spoils his dignity; and it is a sign of weak character too, for they are only fit for serving; and if he consorts too much with nobles, generals and civil governors it injures the king's authority; they grow too familiar and become slack in obeying orders and defraud the state of money.[1] On all matters concerning the provinces, the army, finance, cultivation, dealing with enemies of the country, and things of this kind, it is fitting that the king should converse with his vazir. Now these things are all such as increase his fatigue and anxiety and torture his spirit, because wisdom and pride will not, for the sake of the welfare of the state, allow him to take liberties and be facetious with men of this order. It is only through his boon-companions that the king's spirit is set free, and if he wants to live more fully, to refresh himself in sport and jest, to tell stories, jokes and curious tales, he can enjoy these things with his boon-companions without detriment to his majesty and sovereignty, because he keeps them for

this very purpose. But we have already written a chapter on this subject.

Chapter XXX

On slaves and servants standing in order when they are on duty

1 The order in which nobles, commoners and slaves stand must be laid down. Each one must have a definite place, for standing and sitting in the presence of kings are both alike [in having different degrees]; the same order must be observed in standing as in sitting. The principal members of his private staff stand near and around the throne, such as arms-bearers, cup-bearers and the like; and if anyone tries to stand among them the chamberlain of the court will send him away, and likewise if he sees any stranger or unsuitable person among any group he will shout at 'm and not let him stand there.

Chapter XXXI

Concerning the requests and petitions of soldiers, servants and retainers

1 Every request which is made by soldiers must be passed on through the mouths of their troop-leaders and superior officers, so that if a favourable answer is given, it will be received from their hands. By this means they will gain the respect of the men, for when the men state their wants themselves, there is no need

for an intermediary and so the troop-leader loses respect. If any member of a troop is insolent to his superior officer or fails to give him due respect and oversteps his bounds, he must be punished so that the proper distinction between superiors and subordinates is maintained.

Chapter XXXII

On preparing arms and equipment for wars and expeditions

1 Senior officers who receive large allowances must be told to have arms and equipment ready for war and to buy pages, for their grandeur and splendour consist in these things, not in the magnificence of their household decorations and furniture. The man who has more of the former will be more acceptable in the sight of the king, and will acquire greater prestige and power among his equals and his subordinates.

Chapter XXXIII

On reprimanding those in high positions when they are guilty of mistakes or wrongs

1 When men are promoted and elevated to high rank, much time and trouble has to be spent in the process, and when, as sometimes happens, they make a mistake or omission, if they are publicly reprimanded they suffer loss of honour and no amount of

goodwill or favour will restore them to their positions. It is better that when one commits a fault, it should be overlooked at the time; later on he should be summoned privately and told, 'You did such-and-such, but because we do not wish to bring low one whom we ourselves raised up, nor cast down one whom we promoted, we have pardoned you'; thereafter he should take more care and not make such a mistake again; otherwise he would fall from his position within the retinue, and that would be entirely his own doing.

2 They asked The Commander of the Faithful 'Ali (upon him be peace), 'Who is the bravest of heroes?' He said, 'He who can control himself in time of anger and does no action which he will regret afterwards when he has calmed down and regret is of no avail.'

3 It is the perfection of wisdom for a man not to become angry at all; but if he does, his intelligence should prevail over his wrath, not his wrath over his intelligence. Whoever allows his lusts to prevail over his common sense, if he becomes distraught, his passion veils the eye of wisdom, and he does and says things which are characteristic of madmen; but when a man lets wisdom restrain his lusts, in the time of wrath wisdom will overcome his selfish desires and he will do and say nothing that is not acceptable to all the sages, nor will anyone know that he has been in anger.

4 One day Husain ibn 'Ali (peace be upon them both) was sitting at table and eating bread with a group of Companions of The Prophet and chiefs of the Arabs. He was wearing a costly new cloak of Byzantine brocade and had wound an extremely fine barakānī[1] [turban] on his head. A page was going to put a dish of food in front of him, and was standing right behind him, when the dish chanced to slip from his hand and fell on Husain's head and shoulders, soiling most of his turban[2] and cloak. Human nature manifested itself in Husain, and his cheeks flushed with rage and confusion; he raised his head and looked at the page. The page, seeing him thus, was afraid that he would punish him; he said [quoting the Qu'ran 3. 128], 'And those who curb their wrath and are forgiving towards mankind.' Husain's features brightened and he said, 'O page, I make you free, so that you may be for ever safe from my wrath and my rod.' All those present were amazed and pleased at Husain's clemency and magnanimity in such circumstances.

5 They say that Mu'awiya was extremely forbearing and merciful. One day when he was giving audience and all the nobles were sitting and standing in his presence, a young man came in wearing tattered clothes; he greeted Mu'awiya and sat down impudently in front of him and said, 'O Commander of the Faithful I have come today with an urgent request; if you [promise to] grant it I will tell you what it is.' Mu'awiya said, 'Anything that is possible I will grant.' The youth said, 'Know that I am a bachelor and have no wife; and your mother has no husband. Give her to me in marriage, so that I may have a wife, she a husband and you gain the reward.' Mu'awiya said, 'You are a young man and she is an old woman, so old that she has not a single tooth in her head. What do you want her for?' He said, 'Because I have heard that she has a large bottom, and I always like large bottoms.' Mu'awiya said, 'By Allah, my father married her for the very same thing, and it was the only virtue she had. Anyway I will speak to my mother about this and if she is willing, I am certainly the best procurer for your purpose.' Mu'awiya shewed no sign of agitation and remained completely unmoved. All agreed that one could not be more forbearing than he.

6 Wise men have said that forbearance is good, but it is better still in time of success; knowledge is good, but with skill better; wealth is good but with gratitude and enjoyment better; worship is good but with understanding and fear of God better.

Chapter XXXIV

With regard to night-watchmen, guards and porters

1 The utmost care must be exercised in regard to the king's private watchmen, guards and porters. Those who are responsible for these people must know them all personally and find out about all their affairs private and public; for they are mostly men of

mean estate and covetous, and they are quickly seduced by gold. When a newcomer is seen in their ranks let enquiries be made about his circumstances, and every night when they come on guard and sentry duty, they must all be inspected; this important matter must not be neglected, night or day, for it is a delicate business.

Chapter XXXV

Concerning the arrangements for setting a good table

1 Kings have always paid attention to having well-supplied tables [lit: trays] in the mornings so that those who come to the royal presence may find something to eat there. If the nobles have no desire for it at the time, there is no objection to their eating their own provisions in due course, but it is essential to have the table well spread in the mornings.

2 Sultan Tughril (may Allah have mercy on him) paid the utmost attention to having good tables and various kinds of eatables. If he mounted his horse in the early morning to go for a ride or to hunt, twenty mule-loads of food went with him, and when it was served out in the country, there was so much that all the nobles and amirs were astonished. The khans of Turkistan make it part of their royal function to have abundant food in the hands of servants and in their kitchens. When we went to Samarqand and Uzgand certain meddlesome persons were heard to declare that the Jikilis and people of Transoxiana were constantly repeating that never from the arrival of the sultan until his departure did they break a morsel of bread at his table.[1]

3 A man's magnanimity and generosity can be measured by his household management. The sultan is the paterfamilias of the world; all kings are in his power. Therefore it is necessary that his housekeeping, his magnanimity and generosity, his table and his

largesse should accord with his state and be greater and better than that of other kings.

4 It says in a tradition that providing abundant bread and food for the creatures of God (to Him be power and glory) increases the duration of a king's life, his reign and good fortune.

The story of Moses and Pharaoh

5 It is written in the histories of the prophets (upon them be peace) that Moses was sent to Pharaoh with many miracles, wonders and honours. Now the daily ration for Pharaoh's table was four thousand sheep, four hundred cows, two hundred camels and a corresponding amount of chickens, fish, beverages, fried meats, sweets, and other things. All the people of Egypt and all his army used to eat at his table every day. For four hundred years he had claimed divinity and never ceased providing this food.

6 When Moses (upon him be peace) prayed saying, 'O Lord, destroy Pharaoh', God answered his prayer and said, 'I shall destroy him in water, and I shall bestow all his wealth and that of his soldiers on you and your peoples.' Several years passed by after this promise, and Pharaoh, doomed to ruin, continued to live in all his magnificence. Moses was impatient for God to destroy Pharaoh quickly, and he could not endure to wait any longer. So he fasted for forty days and went to Mount Sinai, and in his communing with God he said, 'O Lord, Thou didst promise that Thou wouldest destroy Pharaoh, and still he has forsaken none of his blasphemies and pretensions. So when wilt Thou destroy him?' A voice came from The Truth saying, 'O Moses, you want Me to destroy Pharaoh as quickly as possible, but a thousand times a thousand of My servants want Me never to do so, because they partake of his bounty and enjoy tranquillity under his rule. By My power I swear that as long as he provides abundant food and comfort for My creatures, I shall not destroy him.' Moses said, 'Then when will Thy promise be fulfilled?' God said, 'My promise will be fulfilled when he withholds his provisions from My creatures. If ever he begins to lessen his bounty, know that his hour is drawing near.'

7 It chanced that one day Pharaoh said to Haman, 'Moses has gathered The Sons of Israel about him and is causing us disquiet.

We know not what will be the issue of his affair with us. We must keep our stores full lest at any time we be without resources. So we must halve our daily rations and keep the saving in reserve.' He deducted two thousand sheep, two hundred cows and a hundred camels, and similarly every two or three days reduced the ration. Moses then knew that the promise of The Truth was near to fulfilment, for excessive economy is a sign of decline and a bad omen. The masters of tradition say that on the day when Pharaoh was drowned only two ewes had been killed in his kitchen.

8 Abraham (upon him be peace) was praised by God for his munificence and hospitality; and God (to Him be power and glory) guaranteed the body of Hatim Ta'i against the fire of hell because of his liberality and hospitality; and as long as the world exists his generosity will be remembered. Then there is the case of The Commander of the Faithful 'Ali (may Allah ennoble his visage), who while he was at prayer gave his ring to a beggar, and so satisfied several hungry persons; God has mentioned him in several passages in the Qur'an and praised him, and until the resurrection people will speak of his valour and generosity.[2]

9 Nothing is better than generosity, kindness and hospitality. The provision of bread is the best of all acts of charity, as 'Unsuri[3] says:

Generosity is the best of qualities;
generosity is of the nature of a prophet.
Two worlds are assured to the generous man;
be generous and two worlds are yours.

If a man is rich and desires, without a royal charter, to act like a lord; if he wants men to humble themselves before him, to revere him and call him lord and prince, then tell him every day to spread a table with victuals. All those who have acquired renown in the world, have gained it mainly through hospitality, while the miserly and avaricious are despised in both worlds.

10 A tradition is preserved which says [in Arabic], 'The miser will not enter the garden' (meaning that misers will not go to paradise). In all ages in paganism and Islam there has never been any quality more esteemed than hospitality.

Chapter XXXVI

On acknowledging the merits of worthy servants and slaves

1 Whenever a domestic servant performs some praiseworthy service he should at once receive some mark of appreciation and reap the fruits of his zeal; and one who commits an offence, unnecessarily and not by mistake, should be punished according to the gravity of his transgression, so that the other slaves will be more diligent in their service, while the guilty ones will be more afraid. Then work will proceed correctly.

2 A boy of the family of Hashim, being drunk, quarrelled with a certain group of men, and they went to his father and complained. His father was going to punish him, but the boy said, 'O father, I committed a fault and I was foolish; do not you punish me when you are wise.' This pleased the father and he pardoned him.

3 [Ibn] Khurdadbih[1] relates that King Parviz was angry with one of his courtiers and confined him. Nobody dared to go near him except Barbad the minstrel who everyday took him food and drink. King Parviz was informed of this. He said to Barbad, 'When we have put a man into confinement, how have you the audacity to attend to him? Do you not know this much, that when we are displeased with a man and confine him, he is not to be paid any attention?' Barbad said, 'O king, that which you have spared him is worth more than what I am doing for him.' He said, 'What have I spared him?' He said, 'His life, and that is better than the things I send him.' The king said, 'Bravo! thou hast said well. Now go; I forgive him for your sake.'

4 It was the custom of the kings of the Sasanian line that whenever anyone in their presence said any word or shewed any skill which pleased them, they would utter the word 'Bravo'; immediately on hearing this the treasurer would give that person 1,000 dinars. The Chosroes surpassed all other kings in justice, humanity and magnanimity, especially Nushirvan The Just.

5 One day Nushirvan The Just had mounted his horse and was going to the chase with his retainers. Passing by the edge of a

village, he saw an old man of ninety years planting walnuts in the ground. Nushirvan was astonished because it takes ten or twenty years after planting for a walnut to give fruit; he said, 'O greybeard, are you planting walnuts?' He said, 'Yes, O sovereign.' The king said, 'Will you live long enough to eat the fruit?' The old man said, 'Others have sown and we have reaped; we sow and others will reap.' Nushirvan was pleased and said, 'Bravo!' Immediately the treasurer gave 1,000 dinars to the old man, who said, 'O sovereign, nobody will eat the fruit of these trees sooner than my humble self.' The king said, 'How so?' The old man said, 'If I had not planted these walnuts, and if Your Majesty had not passed this way, and had not asked me that question, and if I had not given that answer, where should I have got these 1,000 dinars[2] from?' Nushirvan exclaimed, 'Bravo, bravo!' And instantly the treasurer gave him another 2,000 dinars because Nushirvan had twice uttered the word 'Bravo'.

6 One day al-Ma'mun was holding court for the redress of wrongs. He received a petition concerning some need. Al-Ma'mun gave the petition to Fadl ibn Sahl who was his vazir, and said, 'Fulfil this man's want soon, for this sphere turns too quickly to stay in one position, and the world is too soon sated to remain constant to any friend. Today we can do a good work, but tomorrow it may be that if we want to do good to someone, we shall be unable to do it for reasons outside our control.'

Chapter XXXVII

Concerning precautions to be taken with regard to assignments and the condition of the peasants

1 If reports come in from any district shewing that the peasants are being ruined and scattered abroad, and if it seems likely that the informants are actuated by self-interest, one of the private staff should be appointed unexpectedly so that no one will guess

the purpose of his mission, and sent on some pretext to that place, to tour the district for a month and see the state of the towns and villages, whether they are prosperous or ruined; he should listen to what people have to say concerning assignees and tax-collectors and bring back verified reports, because officials [when they are questioned] always bring up the pretext and excuse that those [who accuse them] are their enemies. They should not be listened to for they are getting audacious and doing and saying whatever they like; while trustworthy informants are refraining from advising the king or the assignee for fear lest they be thought self-interested. This is even now a cause of decline in population; the peasants are becoming impoverished and uprooted, and taxes are being unfairly levied.

Chapter XXXVIII

On the inadvisability of hastiness in affairs on the part of kings

1 One should not be over-hasty in matters, and when one hears some news or suspects some possibility, one should act calmly so as to learn the real state of affairs and distinguish the false from the true. For hastiness is a mark of weakness, not a sign of strength. When two contestants come before the king and dispute with one another, the king should not let them know which side he inclines to, for then the man who is in the right may be afraid and not dare to speak, and the one who is in the wrong may increase in audacity and mendacity. It is the command of The Truth (be He exalted) in the Qur'an [49. 6] that when somebody makes a statement, you should not listen to it until you have verified it; you should not be precipitate and then suffer remorse and regret, for regret is of no avail.

2 There was a certain scholar[1] in the city of Herat, a man of some renown; in fact he was that old man whom Bikrak[2] once

introduced to The Master of the World. Now it happened that The Martyr Sultan (may Allah illumine his proof) went to Herat and stayed there for a time, and 'Abd ar-Rahman Khal was lodging in the house of this learned old man. One day during a drinking bout he said in front of the sultan, 'This old man has a room into which he goes at night; I am told that he prays all night long. Today I opened the door of that room, and saw a jar of bitter[3] wine and a brazen idol; [evidently] he drinks wine all night and bows down before this idol.' And he had brought a jar of wine and a brazen idol with him. This 'Abd ar-Rahman supposed that if he told this story in front of the sultan, the sultan would order the man to be put to death that very hour. The sultan sent a page to look for the old man, and another page to me telling me to send someone and call the old scholar. I did not know why he was asking for him. But within the hour the messenger came back and told me not to send for him.

The next day I asked the sultan, 'What was the reason for calling that old scholar yesterday and then not calling him?' He said, 'Because of the impudence of 'Abd ar-Rahman Khal.' Then he related this story to me and went on to say that he said to 'Abd ar-Rahman, 'In spite of what you have told me and although you have produced the jar of wine and the brazen idol, I do not intend to do anything about it without being sure of the truth. So give me your hand and swear by my life and head that what you say is true – or false.' 'Abd ar-Rahman said, 'It was false.' The sultan said, 'Wretched fellow, why did you speak falsely against this old scholar, and seek to shed his blood?' He said, 'Because he has a fine house and I am lodging there. If you put him to death, you could give me his house.'

3 Elders of religion have said [in Arabic], 'Haste is from Satan, deliberation is from The Merciful.' (Precipitancy is from the devil and slowness is from God.) Works undone can be done but that which is done cannot be retrieved.

Buzurjmihr says, 'Precipitancy comes from light-mindedness; he who is hasty and has not calmness, is for ever sorry and sad. Frivolous people are contemptible in the eyes of men.'

I have seen several tasks done almost right but spoilt through overhastiness. The hasty man is always reproaching himself; he is continually repenting, begging to be excused, suffering blame, and paying for his mistakes.

The Commander of the Faithful 'Ali (may Allah be pleased with him) says, 'Slowness is to be praised in all actions, except works of charity.'

Chapter XXXIX

Concerning commanders of the guard, mace-bearers, and the instruments of punishment

1 In all ages the office of commander of the guard was one of the most important posts; in fact apart from the great amir-chamberlain no one at the court was higher and grander than the commander of the guard, because his office is concerned with punishment. Everyone fears the wrath and chastisement of the king, and when the king is angry with anyone it is the commander of the guard whom the king orders to cut off his head, to chop off his hands and feet, to hang him on a gibbet, to give him the bastinado, to put him in prison, or to throw him into a pit; and to save their skins and lives people do not hesitate to sacrifice their money. The commander of the guard was always provided with drums and flags and music, and the people feared him more than the king. But in our epoch this post has fallen into disuse and has been robbed of its prestige. There should be at least fifty mace-bearers constantly at the court, twenty with golden maces, twenty with silver ones and ten with large clubs. The equipment and outfit of the commander of the guard must be of the finest, and he must be surrounded with the utmost possible pomp. If the present occupant of the post can manage this it is well; otherwise he must be changed for someone else.

The story of al Ma'mun and the two guard-commanders

2 The caliph al-Ma'mun one day was sitting with his boon-companions, and he said, 'I have two commanders of the guard who are occupied from morning till night in cutting off people's

heads, hanging people, chopping off hands and feet, giving the bastinado and putting men in prison. One of them is constantly spoken well of and praised by everybody; people are satisfied with him; the other one is reviled; people curse and swear when they hear his name, and they are constantly complaining about him. I do not know what is the reason for this. I need someone to inform me why, these two men having the same job, people praise one and complain of the other.' A certain companion said, 'If my lord instructs me and allows me three days, I will find out about this matter.' The caliph said, 'Very well.'

3 The boon-companion went home and said to a trustworthy servant, 'I have a task for you. There are this day in Baghdad two guard-commanders, one old and one middle-aged. I want you to get up tomorrow morning while it is still dark and go to the house of the elder of these two, and when he comes out of his room into the courtyard see how he behaves, what he does and what he says; and when people go before him and criminals are brought in, see what happens and what sort of orders he gives. Remember all that you see and come and give me an account of it. The day after tomorrow likewise go early to the house of the middle-aged one and note everything of his speech and behaviour from first to last and then report to me.' The servant said, 'To hear is to obey.'

4 The next day the servant got up early and went to the house of the elder guard-commander and there sat down. Some time passed. Then a servant came and placed a candle on a ledge and spread a prayer-mat and put some volumes of the Qur'an, prayer books and rosaries on top of the mat. The old man came out and performed several *rak'ats* of prayer, while people kept coming in. Then the imam announced the commencement of the service and they prayed in congregation. The old man took up a Qur'an and read a portion of the scripture and recited some prayers. When he had finished his litany he took his rosary and telling the beads, chanted 'Praise be to Allah' and 'There is no god but Allah.' People were still coming in and greeting him; some went out and others sat down, until the sun rose. Then he asked, 'Have they found any criminals today?' They said, 'Yes, they have brought in a youth who has killed a man.' He said, 'Is there any witness against him?' They said, 'No, he confesses it himself.' He said, 'There is no power and no strength except with Allah The Mighty.[1] Bring him in; let me see him.' The youth was brought in.

5 When the old man's eyes lighted on the youth, he said, 'Is this the man?' They said, 'Yes.' He said, 'This man has not the countenance of a sinner; rather does the lustre of humanity and the light of Islam shine forth from him. It is unlikely that his hands should commit such a crime. I think people are lying. I will not hear a word against him. What a story! Never would this youth do such a deed. See, his whole face testifies to his innocence.' He said these words so that the youth could hear. Then someone said, 'O amir, he himself confesses his guilt.' The amir shouted at the man and said, 'Silence, who asked you to speak? Have you no fear of God? Do you wantonly seek to shed the blood of a Muslim? This young man is too intelligent to do or say anything that would cause his own destruction.' His intention was to try and make the youth contradict himself and renounce his statement. Then he turned to the youth and said, 'What have you to say?' The youth said, 'It was decreed by God that such a deed should come to pass at my hand – by mistake. This world is followed by another; I have not the strength to endure God's punishment in the next world. So carry out God's judgment upon me.' The guard-commander pretended to be deaf and turning to the people said, 'I cannot hear what he is saying. Does he confess or no?' They said, 'Yes, he confesses.' He said, 'My son, you have not the face of an evil-doer. Perhaps one of your enemies has put you up to saying this, someone who desires your destruction. Consider well.' He said, 'O amir, nobody has put me up to this; I am a sinner. Carry out God's judgment upon me.'

6 When the guard-commander realized that the youth would not withdraw his declaration, and that he had resigned himself to death, and that his own suggestions were having no effect, he said to him, 'So it is as you say?' He said, 'It is so.' He said, 'Am I to execute God's judgment upon you?' The youth said, 'Do so.' Then he turned to the people and said, 'Have you ever seen such a God-fearing, far-seeing young man as this? I never have at any rate. The light of blessedness, of Islam, and of nobility radiates from him as light from the sun. Through fear of God he makes this confession knowing that [in any case] he must die; he prefers that he should appear before God as a saint and a martyr. There is but one footstep between him and paradise with its virgins and palaces. Behold, such are the lucky people who are pardoned and due for paradise.' To the youth he went on, 'Go, wash your head

and body; come and perform two *rak'ats* of prayer, and ask for your [book of deeds] from God; repent and ask forgiveness. Then I will execute God's judgment upon you.' The youth went and bathed, and came back and asked for a prayer mat to be spread. He performed two *rak'ats* of prayer, made his repentance and asked forgiveness. Then he came and stood in front of the guard-commander, who said, 'It seems that this youth will even now look upon [Muhammad] The Elect (upon him be peace) and will dwell in paradise with the martyrs, like Hamza,[2] Hasan and Husain.' In this way he made the talk of death so sweet to the young man's heart that he was impatient for them to kill him as quickly as possible. Then the amir ordered them to strip him of his clothes with all gentleness, and to blindfold his eyes; and all the while he went on talking to him as before. An expert executioner came in with his sword [glistening] like a drop of water, and stood silently behind the youth so that he was unaware of his presence. The guard-commander suddenly gave a sign with his eye, and the executioner deftly brought down his sword and cut off the youth's head with one blow. After that the guard-commander sent to prison several persons arrested for various crimes, while their charges were verified. Then he rose and went into his room, and the people dispersed. The servant came back to the boon-companion and reported all that he had seen.

7 The next day he got up and went to the house of the middle-aged[3] guard-commander. He sat down; policemen and other people came in one by one until the courtyard was full. When the sun rose, the guard-commander came out of his room and held court, with his brows knit and his eyes sodden with drink, looking as if he had been killing angels [i.e. engaged in debauchery] all night. The policemen stood in front of him. If anyone greeted him with 'Peace', he did not reply with 'Upon you', or if he did, he said it as if he was angry with that person. After some time he asked if anyone had been brought in. They said, 'Last night a youth was arrested so drunk that he was out of his mind.' He said, 'Bring him in.' The youth was brought before the guard-commander, who looked at him and said, 'Is this the one?' They said, 'Yes.' He said, 'I have been looking for him for a long time. He is an ill-begotten, thoroughly depraved scoundrel, a night-walker, a quarrelsome, impious, seditious rogue who has no equal in all Baghdad. It is not the lash for him but the sword. He does nothing

night or day but harass people's children; sometimes he makes boys infamous, sometimes he disgraces women; and no day passes without ten people coming to me to complain of him. I have been in search of him for some time.' After all that he had said, the youth was ready for them to cut off his head, in order to escape from his abuses. Then the guard-commander ordered several whips to be brought, and said, 'Hold him down and sit on his head and feet, and give him forty lashes, so that he bites the dust.' When they had finished beating him and were going to take him off to prison, more than fifty heads of well-known families came and gave evidence of his honesty, chastity, generosity, hospitality, morality and piety; they pleaded that after beating him the guard-commander should release him and do them all a favour. He took no notice of these old and respected householders and sent the youth to prison. The elders went away mortified and all the people cursed the guard-commander. He for his part rose and went indoors. The servant returned home and recounted to the boon-companion all that had happened.

8 On the third day the boon-companion went to al-Ma'mun and described the conduct and behaviour of these two guard-commanders as it was reported to him. The Commander of the Faithful was astonished and said, 'May Allah pardon the old guard-commander, and curses be upon that dog who treated a noble youth so savagely for being drunk. If he had to deal with a murderer (we take refuge with Allah!), what ever would he do?' Then he gave orders that he was to be deprived of the office of guard-commander, that the youth was to be brought out of prison, and that the old guard-commander was to be confirmed in his appointment, and decorated afresh with a robe of honour and given complete financial independence.

[*Part Two*]

Chapter XL

On shewing mercy to the creatures of God and restoring all lapsed practices and customs to their proper order

1 At any time the state may be overtaken by some celestial accident, or influenced by the evil eye.[1] Then the government will change and pass from one house to another, or the country will be thrown into disorder through seditions and tumults; opposing swords [will be drawn and there will be] killing, burning, plunder and violence. In such days of discord and disaffection men of noble birth will be crushed; base-born men will gain control and whoever has strength will do what he likes; righteous men will have no power or influence and evil-doers will become rich; the least of men will be an amir [army-commander], the basest of persons will become a civil governor. Noble and learned men will be dispossessed, and any wretch will not hesitate to take upon himself titles reserved for the king and the vazir; Turks will adopt titles proper to civil dignitaries and the latter will take those belonging to Turks, while Turks and Taziks [Persians] alike will decorate themselves with titles of scholars and theologians. The king's wives will issue orders; the religious law will be held in contempt; the peasants will become unruly and the soldiers oppressive; all discretion and decency will vanish away and no one will remedy matters. If a Turk keeps ten administrators, it will pass, and if one Tazik is administrator for ten Turks, it will be allowed. All the affairs of the country will lapse (and have lapsed) from their proper order and organization, and the king will be so distracted by expeditions, wars and anxieties that he will not have the opportunity to attend to such matters or even consider them.

2 Later, when through celestial good fortune the evil times pass away, and days of peace and security follow, God (be He exalted) will bring forth a just and wise king from princely stock, and will give him the power to vanquish his enemies, and the wisdom and intelligence to judge matters aright – a king who will enquire from people and read books to learn what were the rules by which former kings directed affairs, so that after a time he may restore

all the proper forms and rules of government. He will test the merit and estimate the rank of every one; those who are worthy he will put in their due positions, and the unworthy he will reduce in rank and appoint them to their proper tasks and trades. He will exterminate any ungrateful people who abuse their privileges. He will be the friend of religion and the enemy of oppression; he will assist the faith and remove vanity and heresy, with the premission of Allah and by His grace.

3 Let us now expatiate a little on this subject; much will then become clear and it will be a guide to those things which have fallen into disorder, so that when The Master of the World (may Allah perpetuate his reign) reflects upon them he may issue a mandate and an order to deal with each, if Allah wills. One of the principles which kings have observed in all ages is to preserve ancient families and honour the sons of kings, not allowing them to be frustrated, neglected and rejected; rather, under their dominion they gave them posts commensurate with their status, so that their families continued to flourish; other competent and deserving persons too were given allotments from the treasury, such as scholars, descendants of 'Ali, righteous and blameless men, fighters for the faith, guardians of the frontiers [of Islam], and people [expositors] of the Qur'an. Thus in the days of their dominion no one was deprived of his due portion and privilege; so they gained blessings and rewards in both worlds.

The story of Harun ar-Rashid

4 They say that a party of deserving persons presented a petition to Harun ar-Rashid saying, 'We are servants of God and Sons of the Age;[2] some of us are scholars and theologians; some belong to noble families; others are sons of men who have deserved well of this dynasty for their past good services; and we too have laboured without stint; and we are all Muslims of pure faith. Our portion is in the treasury and the treasury is under your control because you are the administrator of the world and The Commander of the Faithful. If that money belongs to the people, then spend it on us for we are of the faithful and we have a right to it; you are virtually the treasurer, and not more than a tenth is due to you as king; that is your salary; yet every day you spend so many thousand dinars on services, rations and lustful objects,

while we cannot get a loaf of bread to eat.' The extraordinary thing was, [they thought,] that he should imagine that all the contents of the treasury belonged to him alone; if he assigned them their portion, well and good; otherwise they would go and complain to the court of The Most High and request Him to take the treasury out of his hands and give it to someone else who had some compassion for his fellow Muslims and kept money and wealth for the sake of men, not men for the sake of money.

5 When Harun ar-Rashid read the petition he was disturbed, and he did not answer it the same day. He returned from the audience-hall to his private palace in a state of uneasiness. When Zubaida saw him out of humour she said, 'O Commander of the Faithful, what is the matter?' He told her about the petition which he had received, and said, 'If it were not for the fact that they have threatened me with the name of God I would have had them punished.' Zubaida said, 'You did well not to hurt them. As you inherited the caliphate from your fathers, so they bequeathed you their principles, their qualities and their traditions. Consider what the caliphs before you did for the good of mankind. Do likewise, for nobility and sovereignty are improved by generosity and liberality. There is no doubt that all the money in the treasury belongs to the Muslims, while you spend large amounts of it for yourself. You should take no more liberties with their property than they would with yours. They are quite justified if they complain about you.'

6 That night it happened that they both dreamed that it was the resurrection and people were going to the place of reckoning; one by one they were brought forward, The Elect (the prayers of Allah be upon him and his family) interceded for them and they went towards paradise; an angel took Harun and Zubaida by the hand to bring them to the tribunal; another angel took hold of the first angel and asked where he was taking them; he said that The Elect had sent him and told him, 'As long as I am present do not let them be brought forward, or I shall be ashamed and unable to say anything about them, because they considered the property of Muslims to be their own and deprived them of their rights – and this when they were my lieutenants.' They both woke up in a frenzy. Harun said to Zubaida, 'What has happened to you?' She told him what she had seen in the dream and that she had been afraid. Harun said, 'I too had the same dream.' Then they praised

God that it was not the resurrection and that it had all been a dream.

7 The next day they opened the doors of their treasuries and issued a proclamation saying, 'Let all entitled persons present themselves that we may give them their portion from the treasury and fulfil their needs and desires.' Then people proceeded to Harun's court in immense numbers[3] and he awarded them gratuities and pensions; these benefactions amounted to 3,000,000 dinars. Then Zubaida said to Harun, 'The treasury is in your hands and you will be required to answer for it at the resurrection, not I. By virtue of your recent acts of grace you have discharged some of your responsibilities, in that all you gave was the property of the Muslims which you restored to them. The things which I am going to do I shall do at my own expense for God's sake and for the sake of salvation at the resurrection. I know that I have to depart from this world and leave behind all this gold and wealth; so let me send something in advance to the next world by way of provision for the journey.'

8 Zubaida then withdrew from her own treasury several million dinars' worth of jewels, silver and raiment; and she said, 'All this must be spent on charitable works such that the effect of them will last until the resurrection and my name will be blessed for ever-more.' So she ordered that from Kufa to Mecca and Medina wells were to be dug at every stage; they were to be made wide at the top and lined from top to bottom with stone, baked brick, plaster and lime; tanks and cisterns were also to be built so that pilgrims should suffer no hardship and shortage on their journey, for every year several thousand pilgrims used to perish in the desert for lack of water. After all these wells and tanks had been constructed, much money was still left. She ordered that fortified castles were to be built on the frontiers, that arms and horses, mares and stallions, were to be bought for warriors engaged in holy war, and that sufficient lands and farms were to be purchased so as to pro-vide throughout the year at each fortress food and fodder when-ever required for one or two thousand warriors; horses were to be bred.

9 When all this had been done much money still remained. So on the borders of Kashgar, Bulur and Shuknan they built a city with a strong wall and named it Badakhshan; it is still in existence and flourishing today. On the borders of Khuttalan opposite

Zhasht and Famir and Kumij[4] they built another fortress called Vaishgird which is still in existence and flourishing; its armoury and its herd of horses are still there. Similarly they built a fortified frontier station as big as a city at Isbijab, which is still in existence and flourishing, a fortress on the road to Khwarazm called Farava, a fortress at Darband and a fortress at Alexandria. In all they built ten fortresses in various places, each one like a city. After all this building work there was still a surplus of money. So she arranged for it to be taken and distributed among the inhabitants and indigents of Mecca, Medina and Jerusalem.

A story of 'Umar and the poor woman

10   Zaid ibn Aslam related the following anecdote: One night The Commander of the Faithful 'Umar ibn al-Khattab (may Allah be pleased with him) was on patrol in person in Medina, and I was with him. We went out of the city, and in the fields there was a ruined building in which a fire was burning. 'Umar said to me, 'O Zaid, come, let us go there and see who it is who has lit a fire in the middle of the night.' So we went, and when we got near we saw a woman with two little children asleep on the ground beside her and a small pot set over a fire; she was saying, 'May God Almighty help me to get justice from 'Umar; he has eaten his fill while we are hungry.' When 'Umar heard this he said to me, 'O Zaid, this woman is arraigning me of all people before God. You stay here while I approach her and ask what is the matter.' He went up to the woman and said, 'What are you cooking at midnight out in the fields?' She said, 'I am a poor woman; I have not got a house of my own in Medina and I am penniless; and I feel so ashamed that these two children of mine are weeping and wailing in hunger and I have nothing to give them, and the neighbours know they are crying because they are hungry and I cannot do anything about it; so I have been out here since yesterday. Every time they cry from hunger and ask for food I put this pot on the fire and say, "You go to sleep and by the time you wake up the pot will be ready." By this means I set them at rest and with this hope they go to sleep; when they wake up and find nothing they start howling again. At the moment I have put them to sleep on some pretence; for two days now I have not had anything to eat and neither have they; and there is nothing but plain water in

this pot.' 'Umar (may Allah be pleased with him) took pity on her and said, 'You are justified in cursing 'Umar and appealing to God.' The woman did not recognize 'Umar. He said to her, 'Wait here for a while until I come back.'

11 'Umar then came back to me and said, 'Step out, we are going back to my house.' When we reached his house he went in and I sat down at the door. After some time he came out with two leather bags on his back. He said to me, 'Come, let us go back to that woman.' I said, 'O Commander of the Faithful, if we have got to go back there, put those bags on my back and let me carry them.' 'Umar said, 'O Zaid, if you carry this load, who will take the load of sin off 'Umar's back?' And he ran all the way to the woman and put the bags down in front of her; one of them was full of flour and the other full of rice, peas and fat. He said to me, 'O Zaid, go into the fields, collect all the sticks and wormwood you can find and bring them quickly.' I went to look for firewood. Then 'Umar took a bowl and fetched some water; he washed the rice and peas, put them in the pot and threw in a lump of fat; and with the flour he made a large flat round of bread. I brought the firewood; and with his own hands 'Umar heated the pot and put the bread under the fire.

12 When the bread and the pot were ready 'Umar filled the bowl with broth and sopped bread, and when it was cooled he told the woman to wake up the children for their food; she awakened the children and 'Umar placed the food in front of them. Then he retired to a distance, spread his prayer-mat and began to pray. After a while he looked; mother and children had eaten their fill and were playing together. 'Umar got up and said, 'O woman, you pick up the children, while I take the bags and Zaid carries the pot and bowl, and we will take you home.' This they did. The woman took the children into her house; 'Umar put down the bags and as he turned to leave, he said, 'Be kind and do not curse 'Umar any more; he cannot withstand God's punishment and rebuke, and he is not a clairvoyant to know what everyone's condition is. Use what I have brought and when it is finished let me know and I will bring more.'

The story of Moses and the lost sheep

13 They say that when Moses (upon him be peace) was still the

shepherd of the prophet Shu'aib (upon him be peace) and had not yet received divine inspiration, he was one day feeding his sheep. By chance one ewe became separated from the others. Moses wanted to bring her back to the flock, but the ewe ran off into the desert; not being able to see the sheep, she ran about in terror and Moses chased her for a distance of two or three farsangs, until she had no strength left and fell down exhausted and could not get up. Moses came up to her and was moved with compassion. He said, 'O hapless one, whither are you fleeing? Whom do you fear?' Seeing that she could not walk any more, he picked her up and put her on his shoulders and brought her back to the flock. When the ewe saw the flock her heart was glad and began to throb; Moses put her down on the ground, and she joined the flock. God (be He exalted) called to the angels, saying, 'Saw ye with what tenderness My servant treated that dumb ewe? Because he took trouble and harmed not the ewe, but rather had mercy on her, [I declare] by My glory that I will raise him up and make him My interlocutor; I will grant him prophethood and send him a book, and as long as the world exists, his name will be spoken.' God bestowed all these tokens upon him.

The story of Mayor Hajji and the mangy dog

14 In the city of Marrud there lived a man who was known as Mayor Hajji; he was a distinguished and wealthy man and owned many estates and farms; in fact in his time there was nobody richer than he in all Khurasan. He had served Sultan Mahmud and Sultan Mas'ud, and we had seen him. At the beginning of his career when he was a young man he was extremely cruel, practising torture and inquisition and overthrowing noble families; there was nobody more merciless and disrespectful than he. In the latter part of his life he found enlightenment; he desisted from tyranny and oppression and began to do good works, like comforting the poor and building bridges and inns; he set free many of his slaves, he paid the debts of the bankrupt, he gave clothes to orphans, he provided money for pilgrims and holy-warriors, he built a Friday mosque in his own city and a fine Friday mosque at Nishapur, and lastly after performing all these charitable acts he went on the pilgrimage in the time of Amir Chaghri (Allah's mercy be upon him). When he reached Baghdad he remained

there for about a month. One day he left his house to go to the bazaar; in the street he saw an extremely mangy dog; all its hair had fallen out and the poor thing was distressed by the mange. The man was sorry for it; he said, 'It too is a living being created by God (to Him be power and glory)'; and he told a servant to go and fetch two maunds of bread and a rope. He waited where he was till the servant came back. Then he broke the bread with his own hand and threw it to the dog until it had eaten enough and felt secure; then he put the rope round the dog's neck and handed it to the servant, telling him to take the dog to the house where they were lodging. He too then departed from the bazaar.

15 When he reached the house he gave order for three maunds of fat to be bought and melted. Mayor Hajji took a stick and wrapped a piece of rag and wool round the end of it; he got up and approached the dog; and with his own hand he dipped the rag and wool into the bowl of fat and began to rub it over the dog until its members were thoroughly anointed. Then he said to a servant, 'You are not more respectable than I am; I thought it no disgrace to do what I did; nor should you, being my servant. I want you to knock a nail in the wall and tie the dog to it; every day you should give it one maund of bread in the morning and one in the evening; also let it have the leavings from the table; and treat it with fat twice a day until it gets better.' The servant did as he was told and in two weeks the dog got rid of the mange, began to grow its hair and put on weight; it became so attached to the house that even if it had been beaten it could not have been turned out. Mayor Hajji performed the pilgrimage, travelling by caravan, and he spent much money on the journey; he returned safely to the city of Marrud and a few years later he died. Some time passed.

16 One night an ascetic saw him in a dream, mounted on a Buraq[5] with boys and girls surrounding him on all sides; they were laughing as they led him gently through one of the gardens of paradise. The ascetic ran towards him and greeted him; he drew rein and returned the salutation. The ascetic said to him, 'O Sir, you were once a tyrant, merciless and oppressive; after you found enlightenment you not only desisted from tyranny, but also did more good works and gave more charity than anyone before you; and you performed the Islamic pilgrimage. Tell me what were the acts of piety by which you attained your present state of exaltation?' He said, 'O ascetic, I am lost in amazement at

God's works; you, too, should take this as a lesson, and put no trust in piety nor deceive yourself by acts of worship. Know that I had been assigned to hell for all the sins I had committed in my youth; all the acts of piety and charity which I did were of no avail; all my prayers and fasting were thrown back in my face in the agony of death; all my good works – mosques, inns, bridges, even my pilgrimage – were useless and worthless. I became so despondent that I gave up all hope of paradise and resigned myself to the torments of hell. Of a sudden I heard a voice saying, "You were one of the dogs of the earth, so we have matched you against a dog and considered all your sins as cancelled; you have been admitted to paradise and delivered from hell because you threw off the cloak of pride and took pity on that mangy dog." After that I saw the angels of mercy coming like lightning, and they snatched me from the hands of the angels of torment and took me into paradise. So of all my acts of piety that was the only one which saved me at the last extremity.'

17 Your humble servant has called to mind this story so that The Master of the World (may Allah perpetuate his reign) may know what a good habit it is to be merciful. Because these men had mercy on a ewe and a dog they acquired high degree and esteem in both worlds. So it can be imagined what reward a man will receive from God if he has mercy on a Muslim who is in distress, and gives him a helping hand. If the king fears God and takes heed for the future, he is bound to be just in every case, and the just man is always merciful and kind. When the king is such, his officers and soldiers will become like him and follow his example. Consequently all humanity will enjoy ease and tranquillity and they [the rulers] will reap the fruit of this in both worlds.

18 It has always been the custom of enlightened monarchs to have respect for old and experienced men, and to keep [in office] those who are skilled in affairs and tried in battle, giving each a position and rank; and whenever any matter important for the welfare and prosperity of the state required to be executed, such as promotion, dismissal, erecting lofty buildings, arranging an alliance, getting information about a [foreign] king, enquiring into religious affairs, and suchlike, they discussed it thoroughly with men of wisdom and worldly experience. On the other hand,

whenever an enemy appeared or a battle threatened, they took counsel with men accomplished in warfare and skilled in such arts; with the result that the business was accomplished successfully. If war broke out they despatched to the front a man who had fought numerous battles, broken enemy ranks, captured forts and gained renown in the world for valour; but at the same time they always sent with him a man of ripe and wide experience so that nothing went amiss. But [nowadays] it happens that when a serious matter arises, they appoint inexperienced men and [even] boys and youths [to deal with it], and errors are committed. If due attention were given to these matters in future it would be better and less dangerous.

On the subject of titles

19 There has become an abundance of titles; and whatever becomes abundant loses value and dignity. Kings and caliphs have always been sparing in the application of titles; for it is one of the principles of government to see that titles are kept in relation to each man's rank and importance. When the title of a bazaar merchant or a farmer is the same as that of a civil governor or high official, there is no difference between the two, and the notable and the insignificant are of the same degree. Supposing an imam or a scholar or a judge has the title of Mu'in ad-Din [Supporter of the Faith], and a Turk's apprentice or a Turk's clerk who knows not the first thing about religious law and probably cannot even read or write, also has the same title of Mu'in ad-Din, then what is the difference in rank between judges and Turks' apprentices, learned and ignorant? Both have the same title and this is not right.

20 Likewise the amirs of the Turks have always been given the titles Husam ad-Daula [Sword of the Empire], Saif ad-Daula [Sabre of the Empire], Yamin ad-Daula [Right Hand of the Empire], Shams ad-Daula [Sun of the Empire], and suchlike; while civil dignitaries, civil governors and officials have received titles like 'Amid al-Mulk [Pillar of the Kingdom], Zahir al-Mulk [Protector of the Kingdom], Qiwam al-Mulk [Support of the Kingdom], Nizam al-Mulk [Harmony of the Kingdom] and Kamal al-Mulk [Perfection of the Kingdom]. Nowadays all discretion has vanished and Turks give themselves the titles of

Taziks, and Taziks take those of Turks, and think it no wrong. But titles always used to be dear.

The story of Sultan Mahmud and his titles

21 On his accession to the sultanate Sultan Mahmud asked The Commander of the Faithful, al-Qadir bi'llah, for a title. He was granted the title of Yamin ad-Daula [Right hand of the Empire]. Then after he took possession of the provinces of Nimruz and Khurasan, and captured innumerable cities and states in Hindustan, going to Somnat and bringing back the idol, conquering Samarqand and Khwarazm, coming to Kuhistan of 'Iraq and taking Rayy, Isfahan and Hamadan, and bringing Tabaristan to submission, he sent a messenger to The Commander of the Faithful bearing many gifts and asking for more titles. His request was not granted and it is said that he sent over ten applications without result. Now the khaqan of Samarqand had been given three titles – Zahir ad-Daula [Protector of the Empire], Mu'in Khalifat Allah [Supporter of the Vicar of Allah], and Malik ash-Sharq wa's-Sin [King of the East and China]; and this was a constant cause of jealousy to Mahmud. Once again he sent a messenger and said, 'I have gained so many victories in heathen lands, I am the acknowledged protector of Islam in Hindustan, Khurasan and 'Iraq, I have captured Transoxiana, and I am continually wielding the sword in your name; yet on the khaqan, who is one of my subjects and vassals, you have conferred three titles and on me, your devoted servant, only one, after all my services and favours.'

22 The reply came back in these words: 'Titles are an honour by which a man's dignity is increased, and by which he is known to the world; know also that a man's [first] name is that which his father and mother give him, his *kunya* [surname of relationship] he chooses for himself, and his title is that which the king gives him; anything beyond these three is superfluous and a mockery, and no wise man submits himself to mockery and vanity. When a person is small, he is called by his first name and this pleases his mother and father because they chose that name for him; when he grows up and acquires discretion he chooses a *kunya* for himself in keeping with his intelligence and wisdom, as the saying is [in Arabic],

"Appellations and aspirations go together." Thereafter people treat him like a man and call him by his *kunya*, and this makes him happy. Later, when he has shewn merit and skill in public life, the king bestows upon him the honour of a title suitable to his rank, in order to distinguish him from his fellow men and exalt him above them. Therefore this name which the king or the caliph grants him is better than the one his parents give him and better than the one he chooses himself. So out of respect for his rank and dignity people call him by the name given to him by the king and known as his title. Apart from these three any other designation is superfluous. However, because the khaqan is an ignorant, outlandish Turk, I have granted his request in order to swell his reputation and make up for his lack of wisdom. As for you who are learned in every science and situated close to me, my intentions concerning you are worthier and my trust in you and your virtue is nobler than that you should ask me for something merely spoken or written, and aspire after the same objects as ignorant men.'

23 When Mahmud heard these words, he was confounded. Now there was a certain woman of Turkish birth who often used to come to Mahmud's palace; she was educated, well-spoken and knew several languages; she would talk, joke and play with Mahmud, sometimes reading him Persian books and stories; in fact she was on most familiar terms with him. One day she was sitting with Mahmud and amusing him; he said, 'However much I try to get the caliph to increase my titles, it is of no use; the khaqan who is a vassal of mine, has received several titles while I have got only one. I wish I had somebody who could steal from the khaqan's treasury or otherwise procure the charter which the caliph sent him; if he were successful I would give him anything he demanded.' This woman said, 'O Master, I will go and get that charter, but you must keep your word and give me whatever I want.' He said, 'I will.' The woman said, 'I have not enough money to devote to the attainment of The Master s desire; if you will give me some assistance from the treasury I will either achieve your object or die in the attempt.' The sultan said, 'What do you want?' Then he supplied her with all that she demanded in the way of money, jewels, robes, ornaments, animals and provisions. This woman had a son fourteen years old who was being educated at the hands of a tutor; she took him with her and set out from Ghaznain to Kashghar. There she bought some Turkish pages

and bondmaids, as well as a large supply of choice goods imported from Cathay and China, such as musk and various kinds of silk and cotton.[6] Then she travelled in the company of merchants to Uzgand, and went from there to Samarqand.

24 Three days after her arrival she went to pay her respects to the khatun, offering a very handsome Turkish bondmaid as a gift together with many choice things from China and Cathay; and saying, 'My husband was a merchant; he used to travel throughout the world and take me with him; we were going to Cathay, but when we reached Khotan he died. I turned back and came to Kashghar. I offered a present to the khan of Kashghar and I saw his khatun and told her how my husband had been one of His Excellency's servants and I was an attendant to Her Excellency; they had set me free, given me to him as a wife and I had had this child by him; he had recently died at Khotan and all that he had left me was some capital which Their Excellencies had given him; I hoped that His Excellency in his charity and nobility would extend the hand of succour over the heads of his humble servant and this orphan and despatch us in good company towards Uzgand and Samarqand, for which act of kindness I should thank him and bless him as long as I lived. The khatun treated us very kindly and so did the khan; both of them praised us and gave us a guide and wrote a letter asking the khan of Uzgand to look after us and send us in good company to Samarqand. Now by your grace and favour I throw myself at your feet, knowing that in all the world there is nowhere such justice and equity as at Samarqand. My husband always used to say that if ever he reached Samarqand he would never leave it. It is your name and fame that have brought us here. If you see fit to accept me as your thrall and extend the hand of succour and lordship over my head, then I will settle down here, sell the ornaments which I possess and buy a house and farm large enough to provide me with subsistence; then I will constantly wait upon you and continue the education of this boy, in the hope that with the aid of your blessings God (to him be power and glory) will prosper him.'

25 The khatun said, 'Do not worry at all. I will do everything possible to treat you well and look after you; I will find you a house and a piece of land to suit you and I will not suffer you to be away from me for an instant. I will also tell the khaqan to fulfil all your needs and requests.' The woman bowed to the khatun

and said, 'Now you are my mistress. I do not know anybody else, so I should be grateful if you would bring my presence to the notice of His Excellency the khaqan and introduce me to him, so that I may have the honour of an interview.' The khatun said, 'I will take you to see him any time you like.' The woman said, 'I will present myself tomorrow.' She said, 'All right.' The next day she went to the khatun s house. When the khaqan left the audience-hall and came back to the palace, the khatun spoke to him about the woman; he ordered her to be brought in. The woman bowed to him and offered presents of a Turkish page, a handsome horse, and all sorts of choice things; and she said, 'Your humble servant has explained something of her circumstances to the khatun. In brief, when my husband died – may Your Excellency live for ever! – his partner advised me not to carry back the goods which were destined for Cathay; he took them on to Cathay; out of what remained the khan of Khotan took some, I gave some to the khan of Kashghar, I used some for travelling expenses, and now there is nothing left but your humble servant, this orphan boy, a small quantity of ornaments and a few animals. If Your Excellency will accept me as a thrall, as the noble khatun has accepted me, then I am ready to spend the rest of my life in your esteemed service.'

26 The khaqan spoke very kindly to her and accepted her. Thereafter she went to see the khatun every two or three days, presenting gifts of either a pair of ruby rings, or a turquoise, or a silk veil, or some other choice and costly article; she entertained her with pleasant tales and romances, and so captivated her that she could not bear to be without her. She made them feel embarrassed, because whenever they offered her villages and farms she declined to accept. Every few days she left the house in which she was lodging and went three, four or five farsangs out into the country ostensibly for the purpose of buying a farm; she would stay there for three or four days; then she would find some fault with it, excuse herself from buying it, and return home. When the khatun and khaqan sent someone to find out why she had forsaken them and ceased coming to see them, they were told that she was buying an estate in such-and-such a village and had been gone for two or three days. They were delighted and assumed that she had decided to stay there. She was in their constant service for a period of six months; and the khatun said to her several times, 'The khaqan keeps saying that whenever he sees you he feels ashamed,

because you do so many things for us; every few days you bring us presents, and whatever we offer you, you decline to accept; he has never met a woman as kind as you; and he wonders what we should do for you after all this; and I feel a thousand times more ashamed than he.' The woman said, 'For me the greatest blessing in the world is the sight of my master and mistress, whom God (to Him be power and glory) has made the providers of my daily bread. I see you every day, and I cannot do without you; so when I need something I will not hesitate to ask for it.' Meanwhile she was preparing her horses; she secretly gave the gold, jewels, carpets and robes which she had to a merchant who habitually travelled between Samarqand and Ghaznain on business; and she sent out five good horses and five riders on to the road to Balkh and Tirmidh with instructions that each rider with horse was to remain at a certain stopping place until she arrived.

27 Then she approached the khatun at a time when she and the khaqan were sitting together; after regaling them both with much eulogy and flattery, she said, 'Today I have come with a request; I do not know whether I should ask you or not.' The khatun said, 'This is a strange thing to hear from you; by this time we ought to have fulfilled a hundred requests of yours. But tell us what it is that you require.' She said, 'You know that this boy is all that I have in the world; I am devoted to him and I am looking after his education; he has already learned the whole of the Qur'an, and now he is studying literature with a tutor and reading treatises in Arabic and Persian; I hope that by the grace of my master and mistress he will be fortunate. Now after the writ of God and The Prophet there is nothing on the face of the earth more venerable than the writs of The Commander of the Faithful which are received by kings; the person who composes these documents is the most learned of all secretaries; so the language and purport which they contain should surely be of the most exquisite. If Your Excellencies think it fit, would you kindly allow your humble servant for two or three days to take the document known as the caliph's charter, so that this boy may read it a few times with his tutor; if he learns only five words from it, it may be that he will win good fortune through its influence.' The khaqan and khatun said, 'What a request is this to put to us! Why do you not ask us to grant you a city or a district? All this time you have made no request; now that you have done so, you have asked for something

of which we have fifty put away in the treasury, all rotting under a layer of dust. What virtue is there in a piece of paper? If you like we will make you a present of all those papers.' The woman said, 'Just the document which the caliph sent will be enough.' A servant was ordered to go with her to the treasury and give her any papers she wanted.

28 So the woman went to the treasury, received the charter and took it back home. The next day she had all her horses saddled and her mules loaded, giving out that she was going to such-and-such a village to buy an estate and would be away for a week. She rode away and went straight to that village; before leaving she had taken a safe-conduct stating that wherever she and her party went in the province of Samarqand and Bukhara, whether buying a farm or acquiring an estate or taking up abode, she was to be treated with respect and esteem; tax-collectors, mayors and other officials were instructed to afford her all assistance within their power and to provide her with lodging and anything she might require.

29 Then one night she stole away from the village in the middle of the night, and passed three farsangs away from the city of Kish. In five days she reached Tirmidh; whenever the need arose she presented the safe-conduct and she had a constant supply of fresh mounts. The khaqan was not aware of her going until she had crossed the Oxus and reached Balkh, and he never thought anything more about the caliph s charter. From Balkh she went to Ghaznain and laid the charter in front of Sultan Mahmud. Mahmud sent it by the hand of a certain scholar, known to be skilled in debate, to The Commander of the Faithful al-Qadir bi'llah together with many presents; he also sent a letter in which he wrote as follows: 'One of my servants was walking in the bazaar at Samarqand, and he passed by a mosque, where a master was holding a Qur'anic school and teaching some boys; there he saw this writ of The Commander of the Faithful in the hands of small boys; without the slightest respect or regard they were passing it from one to the other and rolling it in the dust. My servant recognized that illustrious document and wished to rescue it. So he gave a few raisins to the boys and bought the charter from them for the price of waste paper; he brought it to Ghaznain and shewed it to me. I now respectfully forward it for the attention of The Master of the World, and humbly submit that if after all my deference

and devotion to duty you were to condescend to grant me some titles, I should hold your patents dearer than my own eyesight, regarding them as the crown on my head and giving them the most honourable place in my treasury; yet in spite of all my past services and future expectations you refuse to grant me any titles, and you give them to persons who fail to understand the solemnity of your decrees, who treat all honours and patents with contempt, and who merely despise the titles which they receive.'

30 When this scholar arrived at Baghdad and delivered the presents and the letter the caliph was very surprised, and ordered a letter of reproach to be written to the khaqan. Mahmud's envoy remained for six months on the caliph's doorstep, continually sending in petitions and requesting titles on behalf of Mahmud; but he got no decisive answer. So one day he wrote a proposition in the following terms: 'If a king were to emerge in the furthest parts of the world, and wield the sword for the glory of Islam, and make war on infidels and pagans who are the enemies of God and The Prophet, and make idol-temples into mosques, and turn the abode of unbelief into the abode of Islam; and supposing he were distant from The Commander of the Faithful, being separated by great waters, lofty mountains and fearful deserts, and were unable at all times to report the events which happen, and all his requests met with no response from the caliph; would then it be lawful for him to install a descendant of The Prophet as the caliph's deputy and to submit to his authority, or not?' He gave this proposition to somebody to hand to the chief judge of Baghdad. The judge read it and pronounced that it was lawful. The scholar took a copy of this judgment, and enclosed it with a petition which he wrote to the caliph, saying, 'Your humble servant's stay has become protracted; Mahmud with a hundred thousand acts of devotion and service entreats the favour of one or two titles; but The Master of the World withholds them from him, disappointing The Warrior King's hopes and cruelly wounding his feelings. If hereafter Mahmud acts in accordance with the decree and licence which he has lawfully obtained from the chief judge of Baghdad, will he be excused, or not?'

31 As soon as the caliph read this petition and the decree, he sent the chief chamberlain to the vazir with instructions that Mahmud's envoy was to be summoned immediately and set at ease with assurance; then he was to be given such robes of honour,

banners and titles as the caliph authorized, and sent on his way satisfied. In spite of all Mahmud's services and attempts to curry favour with the caliph, and despite the clever advocacy of the scholar, he received only one additional title – Amin al-Milla [Trustee of the Nation]; and as long as he lived Mahmud's only titles were Yamin ad-Daula and Amin al-Milla.

In these days the lowest official is angry and indignant if he is given less than seven or ten titles.

32 The Samanids who for so many years were the greatest kings of their time and ruled over the whole of Transoxiana and over Khurasan, 'Iraq, Khwarazm, Nimruz and Ghaznain, each had one title. Nuh was called Shahanshah [King of Kings]; Nuh's father, Mansur, was called Amir Sadid [The Good Commander]; Mansur's father, Nuh, was called Amir Hamid [The Praised Commander]; Nuh's father, Nasr, was called Amir Rashid [The Rightly Guided Commander], Isma'il ibn Ahmad was known as Amir 'Adil [The Just Commander] and in the history books as Amir Madi [The Late Commander] and Ahmad was called Amir Sa'id [The Fortunate Commander], and so on. Titles must suit the persons who hold them: judges, theologians and scholars have had titles like Majd ad-Din [Glory of the Faith], Sharaf al-Islam [Honour of Islam], Saif as-Sunna [Sword of the Ordinance], Zain ash-Shari'a [Ornament of the Religious Law], and Fakhr al-'Ulama [Pride of Scholars]; because scholars and theologians are concerned with knowledge, 'Islam', 'the faith', 'the religious law' and 'the ordinance'. If anyone who is not a scholar takes these titles upon himself, not only the king but all men of discretion and learning should refuse to countenance it, and that person should be punished so that everyone observes his rank and station. Likewise the titles of army-commanders, amirs, assignees and commissioners have been distinguished by the word *daula* [empire], for instance, Saif ad-Daula [Sabre of the Empire], Husam ad-Daula [Sword of the Empire], Zahir ad-Daula [Protector of the Empire], Jamal ad-Daula [Grace of the Empire], Shams ad-Daula [Sun of the Empire] and suchlike; while civil governors, tax-collectors and officials have been given titles with the word *mulk* [kingdom], like 'Amid al-Mulk [Pillar of the Kingdom], Nizam al-Mulk [Harmony of the Kingdom], Kamal al-Mulk [Perfection of the Kingdom], Sharaf al-Mulk [Honour of the Kingdom],

Shams al-Mulk [Sun of the Kingdom], and so on. It was never the rule that Turkish amirs should take upon themselves the titles proper to civil dignitaries.[7] Titles including the words *din* and *Islām* are for scholars; *daula* is for amirs and *mulk* is for civil dignitaries. Apart from these whoever introduces the words *din* and *Islām* into his titles should be punished, so that others may take warning.

33 The principal object of titles is that people may be recognized by them. For example, there may be a hundred persons in a certain company or gathering; of that number perhaps ten may be called Muhammad. Suppose someone calls, 'O Muhammad'; all ten Muhammads will have to answer '*Labbaik*' [Here I am], for each will think that he alone is being called. But if one Muhammad is called Mukhtass [Special], another Muwaffaq [Successful], another Kamil [Perfect], another Kafi [Capable], another Rashid [Correct], and so on, then when they are called by their titles, they will know at once who is meant.

34 Apart from the vazir, the head of the correspondence department, the accountant-general, the head of the military department and the civil governors of Baghdad, Khurasan and Khwarazm, nobody else in the country should be given titles other than those without the word *mulk*, such as Khwaja Rashid [The Correct Chief], Khwaja Mukhtass [The Special Chief], Khwaja Sadid [The Good Chief], Ustad Amin [Trusted Master], Ustad Khatir [Honoured Master], and Ustad Tagin [Brave Master] and the like; thus the degrees and ranks of high and low, great and small, nobles and commons will be distinct, and the prestige of the administration will remain undiminished. When there is stability in the country, when the king is just and vigilant, when he gives diligent attention to affairs, and seeks to learn about the customs and manners of his predecessors, and when he has a successful, knowledgeable and skilful vazir, then he will restore all matters to good order, he will reinstate the proper rules with regard to titles, and he will abolish all new-fangled customs through the exercise of his judgment, his authority and his sword.

Chapter XLI

On not giving two appointments to one man;
on giving posts to the unemployed and not leaving
them destitute; on giving appointments to men
of orthodox faith and good birth, and not employing
men of perverse sects and evil doctrines; keeping the latter
at a distance

1 Enlightened monarchs and clever ministers have never in any
age given two appointments to one man or one appointment to
two men, with the result that their affairs were always conducted
with efficiency and lustre. When two appointments are given to
one man, one of the tasks is always inefficiently and faultily performed, because if the man performs one task properly and dili-
gently, the other one will be spoiled and neglected; and if he
carries out the other task well and attentively, the first one will be
sure to suffer damage and failure; and in fact you will usually find
that the man who has two functions fails in both of them, and is
constantly suffering censure and complaint from his dissatisfied
manager. And further, whenever two men are given a single post
each transfers [his responsibility] to the other and the work
remains forever undone. On this point there is a proverb which
runs, 'The house with two mistresses remains unswept; with two
masters it falls to ruins.'[1] Each of the two thinks to himself, 'If I
take pains to do the work expediently, and take care not to let
anything go wrong, our master will think that this is due to the
capability and skill of my partner, not to my own diligent and
patient efforts.' The other one has the same idea and actually there
will be constant confusion in the work; if the manager says, 'What
is the cause of this inattention and inefficiency?' each man will
excuse himself by saying that it is the other's fault and putting the
blame on him. But when you go to the root of the matter and
think intelligently, it is not the fault of either of them; it is the
fault of the man who gave one appointment to two persons.
And whenever one officer is given two posts – or three or five or
seven – by the divan it is a sign of the incompetence of the vazir

and the negligence of the king. Today there are men, utterly incapable, who hold ten posts, and if another appointment were to turn up, they would apply for it, giving bribes if necessary, and get it; and nobody would consider whether such people are worthy of the post, whether they have any ability, whether they understand secretaryship, administration, and business dealings, and whether they can fulfil the numerous tasks which they have already accepted. And all the time there are capable, earnest, deserving, trustworthy and experienced men left unemployed, sitting idle in their homes; and no one has the imagination or discernment to enquire why one unknown, incapable, base-born, ignorant fellow should occupy so many appointments, while there are well-known noble and trusted men who have no work at all, and are left deprived and excluded, particularly men to whom this dynasty is greatly indebted for their satisfactory and meritorious services.

2 Even more extraordinary is the fact that in all previous ages a public appointment was given to a man of the same religion and the same rite, who was pure alike in religion and origin; and if he was averse and refused to accept it, they used compulsion and force to make him take the responsibility. So naturally the revenue was not misappropriated, the peasants were unmolested, assignees enjoyed a good reputation and a safe existence, while the king lived a life of mental and bodily ease and tranquillity. But nowadays all distinction has vanished; and if a Jew administers the affairs of Turks, it is permitted; and it is the same for Zoroastrians, Rafidis, Kharijis and Qarmatis. Everywhere indifference is predominant; there is no zeal for religion, no concern for the revenue, no pity for the peasants. The dynasty has reached its perfection; your humble servant is afraid of the evil eye and knows not where this state of affairs will lead. In the days of Mahmud, Mas'ud, Tughril and Alp Arslan no Zoroastrian or Christian or Rafidi would have dared to appear in a public place or to present himself before a Turk. Those who administered the affairs of the Turks were all professional civil servants and secretaries from Khurasan, who followed the orthodox Hanafi or Shafi'i schools. The heretics of 'Iraq were never admitted to their presence or allowed to work as secretaries and tax-collectors; in fact the Turks never used to employ them at all; they said, 'These men are of the same religion as the Dailamites and their supporters; if they get a firm footing they will injure the interests of the Turks and cause distress to the

Muslims. It is better that enemies should not be in our midst.'
Consequently they lived free from disaster. Now things have
reached such a state that the court and the divan are full of them,
and every Turk has two hundred of these individuals running
after him, and their object is to prevent any Khurasanis from
entering the service of this court and earning a living here. One
day the Turks will realize the iniquity of these people and recall my
words, when the divan becomes empty of Khurasani secretaries
and officials.

In former times if a man offered himself for service to a Turk as
an administrator or a cleaner or a stirrup-holder, they used to ask
him what province and city he came from and what rite he professed; if he said that he was of the Hanafi or Shafi'i persuasion
and from Khurasan, Transoxiana or a Sunni city, he was accepted;
but if he said that he was a Shi'ite[2] from Qum, Kashan, Aba or
Rayy[3] he was refused and told, 'Be gone; we kill snakes not nour-
ish them.' Even if money and presents were offered, the Turk
would not accept them, but would say, 'Go in safety; take these
gifts back to your own house and use them for yourself.' If ever
Sultan Tughril and Sultan Alp Arslan heard that a Turk or an
amir had admitted a Rafidi into his presence, they would be angry
and reprimand him for the error.

3 One day it was reported to The Martyr Sultan Alp Arslan
that Ardam was going to appoint Dihkhuda Abaji[4] as his secretary. He was enraged to hear it, because Dihkhuda was said to be
a Batini. He spoke to Ardam in the audience-hall and said, 'Are
you my enemy and the foe of the state?' Ardam fell on the ground
and said, 'O Master, what is this you say? I am the least of your
slaves; till now what fault have I committed in service and loyalty
to my lord?' The sultan said, 'If you are not my enemy why have
you taken my enemy into service?' Ardam said, 'Who is that?'
He said, 'The wretched Dihkhuda who is your secretary.' He said,
'What in the world is wrong with him? and even if he turned into
pure venom, what could he do to this empire?' He said, 'Go and
bring that man here.' He was brought in immediately. The sultan
said, 'Thou wretch, thou sayest that the caliph of Baghdad is not
the lawful caliph; thou art a Batini.' The wretched man said, 'O
Master, your slave is not a Batini; I am a Shi'ite'[5] – that is, a·Rafidi.
The sultan said, 'O cuckold, what is so good about the Rafidis
that you make them a screen for the Batinis? The one is bad; the

other is worse.' He commanded the mace-bearers to beat the man, and they threw him half dead out of the palace.

4 Then the sultan turned to the nobles and said, 'It is not this wretched man's fault; it is Ardam's fault for taking an infidel into his service. I have told you over and over again that you Turks are the army of Khurasan and Transoxiana and you are foreigners in this region; we conquered this country by the sword. We are all pure Muslims; but the Dailamites and people of 'Iraq are mostly infidels and heretics. Enmity and opposition between the Turks and the Dailamites is not something recent; it is ancient. Today God (to Him be power and glory) has favoured the Turks and given them dominion because they are orthodox Muslims and do not tolerate vanity and heresy. We Turks hate the Dailamites for their heresy and bad religion; as long as they are weak they will remain in submission and obedience but if ever they gained power and the fortunes of the Turks declined, both for religious and for political reasons they would not leave one of us Turks alive. People who do not know their own friends and enemies are less than asses and cows.' He then called for two hundred dirams-weight of horse hair; he pulled out one strand and told Ardam to break it. Ardam took it and broke it. He gave him five hairs and then ten hairs, and Ardam broke them easily. Then he called a servant and said, 'Twist all this into a rope.' He made a rope three yards long and brought it; the sultan gave it to Ardam. However much he tried and strained he could not break it. The sultan said, 'So it is with enemies; in ones and twos and fives they can easily be eliminated but when they become numerous and combine together they cannot be rooted out; they cause us trouble. This is the answer to your question, "If this wretched fellow were pure poison what could he do to the state?" If they infiltrate one by one amongst the Turks, and are allowed to administer their business and get to know about their affairs, then the very moment that revolt breaks out in 'Iraq, or if the Dailamites attack this country, all these people will secretly and openly make common cause with them and seek to destroy the Turks. You are a Turk; you need Khurasanis in your retinue; your administrators, secretaries and officials should all be Khurasanis; and the same should apply to all the Turks, if their interests are not to be damaged. When you make an alliance with the king's enemy and your own enemy, it is a treason committed against your person and against

the king; and even if you may do what you like to your own person, it is impossible for the king to relax his vigilance and caution, and to spare the traitor. I must protect you; you do not protect me, for God (to him be power and glory) has made me king over you, not you over me. Do you not know this, that whoever makes friends with the king's enemies, is himself an enemy of the king; and he who has converse with thieves and evil-doers is to be reckoned one of their number.'

5 On this occasion when the sultan was uttering these words Khwaja Imam Mushattab[6] and the judge of Lukar[7] were present. He turned to them and said, 'The Master of the World has said what God and The Prophet say concerning Rafidis, Batinis, heretics and non-Muslims.'

6 Then Mushattab said: 'Abd-Allah ibn 'Abbas says that one day The Prophet (upon him be peace) said to 'Ali (may Allah be pleased with him) [in Arabic], 'If you meet a people nicknamed Rafidis professing Islam, slay them for they are polytheists.' (The Persian translation is as follows: If you find a people called Rafidis, they will have abandoned Islam; when you meet them you must kill them all for they are unbelievers.)

7 The judge of Lukar said: Abu Umama relates that The Prophet (upon him be peace) said [in Arabic], 'At the end of time a people called Rafidi [will arise]; when you meet them, kill them.' (The Persian translation . . .)

8 Then Mushattab said: Sufyan ibn 'Uyaina called the Rafidis infidels and he adduced this verse [Qur'an 48. 29], 'That the unbelievers may be enraged at them. . . . [They are] most vehement against the unbelievers.' And he used to say that whoever slanders The Companions of The Prophet is an unbeliever, on the authority of this verse which has been quoted. And The Prophet (upon him be peace) said [in Arabic], 'Allah (be he blessed and exalted) has given me companions and ministers and relations by marriage; whoever abuses[8] them, upon him be the curses of Allah, of the angels, and of all the human race. Allah will not accept their requital nor their repentance.' (The Persian translation is: God has given me friends who are my ministers, fathers-in-law[9] and sons-in-law . . .) God says [in the Qur'an 9. 40] concerning Abu Bakr (may Allah be pleased with him), 'The second of two, when they two were in the cave, and he said to his companion: Grieve not; verily Allah is with us.' (The interpretation of this is as

follows: If no one helps us, O Abu Bakr, do not grieve for God is with us.) 'Our whole life is just a spectacle.'[10]

9 The judge of Lukar said: 'Uqba ibn 'Amir relates that The Prophet of Allah (may Allah bless and save him) said [in Arabic], 'If there were a prophet after me, it would be 'Umar ibn al-Khattab.' (The Persian translation . . .)

10 Mushattab said: Jabir ibn 'Abd-Allah (may Allah be pleased with him) relates [in Arabic] that The Prophet (may Allah bless him) was present at a funeral and did not pray over the corpse; they said, 'O Prophet of Allah, we never saw you omit to pray over any but this.' He said, 'He hated 'Uthman; may Allah hate him.' (The Persian translation . . .)

11 The judge of Lukar said: Abu 'd-Darda relates (may Allah be pleased with him) that The Prophet (upon him be peace) said concerning 'Ali (may Allah be pleased with him) [in Arabic], 'They who rebel against you are the dogs of hell.' (The Persian translation . . .)

12 Mushattab said: 'Abd-Allah ibn 'Abbas and 'Abd-Allah ibn 'Umar (may Allah be pleased with them both) say that The Prophet (upon him be blessing) said [in Arabic], 'The Qadaris and the Rafidis have no portion in Islam.' (The Persian translation . . .)

13 The judge of Lukar said: Sahl ibn Sa'd relates (may Allah be pleased with him) that The Prophet (upon him be peace) said [in Arabic], 'The Qadaris are the Magians of this community; if they are ill, do not visit them; and when they die, be not present at their funerals.' (The Persian translation . . .) And all Rafidis hold the same doctrine as the Qadaris.

14 Mushattab said: Umm Salama relates about The Prophet (may Allah bless and save him) as follows: One day The Prophet (upon him be peace) was with me; Fatima and 'Ali (may Allah be pleased with them) came to see him and ask after his health. The Prophet (upon him be prayers and peace) raised his head and said, 'O 'Ali, greeting to you, for you and your kinsmen will be in paradise. But after you a people will rise up professing to love you, pronouncing the creed and reciting the Qur'an; and they will be called Rafidi. If you find them wage holy war against them for they are polytheists, that is, unbelievers.' 'Ali said, 'O Prophet of Allah, what shall be their sign?' The Prophet said, 'They will not be present at the Friday prayers; they will not congregate for

worship; neither will they pray at funerals; and they will slander their forefathers.'

15 On this subject there are many traditions and verses of the Qur'an; if I were to mention them all, it would be a book in itself. At all events such are the characteristics of the Rafidis. As for the Batinis, which are worse than the Rafidis – just consider how vile they must be. At whatever time they may appear, the ruler of that time will have no more obligatory duty than to wipe them from the face of the earth and make his country free and clear of them, so that he may enjoy his rule and live happily. Similarly it is prohibited to employ Jews, Christians and Zoroastrians, and to give them charge over Muslims.

16 The Commander of the Faithful 'Umar (may Allah be pleased with him) was sitting in the mosque at Medina; Abu Musa Ash'ari (may Allah be pleased with him) was sitting in front of him, and was presenting the accounts for Isfahan – written in a fair hand and exactly reckoned, so that all who saw admired them. Abu Musa was asked, 'Whose writing is this?' He said, 'My secretary's.' They said, 'Send someone to bring him here for us to see him.' He said, 'He cannot come into the mosque.' The Commander of the Faithful 'Umar said, 'Is he unclean then?' He said, 'No; he is a Christian.' 'Umar gave Abu Musa a slap on the thigh – so hard that he said he thought his thigh was broken – and said, 'Have you not read the command of The Lord of Majesty where He speaks [Qur'an 5. 56]: O ye who believe, take not Jews and Christians as friends; they are friends to one another?' Abu Musa said, 'This very hour will I dismiss him and give him leave to return to Iran.'

Hakim [Sana'i] has composed a nice epigram on this subject:

'Tis right to beware of friendly enemies;
friendship with friendly friends is better.
Be not heedless of two kinds of men –
hostile friends and friendly foes.

17 After that Sultan Alp Arslan did not speak to Ardam for a whole month but only looked severely at him; until at last the nobles interceded during a party and persuaded him to forgive him and restore him to favour.

Now let us return to our discourse.

18 Whenever appointments are given to ignoble, unknown and

untalented persons, while famous, learned and high-born men are left unemployed and wasted – when five posts are vested in a single man while another receives none at all, this is a sign of the ignorance and incompetence of the vazir; if the vazir is incompetent and ignorant it is indicated by the fact that he tries to cause the empire's decline and seeks to damage the king's interests; in fact he is the worst of enemies because when he gives ten appointments to one man and leaves nine men without work, there are more people in the country unemployed and deprived than there are employed. When this is so the unemployed start working together; this is a situation which it may be possible to remedy; on the other hand it may not.

19 Now in actual fact there is just such a one[11] who is seeking to ruin this country by recommending economies; to The Master of the World he has alleged that the world is subdued; that there is nowhere any enemy or opponent who can withstand him; that he has nearly 400,000 men on his pay-roll; that 70,000 would be enough to keep and he could detail them to deal with any emergency; let him suppress the pay and allowances of the remainder; this would represent an economy of so many million dinars a year, and in a short time the treasury would be full of gold. When The Master of the World spoke in these same terms I knew whose words they were – the words of one who wishes to ruin the country. I replied: It is for The Master to command; but if he gives pay and allowances to 400,000 men, then it follows that he will have Khurasan; he will have Transoxiana as far as Kashghar, Balasaghun and Khwarazm; he will have Nimruz, 'Iraq [Jibal] and 'Iraqain [Kufa and Basra]; he will have Pars, Mazandaran and Tabaristan; he will have Adharbaygan, Armenia and Arran; and he will have Syria as far as Antioch and Jerusalem. I would have preferred that instead of 400,000 he had 700,000, because if he had more men, Ghaznain, Sind and India would be his; he would also have the whole of Turkistan, China and Machin; he would also have Yemen, Abyssinia, Barbar and Nubia; and in the Maghrib [N. Africa] and Spain he would rule as far as Qairuwan (of the Maghrib); and the whole of Rum would be under his sway. For the more troops a king has, the wider his realm; the fewer troops he has, the smaller his dominion; as soon as he lessens his army his territory shrinks, and when he increases his army his territory expands. Moreover The Sublime Intellect is aware that if he keeps

70,000 men in place of 400,000 the names of 330,000 must be erased from the register. Obviously 330,000 men are more than 70,000, and those 330,000 are all active men of the sword. When they have nothing more to hope for from this empire, they will find some other master or make one of themselves their leader. Then they will cause such trouble that the riches of many years will all be dissipated and still, maybe, the matter will not be put to rights. For countries are held by men, and men by gold. If someone says to the king, 'Take gold, and leave men', that person is in truth the king's enemy and is seeking to destroy the country, for gold is acquired only by men; his words must not be heeded.

20 The case of deprived and destitute civil officials is exactly the same. When people have performed great works and difficult tasks for this empire, have achieved celebrity and fame, and deserved reward for their services, it is not proper to disregard their claims, to leave them ruined, disappointed and dispossessed; to keep them unemployed is not right, nor is it compatible with humanity. It has always in the past been thought proper to offer them appointments, or allow them some livelihood according to their capabilities, so that at least a part of their dues of service will be paid, and they will not remain without any portion from this empire. Then there is another body of men – doctors, scholars, noblemen and men of valour – whose portion lies in the treasury. They are entitled to consideration and remuneration, yet no one offers them any work, and they get neither remuneration nor consideration. If all these remain deprived of their livelihood and disappointed of their portion from the empire, a time may come when the king's agents, being ignorant and graceless, fail to represent the cases of these deserving people to the king, neglect to give these officials any work and omit to provide salary and sustenance to such noble and learned men; in that time this party, cutting off their expectations from this empire, will become disaffected to the government; if they are aware of any faults committed by tax-collectors, scribes or king's intimates, they will expose them publicly rather than report them to the king privately; and they will spread false rumours. Then, whoever amongst them is best provided with stores, troops and funds, will be put at their head, and they will cause disturbances and rise against the king, throwing the country into confusion, just as they did in the time of Fakhr ad-Daula.

The story of Fakhr ad-Daula

21 They say that in the city of Rayy in the time of Fakhr ad-Daula, whose vazir was the Sahib Isma'il ibn 'Abbad, there was a fire-worshipper, a rich man, who was called Buzurjumid Dizu. He had built a sepulchre[12] for himself on the hill of Tabarik,[13] and it is still in existence today; now it is called The Generals' Look-out, and it is situated above The Dome of Fakhr ad-Daula. Buzurjumid took great pains and spent much money on completing this sepulchre with two envelopes[14] on top of that hill. Now there was a man called B'akhir-asan [Easy-at-the-end], who was the municipal censor of Rayy; on the day that the tower was finished, he went up it on some pretext and proclaimed the [Islamic] call to prayer; the sepulchre was thus desecrated. Thereafter it came to be known as The Generals' Look-out.

22 It so happened that in the latter part of the reign of Fakhr ad-Daula they had couriers; one day they reported that thirty or forty people were leaving the city every morning and ascending that tower; they would stay up there until sundown and then come down and disperse in the city; if anyone asked them why they were going there every day, they said it was for recreation. Fakhr ad-Daula ordered that the men were to be brought before him together with any things they had with them. A party of courtiers went and climbed the hill; they shouted at the foot of the tower because they could not get up. The men heard them and looked down; they saw the chamberlain of Fakhr ad-Daula with a party of attendants. They let down ladders for the party to ascend. When they got to the top they saw a chess-board laid out, and a backgammon-board; there were pens, ink and paper; there was a cloth with bread on it, two jugs of water, a pitcher and a rush mat[15] spread out. The chamberlain said, 'Get up; Fakhr ad-Daula summons you.' The men were brought in front of the king; as it happened The Sahib was present. Fakhr ad-Daula asked them who they were and why they went up the tower every day. They said they were having an outing. The king said, 'An outing may be for one or two days; you have been carrying on this business for a long time. Tell me the truth.' They said, 'There is no secret about the fact that we are not robbers, or murderers, or seducers of women and children; nor has anybody ever complained to

167

Your Majesty about us on account of any objectionable or unreasonable behaviour. If Your Majesty will guarantee our lives, we will tell you what we are.' Fakhr ad-Daula said, 'I give you security for your lives and property'; and he took an oath upon it, because he recognized most of them.

23 When they had been assured of security for their lives, they said, 'We are a group of secretaries and officials who have been left unemployed in Your Majesty's reign and deprived of a portion from your government; nobody offers us any work and nobody pays any attention to us. We hear that in Khurasan a king has appeared whom they call Mahmud, and he welcomes men of merit, learning and talent, and does not allow them to be wasted; abandoning all hope in this country we have now pinned our faith upon him. Every day we go up this tower and condole with one another upon our misfortune; whenever anyone arrives from a distance we seek information about Mahmud, and we constantly write letters and overtures to our friends in Khurasan, explaining our circumstances and inquiring after companions for the journey to Khurasan; for we are all family men, and being reduced to poverty we are compelled by necessity to leave the land where we were born and go abroad in search of work. Now we have explained our circumstances; it is for The Master to command.'

24 When Fakhr ad-Daula heard these words he turned to The Sahib and said, 'What is your opinion? what ought we to do?' The Sahib said, 'Your Majesty has given them security, and moreover they are professional secretaries, respectable men, and I know some of them. The affairs of secretaries are my concern; leave the matter of their employment to me; I will do all that is required to provide for them adequately and will ensure that a report reaches Your Majesty's auspicious hearing tomorrow.' So they ordered the chamberlain to conduct the men to The Sahib's house and leave them there. The chamberlain did so and came back to Fakhr ad-Daula's palace. Meanwhile the men were gloomy and apprehensive, wondering what punishment The Sahib would give them. When The Sahib returned from the palace he took a look at them. Some time elapsed; then a servant entered and led them all into another room decked out like paradise and strewn with costly carpets and cushions. The servant said, 'Go and sit wherever you like.' So they went and seated themselves on the mattresses. Sherbet was brought in; when they had drunk that, trays of food were

brought; and when they had eaten the food and washed their hands, wine was served and salvers were set out; and as they drank the wine minstrels played and sang. Apart from the three servants who were serving them nobody was allowed into that room, and nobody outside knew what had happened to them; throughout the city men and women were worried about them and their wives and children wept.

25 After three or four rounds[16] one of The Sahib's chamberlains entered the room and said, 'The Sahib says you are to understand that he does not wish his house to become a prison; today and tonight you are his guests. If they had wanted to do you any harm they would not have sent you to his house.' When The Sahib came back from the office he began to make arrangements for their employment. He fetched a tailor, and ordered twenty brocade cloaks to be cut; he also called for twenty horses saddled and caparisoned. At sunrise the following day everything was ready. The Sahib summoned all the men; he invested each with a cloak and turban, gave every one a horse with trappings and appointed them all to various official posts; some were given pensions and all were given presents; then they were sent to their homes satisfied. The next day they all came to call on The Sahib; The Sahib said, 'Now be kind and complain no more; send no more letters to Mahmud and stop trying to bring about the decline of our country.'

26 When next Fakhr ad-Daula received The Sahib, he asked him what he had done with that group of men. He said, 'O Master, I gave each one a horse with trappings, a suit of clothes and money for expenses; and wherever I found one man holding two posts in the administration, I relieved him of one and gave it to one of these men, so when I sent them back home they had all become government officials.' Fakhr ad-Daula was pleased and approved his action, saying, 'If you had done otherwise it would not have been right; would that what you have done this year you had done ten years ago, and then they would not have had recourse to our enemies. Hereafter one man is not to be given two posts; everyone is to have one post only, so that all civil servants may be employed and the prestige of all the posts may be maintained. Moreover, when two or three posts are allotted to one man, it becomes difficult for all civil servants to make a living; and foreigners and critics will say that we have no men left in our cities and our country

because we give two posts to one man; so they will infer that we are incompetent. Do you not know that wise men have said [in Arabic], "There are men for every work." (That is to say: one man one job.) In our country there are high, low and middle grade appointments; and each official and professional civil servant should be given only one appointment according to his capacity, knowledge, suitability and resources; if anyone who has an appointment asks for another, his request should be disregarded and refused; then this improper practice will be discontinued, and when there are no officials unemployed, the country will become prosperous.'

27 Furthermore the kingdom is kept in order by its tax-collectors and army officers; and the head of all the tax-collectors and civil servants is the vazir. Whenever the vazir is corrupt, treacherous, oppressive and unjust, the tax-men are all likewise, nay worse. A tax-man may be well versed in his duties, he may be a secretary, an accountant or a business expert such that he has no peer in all the world; but if he is a member of a bad sect or bad religion, such as Jew, Christian or Zoroastrian, he will despise the Muslims and afflict them with hardships on the pretext of taxes and accounts. If the Muslims are oppressed by that heretic or infidel and complain about him he must be dismissed and punished. One must not be concerned with what his intercessors may say – they may say there is no secretary or accountant or tax-collector in the world like him; they may say that if he is removed from office, the work will all come to grief, and there is nobody to take his place. This is all lies and such words must not be heeded; it is imperative to change that man for another, as The Commander of the Faithful 'Umar once did (may Allah be pleased with him).

The story of 'Umar and the Jewish tax-collector

28 It so happened that in the days of Sa'd [ibn Abi] Waqqas[17] in the area of Baghdad, Wasit, Anbar and those districts as far as Basra and the boundary of Khuzistan, there was a Jewish tax-collector. Now the people of these districts wrote a petition to The Commander of the Faithful 'Umar (may Allah be pleased with him) and complained against that Jewish collector, saying,

'This man is troubling us unjustly and is humiliating and mocking us on the pretext of tax-collection; we cannot endure it further. If there is no other alternative, appoint a Muslim collector over us; being of the same religion as ourselves perhaps he will not exceed his authority and oppress us; if however he does so at least we would prefer to suffer such injustice and indignity from a Muslim than from a Jew.' When 'Umar read the petition he said, 'Is it not enough for a Jew that he should be alive in the world? Does he also expect preference over the Muslims?' He immediately ordered a letter to be written to Sa'd Waqqas telling him to dismiss the Jew and give the appointment to a Muslim.

29 On reading the letter, Sa'd Waqqas detailed a horseman to go and bring the Jewish collector to Kufa, and he sent several other riders to summon all the Muslim tax-collectors in the province of Iran. The Jew arrived and the other tax-collectors. On inspection none of the Arabs was found to possess the knowledge to fulfil the post, and of the Persian collectors who were Muslim not one was discovered who had the same ability as the Jew, nor did anybody understand as well as he the various aspects of the work, such as collecting revenue, developing the country, dealing with people, and keeping up with taxes and arrears. Sa'd Waqqas was at a loss to know what to do. Of necessity he kept the Jew in the appointment and wrote to The Commander of the Faithful saying, 'I attended to your command and brought the Jew here and assembled together all the tax-collectors and civil servants, both Arab and Persian; but I found nobody among the Arabs who was acquainted with Persian affairs; and I weighed up all the Persian tax-collectors, but there was no one at all who was as competent and understood the duties of tax-collection and administration as well as the Jew. I was obliged to keep him at his post to prevent disorganization of business and breakdown in the collection of taxes. What is your command?'

30 When the letter reached 'Umar (may Allah be pleased with him) he was angry, and said, 'This is most extraordinary, that a man should overrule my authority and countermand my order.' He took up his pen and wrote at the top of the letter [in Arabic], '*Māta 'l-Yahūdī*' and sent it back to Sa'd Waqqas. '*Māta 'l-Yahūdī*' means in Persian, 'The Jew is dead'. What he meant was, 'Every man has to die; and death causes dismissal. Know that if a tax-collector dies or is dismissed, his work cannot be allowed to lapse.

In the end someone else has to be appointed; why are you so weak and helpless? Suppose the Jew is dead.' When Sa'd received the letter and saw 'Umar's postscript on it, he immediately dismissed the Jew and gave the post to a Muslim. After a year had passed it was observed that the Muslim discharged his duties even more efficiently than the Jew; and public works increased. Sa'd Waqqas then said to the Arab nobles, 'What a great man is The Commander of the Faithful 'Umar! We wrote a long letter on the subject of that Jew and the province's taxes; he gave the answer in two words; and it turned out as he said, not as we thought: and he got us out of difficulty.'

31 Two persons spoke two sayings; both were applauded and among Arabs and non-Arabs will be cited as proverbs by Muslims until the resurrection. One was that saying of The Commander of the Faithful 'Umar (may Allah be pleased with him): '*Māta 'l-Yahūdī.*' Whenever it is desired to dismiss a tax-collector or other official who knows well the duties of a secretary and is an efficient administrator, but is extortionate and unjust or a heretic, and some people favour him and support him saying, 'We cannot do without him; he is a good secretary and a clever official, and nobody knows more about business than he', and suchlike, then the manager must say at once, '*Māta 'l-Yahūdī.*' All their arguments will be confounded by these two words, and the collector will be dismissed. Secondly, when our Prophet (upon him be peace) went out from the world, not one of his Companions dared to say that The Prophet was dead; after Abu Bakr Siddiq (may Allah be pleased with him) was installed as his successor, he mounted the pulpit to preach, and said [in Arabic], '*Māta Muhammad.*' Then he said, 'O Muslims, if you were worshipping Muhammad, Muhammad is dead; and if you were worshipping the God of Muhammad, He is still there and always was and always will be; He it is who will never die.' The Muslims approved this speech, and it became a proverb among the Arabs; and whenever any great affliction befalls the Arabs or a dear one passes away, and they want to ease the burden of suffering for the unfortunate relative, people cry out, '*Māta Muhammad*', that is 'Muhammad is dead!'; for of all mankind had it been possible for one man not to die, then that person should have been Muhammad The Elect (upon him be peace).

Now let us return to our discourse.

32 We said that tax-collectors and their work are the concern of the vazir. The good vazir enhances the fame and character of his sovereign; and the kings who have become great rulers of the world and whose names will be blessed until the resurrection, have all been those who had good vazirs, and the same is true of the prophets (the prayers of Allah be upon them all): Solomon (upon him be peace) had one like Asaf ibn Barkhiya, Moses (upon him be peace) had his brother Aaron (upon him be peace), Jesus (upon him be peace) had Simon, and Muhammad The Elect (upon him be peace) had Abu Bakr Siddiq (may Allah be pleased with him). Among great kings there was Kai Khusrau who had a vazir like Gaudarz, Manuchihr had Sam, Afrasiyab had Piran-i Visa, Gushtasp had Jamasp, Rustam had Zavara, Bahram Gur had Khuraruz, and Nushirvan had Buzurjmihr; while the 'Abbasid caliphs had such ministers as the Barmakids [Barmecides], and the Samanids had the Bal'amis, Sultan Mahmud had Ahmad ibn Hasan, Fakhr ad-Daula had The Sahib Isma'il ibn 'Abbad, Sultan Tughril had Abu Nasr Kunduri.[18] Thus the lives of prophets and the histories of kings became celebrated in the world; and there are many more like these.

33 Now a vazir needs to belong to a pure religion, to have sound faith and to adhere to a good school of doctrine – either Hanafi or Shafi'i, and he must be efficient, shrewd, a fluent writer, and loyal to his king; if he also be the son of a vazir so much the better and more blessed, for from the time of Ardashir Papakan to Yazdijird ibn Shahryar (the last of the kings of Iran) vazirs needed to be sons of vazirs just as kings had to be sons of kings; and this remained so until the coming of Islam. When the kingship passed out of the house of the kings of Iran, the vazirship departed from the house of the vazirs.

The story of Sulaiman ibn 'Abd al-Malik and Ja'far ibn Barmak[19]

34 They say that one day Sulaiman ibn 'Abd al-Malik was giving audience and all the nobles of the state and all his boon-companions were present. [In the course of the proceedings] the caliph voiced the following idea: 'If my dominion is no greater than that of Sulaiman ibn Davud [Solomon son of David] (upon them both be peace) it is not less, except for the fact that he had command

over winds, demons, fairies, wild beasts and birds, and I have not; as for treasure, magnificent equipage, territorial possessions, military strength and personal authority, who in all the world now has, or who before me has ever had, the equal of what is mine at this moment? In this kingdom of mine do I lack anything which I ought to have?' One of the nobles said to him, 'The most important thing which countries need and kings have always had, Your Majesty has not.' Sulaiman said, 'What is that?' He said, 'You have not a vazir who is worthy of you.' He said, 'How so?' He said, 'You are a king, born of royal stock; you should have a vazir who is sprung from a line of vazirs, besides being blessed with talents and good fortune.' Sulaiman said, 'Can there be found in all the world a vazir such as you have described?' He said, 'Yes.' He said, 'Where?' He said, 'At Balkh.' He said, 'Who is he?' He said, 'Ja'far ibn Barmak, whose ancestors back to the time of Ardashir Papakan have been vazirs and sons of vazirs; the ancient fire-temple at Nau-bahar [near] Balkh[20] is a pious foundation vested in that family. When Islam spread and fortune deserted the dynasty of the kings of Iran, Ja'far's ancestors settled at Balkh, and remained there. Vazirship is hereditary in their family and they possess books about the functions and duties of a vazir; when their children were taught writing, literature and secretaryship, they used to be given these books to read, learn and act upon; thus sons assimilated the character of their fathers in all respects. Ja'far is the most suitable man in the world to be Your Majesty's vazir. Hereafter Your Majesty knows best.' Yet of the Umayyads and Marwanids there was no greater or more powerful ruler than Sulaiman ibn 'Abd al-Malik.

35 When he heard these words he determined to bring Ja'far ibn Barmak from Balkh and give him the vazirship. He wondered whether he might not still be a fire-worshipper; he made enquiries and when he found out that he had been born a Muslim he was glad. He sent a letter to the governor of Balkh instructing him to send Ja'far to Damascus, and even if it cost 100,000 dinars to equip him for the journey he was to spend the money and send him with all possible pomp to the capital. So Ja'far was sent to Damascus. The nobles of every city on the way came out to meet him and give him hospitality. When he reached Damascus, all the highest officers of state and army, apart from Sulaiman ibn 'Abd al-Malik himself, went to welcome him; they escorted him into

the city with the utmost pomp and circumstance and installed him in a most palatial residence. After three days he was taken before Sulaiman ibn 'Abd al-Malik; when Sulaiman first saw him as he came into the palace, he was pleased with his appearance and bearing. Ja'far went up onto the dais and the chamberlains conducted him gradually towards the throne; having shewn him to his seat they retired. The moment that Ja'far sat down, Sulaiman looked sharply at him; then he scowled and said angrily, 'Be gone from my sight!' The chamberlains hurriedly seized him and whisked him away; nobody knew what the reason was; until later in the day after the noon prayer there was a drinking party attended by nobles and boon-companions; several rounds were drunk and there was general merriment.

36 When it was seen that Sulaiman had recovered his temper, one of the courtiers said, 'Your Majesty commanded Ja'far to be brought from Balkh with all this dignity and ceremony for a high office. When he appeared before Your Majesty you suddenly looked coldly upon him and ordered him to be taken away; what was the reason for that? We your humble servants were struck with amazement.' Sulaiman said, 'Had it not been for the fact that he is of noble birth and has come from afar, I would have had him executed there and then, because he had deadly poison with him – the very first time he came into my presence he brought poison as a gift!' One of the nobles said, 'Would you permit me to go and question him about this, to see what he says – whether he confesses or denies?' He said, 'You may go.' So he got up and left the company to go and see Ja'far; he asked him, 'When you came before Sulaiman today, did you have poison with you?' He said, 'Yes, and I still have it; here it is, underneath the gem of my ring. My forefathers had similar rings and this one came to me from my father. I and my ancestors have never harmed so much as an ant with this ring, let alone a human being. Rather we kept it for prudence and precaution's sake, for my ancestors were many times subjected to hardship and torture for financial ends; and in this case when Sulaiman summoned me, I did not really know the reason for the call; I considered that if he were to ask for treasure-lists or make some other demand which I could not fulfil, or if he molested me in any way that I could not endure, I would remove the gem of the ring with my teeth and swallow the poison in order to escape from all the suffering and misery.'

37 Having listened to this explanation from Ja'far, the courtier immediately went back and told Sulaiman what had transpired; he was amazed at his prudence and foresight; he had no more doubt about him, and accepted his explanation. Then he ordered all the nobles to take his private horse, go to the door of Ja'far's house and bring him with honour and dignity to the court. The next day this was done. When Ja'far came before Sulaiman, Sulaiman held out his hand to him, enquired about his journey, and welcomed him warmly; he made him sit down and invested him there and then with the robe of the vazir's office; then he placed the inkpot in front of him for him to sign a few official documents in his presence. Sulaiman had never been seen in such a good humour as he was on that day; after the audience was over, he held a drinking party and the presence-chamber was decorated with gold, jewels and carpets woven with gold thread, the like of which had never been seen before.

38 So they settled down to their drinking; and in the course of the merry-making Ja'far asked Sulaiman, 'How did Your Majesty know that I, out of so many thousand people, had poison with me?' Sulaiman said, 'I have with me something more precious to me than all my treasuries and all my possessions, and I never go without it; this is a couple of beads, like onyx but not in fact onyx; I acquired them from the treasury of the kings and I wear them fastened on my arm; they have this property, that wherever poison may be, whether with a person or in food or drink, as soon as the smell of it reaches them, they immediately start moving and knocking against one another restlessly; then I know that there is poison somewhere in the room and take steps to guard against it. When you set foot onto the dais the beads began to move; the nearer you came the more their agitation increased; by the time you sat down in front of me they were rattling together. I had no doubt at all that you were carrying poison, and had anyone else been in your place I would not have spared him. When they took you away the beads calmed down, but they did not cease moving altogether until you had left the palace.' Then he loosed the beads from his arm and shewed them to Ja'far saying, 'Have you ever seen anything more wonderful than this?' All the nobles looked at the beads in astonishment. Then Ja'far said, 'In the course of my life I have seen two unparalleled marvels; one is this which I now see with Your Majesty; the other is something I

saw with the king of Tabaristan.' Sulaiman said, 'What was that? Tell me; I would like to hear.'

39 Ja'far related the following story: When Your Majesty's decree reached the governor of Balkh instructing him to despatch your humble servant to Damascus, I packed my things for the journey and bent my steps towards your presence. From Nishapur I took the road to Tabaristan because I had some goods there. When I reached Tabaristan, the king of Tabaristan came out to meet me and escorted me to his palace in the city of Amul where I was entertained. Every day the king and I used to eat and sit together, and we made daily excursions to different places. One day in a jovial mood he said to me, 'Have you ever taken a trip on the sea?' I said, 'No.' He said, 'Tomorrow you are my guest for a sea trip.' I said, 'It is for you to command.' He ordered boatmen to prepare boats and hold themselves ready. On the following day the king took me down to the sea and we got into a boat; minstrels struck up a tune and the boatmen rowed us out to sea, while cupbearers plied us all the while with wine. The king and I were sitting close to one another with nobody in between us; on his finger he had a ring the gem of which was a red ruby of the most exquisite beauty and brilliance that I had ever seen; and on account of its splendour I could not keep my eyes off it.

40 When the king noticed that I was constantly looking at the ring, he took it off his finger and tossed it into my lap. I bowed to him, kissed the ring and laid it in his lap. The king picked it up and gave it to me again, saying, 'A ring which has left my finger by way of being a present freely given does not come back on my finger again.' I said, 'This particular ring is worthy of Your Majesty's finger'; and I gave it back to the king. The king gave it to me again. Considering that the ring was so beautiful and valuable, I said, 'Your Majesty says this in his cups: I would not wish him to regret it and be distressed when he is sober.' I put the ring back in the king's lap. The king took it and threw it into the sea. I exclaimed, 'Oh! what a pity! if I had known for certain that Your Majesty would not put the ring on his finger again and was going to throw it into the sea, well – I would have accepted it, for I had never seen such a ruby.' The king said, 'I offered it to you several times; when I saw your eyes fixed on it, I took it off my finger and presented it to you; although I liked the ring very much, if you had not liked it even more, I would not have given it to you; it

was your fault for not accepting it; now that I have thrown it in the sea you are sorry. However, perhaps I can contrive to get it back for you.' He said to a page, 'Get into a small boat and go back to the shore; when you land take a horse and gallop back to the palace; tell the treasurer that you want a certain silver casket; take it and bring it here with haste.' Before sending the page he told the boatman to drop anchor and keep the boat in the same place until he had further instructions; he did so. Meanwhile we carried on drinking until the page arrived with the casket and laid it in front of the king. The king opened a purse which he kept on his waist and took out a silver key; he undid the lock of the casket and lifted the lid; putting his hand inside he removed a golden fish and threw it into the sea. The fish went under the water and dived to the bottom of the sea, disappearing from sight. After some time it came to the surface, holding the ring in its mouth. At the king's command a boatman hurried to the spot with a small boat, picked up the fish with the ring and brought it like that to the king. The king took the ring from the fish's mouth and tossed it into my lap. I bowed to him, picked up the ring and put it on my finger, while the king put the fish back into the casket, locked it up and replaced the key in his purse.

41 Ja'far was wearing the ring [as he spoke]; he took it off his finger and laid it in front of Sulaiman, saying, 'This is the ring, O Master.' Sulaiman picked it up and looked at it; then he gave it back to him and said, 'You should not lose the souvenir of such a [remarkable] man.'

42 The purpose of this book was not to tell stories such as this; however, when a particular story seemed out of the ordinary and at the same time fitting, it was related.

43 My object in this chapter is to point out that when the good age arrives and the sick time changes, the sign of it is this, that a just king appears and does away with evil-doers; his judgments are right; his vazir and other officers are men of virtue and nobility; every task is allotted to the proper workman; two posts are not given to one man and one post is not given to two men; heretics are put down and the orthodox are raised up; tyrants are repressed and restricted to harmless activities; soldiery and peasantry fear the king; uneducated and base-born men are not given employment; boys[21] are not promoted [to high office]; advice is

sought from men of mature wisdom and intelligence; high command in the army is given to experienced elders not to immature youths: men are in demand for their skill not for their money; religion is not sold for worldly things; all things are restored to their proper order and each person's rank is fixed according to his deserts, with the result that affairs religious and worldly are well arranged and every man has work according to his capability; nothing contrary to this is permitted by the king and all things great and small are regulated by the balance of justice and the sword of governance, by the grace of Allah (be He exalted).

Chapter XLII

On the subject of those who wear the veil

1 The king's underlings must not be allowed to assume power, for this causes the utmost harm and destroys the king's splendour and majesty. This particularly applies to women, for they are wearers of the veil and have not complete intelligence. Their purpose is the continuation of the lineage of the race, so the more noble their blood the better, and the more chaste and abstemious their bearing the more admirable and acceptable they are. But when the king's wives begin to assume the part of rulers, they base their orders on what interested parties tell them, because they are not able to see things with their own eyes in the way that men constantly look at the affairs of the outside world. They give orders following what they are told by those who work amongst them such as chamberlains and servants. Naturally their commands are mostly the opposite of what is right, and mischief ensues; the king's dignity suffers and the people are afflicted with trouble; disorder affects the state and the religion; men's wealth is dissipated and the ruling class is put to vexation. In all ages nothing but disgrace, infamy, discord and corruption have resulted

when kings have been dominated by their wives. Let us discuss a little of this subject in the hope that much will be made clear.

2 The first man who suffered loss and underwent pain and trouble for obeying a woman was Adam (upon him be peace) who did the bidding of Eve and ate the wheat[1] with the result that he was expelled from paradise, and wept for two hundred years until God had mercy on him and accepted his repentance.

The story of Saudaba and Siyavush

3 Saudaba was the wife of Kai Kavus and she had power over him. When Kai Kavus sent messengers to Rustam asking for the return of Siyavush because he longed to see him – Siyavush was his son and Rustam had fostered him until he reached the age of manhood – Rustum sent Siyavush to him. Now Siyavush was exceedingly handsome. Saudaba saw him from behind the curtain and was enamoured of him. She said to Kai Kavus, 'Tell Siyavush to come into the women's apartments so that his sisters may see him.' Kai Kavus said to Siyavush, 'Go into the women's apartments, for your sisters want to see you.' Siyavush said, 'It is my lord's command, nevertheless it were better that they be in their apartments and I in the hall.' When he went into the night-quarters, Saudaba assaulted him and drew him to herself with mischievous intent. Siyavush became angry and wresting himself from her embrace, he left the women's apartment and went to his own house. Saudaba was afraid of what he might say to his father. She said to herself, 'It is better that I anticipate him.' So she went to Kai Kavus and said, 'Siyavush assaulted me and clung to me, and I escaped from him.' Kai Kavus was vexed with Siyavush and there was much fierce and angry talk, until at last it was suggested to Siyavush that he should undergo ordeal by fire to satisfy the king. Siyavush said, 'It is for the king to command; whatever he says, I am ready.' So they collected enough firewood to cover half a farsang square, and set fire to it.

4 When the fire gained strength, Kai Kavus went up a mountain; then he said to Siyavush, 'Go into the fire!' Siyavush was riding Shabrang. He uttered the name of God, made his horse leap into the flames, and disappeared. After some time he emerged from the far side of the fire in safety with not a hair singed either on himself or on his horse, by God's command. All the people

were amazed. The priests took some of that fire and carried it to
the fire-temple; and it is still alive – the fire which gave judgment
correctly.

5 After this judgment Kai Kavus appointed Siyavush to be
amir of Balkh and sent him there. But Siyavush had been offended
by his father on account of Saudaba, and he lived unhappily there.
He was minded not to stay in the land of Iran. He thought of
going to Hindustan, or else to China and Maciin. Piran-i Visa,
who was Afrasiyab's army-commander, came to know Siyavush's
secret intent. He presented himself to Siyavush, paid him compliments on behalf of Afrasiyab and accepted him into Afrasiyab's
allegiance. Piran said that their house was one, and their two
families were one; Afrasiyab would hold him dearer than all his
own sons; and if he ever wished to be reconciled with his father
and return to Iran, Afrasiyab would intercede for him, and make
a firm treaty with Kai Kavus, and then send him to his father with
all honour and respect. So Siyavush went from Balkh to Turkistan. Afrasiyab gave him his daughter in marriage and held him
dearer than his own sons. However, Garsivaz, Afrasiyab's brother,
became jealous of him, and conspired with slanderers and con-
trived to turn Afrasiyab against him. Siyavush was innocent but
he was slain in Turkistan. Wailing arose in Iran and her warriors
were aroused. Rustam came from Sistan to the capital. Without
permission he entered the women's apartments of Kai Kavus and
seized Saudaba by the hair; he dragged her outside and cut her to
pieces with his sword. No man dared to tell him, 'You did well',
or 'You did ill.' Then they girded themselves for war, and went
to Turkistan to take vengeance for the murder of Siyavush. The
war went on for many years, and on both sides many thousand
men were slaughtered. And the cause of all this was Saudaba and
her domination over King Kai Kavus.

6 Kings and men of strong judgment have always ordered their
lives in such a way, and followed such a path that they never let
their wives or maid-servants know their feelings; so they remained free from the yoke of their desires and commands and
did not succumb to them; one such was Alexander.

7 History relates that when Alexander came from Rum and
defeated Darius son of Darius, who was King of Persia, Darius
was killed in flight by one of his own servants. Now Darius had a

daughter perfect in beauty and charm, and she had a sister just as fair; and in his palace there were other girls of his family – all of them beautiful. People said to Alexander, 'It befits you to pass by Darius's night-quarters and see those moon-faced fairy-figured ones, especially his daughter, for in beauty she has no peer.' Those who said this intended that Alexander should see Darius's daughter, and having seen her with all her comeliness, surely marry her. Alexander replied, 'We vanquished their men; let us not be conquered by their women.' He heeded them not, and went not into Darius's night-quarters.

8 Another well-known story is that of Khusrau and Shirin and Farhad. Since Khusrau so loved Shirin that he put the reins of fancy into her hands and did everything that she said, then inevitably she grew bold, and though she was queen to such a great king, she began to prefer Farhad.

9 Buzurjmihr was asked, 'Why was it that the empire of the house of Sasan fell to ruin while you were their counsellor, for today you have no equal in the world for prudence and policy and wisdom and learning?' He said, 'There were two reasons: firstly the Sasanians entrusted weighty affairs to petty and ignorant officers, and secondly they hated learning and learned people. Men of stature and wisdom should be sought out and put into office; I had to deal with women and boys.'

This is the very opposite of prudence and wisdom, for be assured that whenever a king leaves affairs to women and boys, the kingship will depart from his house.

10 There is a tradition that The Prophet (upon him be prayers and peace) says, 'Consult women, but whatever they say, do the opposite, and that will be right.' The words of the tradition are [in Arabic], 'Consult them and oppose them.' Had women possessed complete intelligence, The Prophet (upon him be peace) would not have commanded people to go against their opinions.

11 It is reported in another tradition that when The Prophet's illness became severe at the end of his epoch, he was so weak that when the time came for obligatory prayer, The Companions were all waiting for him to begin the congregational service and he was not strong enough to go to the mosque. 'Ayisha and Hafsa (may Allah be pleased with them both) were sitting at his bedside; 'Ayisha said to The Prophet, 'O Prophet of Allah, it is time for prayer, and you are not strong enough to go to the mosque;

which of The Companions will you command to lead the prayer?'
He said, 'Abu Bakr' (may Allah be pleased with him). Again she
said, 'Whom do you command?' He said, 'Abu Bakr.' Yet again,
she said, 'Whom do you command to lead the prayer?' He said,
'Abu Bakr.' After a time 'Ayisha whispered to Hafsa, 'I have
spoken three times; now you tell him directly that The Commander of the Faithful Abu Bakr is a tender-hearted man and
loves him very much; if he were to see The Prophet's place (that
is the *miḥrāb*) empty, he would be overcome with weeping and
unable to control himself, and that would spoil his own and all
the others' prayers. 'Umar is strong and stout of heart; tell him to
lead the prayer.' So Hafsa spoke in this wise to The Prophet; he
said, 'You are like Yusuf and Kirsuf in the story; I shall not do
what you want; I shall do what is right and proper; go and tell
Abu Bakr to lead the congregation.'

12 The [Arabic] words of the tradition are, 'You are companions of Yusuf and Kirsuf.' And in spite of all the nobility, the
learning, the devotion and the piety of 'Ayisha, The Prophet (upon
him be peace) did the opposite of what she wanted. So imagine
what the opinions of other women are worth.

The story of Yusuf and Kirsuf

13 They say that in the time of The Sons of Israel it was the rule
that if for forty years a man had preserved himself from great sins,
had fasted and prayed at the proper times and harmed no one,
then God would grant him three wishes and he could have anything he wanted. Now there was in those days one of The Sons
of Israel called Yusuf, a good and pious man, and he had a wife
called Kirsuf, as devout and chaste as he. He accomplished this
devotional exercise and worshipped God for forty years without
default. He thought to himself, 'Now what thing shall I ask from
God (to Him be power and glory)? I wish I had a friend to advise
me what to ask for – something beneficial.' However much he
pondered he could not think of anyone suitable. As he entered his
house he caught sight of his wife. He said to himself, 'In all the
world nobody holds me dearer than she; she is my mate and the
mother of my children. My good is her good, and she more than
all people desires my good. The right thing is to consult her in this
matter.'

14 So he said to his wife, 'Know that I have now completed forty years of devotion, and three wishes will be granted to me. No one in all the world desires my good more than you. Tell me what to ask from God.' His wife said, 'You know that I have only you in all the world; my eye rejoices in you; and you know that the wife is a man's recreation ground and sowing field; your heart is always happy at the sight of me, and your life is sweet with me as companion. Ask God to give me, your mate, such beauty as he has given to no other woman, and then whenever you come in at the door and see me so fair and charming, your heart will be glad; as long as we are vouchsafed to remain in this world, we will live in joy and happiness.' The man was pleased at his wife's words. He prayed saying, 'O lord, give this woman grace and beauty such as Thou hast given to no other woman.' God heard and answered Yusuf's prayer. Next day when his wife got up, she was not the woman who had gone to sleep the night before; she had changed into a form of such comeliness as mortals had never seen.

15 When Yusuf saw her so beautiful he was astonished and he nearly jumped out of his skin for joy. Every day his wife's beauty and excellence grew until by the end of a week it reached a point where the beholder could not bear to look upon her; she was a thousand times fairer than the moon and the sun and finer and prettier than houris and fairies. The report of her beauty spread throughout the world; women came from cities and villages and far-off places to catch sight of her, and took back reports of their astonishment. Then one day she looked in the mirror and saw her perfect beauty; she enjoyed the picture of her face, hair, lips, teeth, eyes and eyebrows. Her heart was filled with wonder and pride; she said egotistically, 'Who is like me in all the world today? who has such grace and beauty as I have? what have I got to do with this pauper who eats barley-bread without having enough even of that, and passes a miserable existence without any of the good things of this world? I am fit for the greatest kings and Chosroes of the world, and if they find me they will adorn me with gold and finery.' Vain desires and ambitions of this sort entered the woman's head. She began to be disobedient, bad-tempered and quarrelsome with her husband; she was rude and abusive and often said to him, 'You are not fit for me; you have not even got enough barley-bread to eat.' She had three or four children by Yusuf; she ceased to look after them and gave up

washing and feeding them and putting them to bed; she became so unmanageable that Yusuf was at his wit's end and did not know what to do. He looked up to heaven and said, 'O Lord, turn this woman into a bear.' Immediately the woman turned into a bear and became a scourge, constantly prowling about the walls and roof of his house; it never went away from the house, and all day water ran from its eyes. Yusuf was at a loss to know how to look after his children; he was unable to perform his divine worship, and he constantly missed the time for prayer. Once more he was in distress; he reached such dire straits that he looked up to heaven, raised his hands and said, 'O Lord, turn this bear back into a woman just as she was before; give her a contented mind, so that she will watch over her children and care for them as she used to do; then I, Thy servant, will devote myself to worshipping Thee, O merciful God.' Straight away the woman resumed her original form, and proceeded to attend to her children. She never remembered what had happened, and only thought that she had been dreaming. So the forty years' devotion of Yusuf was [as the Qur'an 25. 25 says] 'blown dust' and come to nothing – all because of the schemes and desires of a woman.

Thereafter this story became a proverbial warning against doing what women say.

16 The caliph al-Ma'mun one day spoke as follows: 'May there never be a king who allows the people of the veil to speak to him about the state, the army, the treasury and the government or to interfere in such matters, or to patronize particular persons; for if they are heeded, at their behest the king may promote one and punish another, or appoint one and dismiss another; [and if this happens] inevitably people will resort to the women's court and present their needs to them since they can be more easily won over. The women, finding themselves the object of attention and seeing their doors thronged with soldiers and peasants, will give way to all sorts of vain desires and initiate all kinds of corrupt practices. Soon evil men and heretics will gain access to them. Then it will not be long before the king's majesty vanishes, and the dignity and splendour of the court and the government depart; the king will lose the respect of all, and reproaches will come in from surrounding countries; the country will lapse into confusion, the

troops will become disaffected, and the vazir will be powerless to prevent it.'

17 So what is the best way for the king to avoid all this anxiety? He should follow the established custom which great and prudent kings have practised and which God (to Him be power and glory) himself has commanded [Qur'an 4. 38]: 'Men are rulers over women.' (He says: We appointed men over women to keep them under control.) If women had been able to control themselves, He would not have set men over their heads. So if anyone places women over men, whatever mistakes and mischiefs occur are his fault, for permitting such a thing and changing the custom.

18 It was a dictum of Kai Khusrau that any king who wants his house to endure, his country not to be destroyed and his own pomp and dignity not to fall to the ground, must never permit people of the veil to have any say in matters concerning his under-lings and servants or give orders to his stewards, tax-collectors and assignees. In this way they will preserve the ancient custom and keep themselves free from all anxieties.

19 The Commander of The Faithful 'Umar ibn al-Khattab (may Allah be pleased with him) said, 'The words of the people of the veil are, like their persons, indecent. Just as it is wrong to display their persons in public, so also it is unseemly to repeat their words.'

20 Let that which has been mentioned on this subject suffice; it will throw light on much else, and it will be seen that these words are full of benefit.

Concerning underlings

21 God (to him be power and glory) has created the king to be the superior of all mankind and the inhabitants of the world are his inferiors; they derive their subsistence and rank from him. He must then keep them in such a position that they always know their places and do not put off the ring of service from their ears nor loose the belt of obedience from their waists. At times he should tell them how they stand whether in merit or demerit, so that they do not forget themselves, and he should not give them so much rope that they do whatever they like. He should know the measure and rank of every one, and be constantly enquiring into their circumstances lest they deviate from the letter of his commands or overstep the limits which are set for them.

22 One day Buzurjmihr Bakhtgan said to Nushirvan The Just, 'The country belongs to the king, and the king has given the country, but not the people of the country, to the army. The army are not interested in the king's country, and have no kindness and mercy towards the people; they are only out to fill their own purses, and they do not care whether the country is deserted or the peasantry impoverished. When the army has power over the country to strike, to fetter, to imprison, to usurp, to extort, to dismiss and to impose taxes, then what difference is there between the king and them? For these things have ever been the king's prerogative, not the business of the army; armies have never been allowed to exercise such power and authority. In all ages the golden crown, the golden stirrup, the throne and the coinage have belonged by right to the king alone.' And he went on, 'If the king wishes to have virtue and glory above all other kings, then let him refine and polish his morals.' The king said, 'How shall I do that?' He said, 'Banish the bad qualities from yourself, and take hold of the good qualities and exercise them.' He said, 'Which are the bad qualities?' He said, 'Hatred, envy, pride, anger, lust, greed, desire, spite, mendacity, avarice, ill temper, cruelty, selfishness, hastiness, ingratitude and frivolity. And the good qualities are these: modesty, good temper, clemency, forgiveness, humility, generosity, truthfulness, patience, gratitude, mercy, knowledge, intelligence and justice.'

23 He who exercises these qualities knows how to regulate all things and in the management of subordinates and the direction of affairs of state will need no guide or director.

Chapter XLIII

Exposing the facts about heretics who are enemies of the state and of Islam

1 Your humble servant wanted to compose a few chapters on the

risings of various rebels, so that all the world might know how great has been my concern for this kingdom, and how sincere my loyalty and devotion to the empire of the Saljuqs, especially to The Master of the World (may Allah perpetuate his reign) and to his children and family (may the evil eye be averted from this epoch).

2 Seceders have existed in all ages, and from the time of Adam (upon him be peace) until now in every country in the world they have risen up in revolt against kings and prophets. Never has there been a more sinister, more perverted or more iniquitous crowd than these people, who behind walls are plotting harm to this country and seeking to destroy the religion. Their ears are alert for the sounds of sedition and their eyes are open for signs of the evil eye. If in any way (we take refuge with Allah!) through some celestial accident any misfortune should befall this victorious empire (may Allah The Mighty strengthen it) these dogs will emerge from their hiding places, and will revolt against this empire. They claim to be Shi'ites and most of their strength and reinforcement comes from the Rafidis and Khurrama-dins, and as far as they can they will leave nothing undone in the pursuit of vice, mischief, murder and heresy. In their speech they claim to be Muslims, but in reality they act like unbelievers; their inward purposes are at variance with their outward appearances; their words are the opposite of their deeds. The religion of Muhammad (upon him be peace) has no worse enemy than them, and the kingdom of The Master of the World has no more vile and more accursed opponent.

3 There are certain persons who on this very day hold privileged positions in this empire and who, having removed their heads from the collar of the Shi'a, are members of this [Isma'ili] faction and secretly do its business, assist its policies and preach its doctrines. They try to persuade The Master of the World to overthrow the house of the 'Abbasids, and if I were to lift the lid[1] from the top of that pot – Oh! the disgraceful things that would be revealed! But – worse than that – as a result of their representations The Master of the World has become weary of his humble servant, and is not prepared to take any action in the matter, because of the economies which these people recommend, thereby making The Master of the World greedy for money. They make out that I am interested in my private advantage and so my humble

advice finds no acceptance. One day The Master will realize their iniquity and treachery and criminal deeds – when I have disappeared. Then will he know the measure of my devotion and loyalty to this victorious empire; for I have not been negligent or ignorant of their characters or their plottings and I have on various occasions made them known to The Sublime Intellect and not concealed them. But when your humble servant saw that his words on this subject were not accepted or believed, he did not repeat them any more.

4 However, I have introduced into this book of Rules [for Kings] a section dealing with the revolts of these Batinis, because it is important to explain as concisely as possible who they are, what sort of beliefs they hold, whence they first originated, how many times they have emerged, and in each case who was responsible for putting them down – so that after my death it may be a reminder for [succeeding] Masters of the Kingdom and the Faith. For this accursed faction has broken out and perpetrated massacres even in the lands of Syria, Yemen and Spain. I will only relate, in the manner of an epitome, what they have done in Persia. Whoever wishes to learn all the facts about them and all the disasters which they have caused to the kingdom and the religion of Muhammad The Elect (upon him be peace) should study the histories, especially the 'History of Isfahan'.

Now I will proceed to describe about one hundredth of what they have done in the land of Persia – for that is the principal part of the kingdom of The Master of the World – so that their story from beginning to end may be known to The Sublime Intellect.

Chapter XLIV

On the revolt of Mazdak and the doctrines of his sect; how Nushirvan The Just destroyed him and his followers

1 The first person in the world to introduce atheistic doctrines was a man who appeared in the land of Persia; he was a Zoroastrian high priest[1] in the time of King Qubad ibn Firuz and Nushirvan The Just; and his name was Mazdak Bamdadan. He plotted to corrupt the Zoroastrian faith to the disadvantage of its adherents, and spread a new way in the world. Now it so happened that this Mazdak was well versed in astrology, and from the motions of the stars he foretold that in that age a man was to appear who would introduce a religion to cancel the Zoroastrian, Jewish, Christian and idolatrous faiths; this new religion he would impose upon the necks of mankind by miracles and by force, and it would last until the resurrection. Mazdak conceived the vain fancy that he would be this person, and he began to ponder how he should convert the people and propagate a new cult. He knew that in the king's council he enjoyed the utmost respect and the highest estate, while his word was supreme among all the nobles; never had he been heard to utter a vain word – until he laid claim to prophethood. What he did was to tell his minions to make a tunnel in a certain place; they gradually bored a hole so that the end of it came up in the fire-temple, just at the spot where the fire was made; it was only a small opening. Then he began to state his claim to be a prophet, and said, 'I have been sent to renew the faith of Zoroaster because people have forgotten the meaning of the Avesta and Zend, and have ceased to obey the commands of The Good One as Zoroaster laid down; just as in the case of The Sons of Israel when they were disobedient and failed to perform the laws of Moses (upon him be peace) which he received from God in the Torah, He sent a prophet, as promised in the Torah itself, to cast out the disobedience[2] from The Sons of Israel, to restore the authority of the Torah and bring the people back to the right way. Now I have been sent to renew the faith of Zoroaster and shew people the right way.' These words reached the ears of King Qubad.

2 The next day he called his nobles and priests and held court for the redress of wrongs. He summoned Mazdak and said to him publicly. 'Do you claim to be a prophet?' He said, 'Yes. I have come because our enemies have corrupted the faith which Zoroaster instituted, and cast it into doubt; I will restore it to health. For the most part the people are wrong in their interpretation of the Avesta and Zend; I will shew them the true meaning.' Qubad said, 'What is your [proof or] miracle?' He said, 'My miracle is this, that I will make the fire speak – the fire which you regard as your *qibla*[3] and sanctuary; and I will ask God (to Him be power and glory) to command the fire to bear witness to my prophethood, so that the king and everyone with him may hear.' The king said, 'O nobles and priests of Iran, what do you say to these words which Mazdak speaks?' The priests said, 'The first thing is this, that he is calling us to our own faith and book, and he is not opposing Zoroaster. It is true that there are passages in the Avesta and Zend which can bear ten different meanings, and every priest and doctor explains and interprets them differently. It is possible that he may give a better interpretation and more fitting meaning to those passages. But as for his saying that he will give voice to this fire which is the object of our worship – this is a marvel which is not within the power of a man. More than this the king knows best.' Then Qubad said to Mazdak, 'If you make the fire speak I will bear witness that you are a prophet.' Mazdak said, 'Let the king appoint a time when he will come to the fire-temple with his priests and nobles, and at my bidding God (to Him be power and glory) will make the fire speak. If he wills, let it be this very day or this very hour.' Qubad said, 'We propose to come to the fire-temple tomorrow.' The next day Mazdak sent one of his minions into that hole and said, 'Each time that I call upon The Good One with a loud voice, you get beneath the hole and say: Let all worshippers of The Good One in Iran adopt and practise the words of Mazdak; thus they will find prosperity and good fortune in both worlds.'

3 So Qubad and the nobles and priests went to the fire-temple. Mazdak was called; he went and stood beside the fire, and called upon The Good One with a loud voice and blessed Zoroaster, and was silent. From out of the fire there came a voice after the manner we have related, so that the king and all the nobles heard it and were amazed; Qubad had it in mind to believe in Mazdak, and

they returned from the fire-temple. Thereafter Qubad drew
Mazdak daily nearer to himself, until at last he believed in him.
He gave him a golden throne inlaid with jewels, and ordered it to
be placed on the dais in the audience-hall. At the time of audience
Qubad would sit on the dais, and Mazdak would sit on the throne,
and Mazdak would be much higher than Qubad. Then people
began to join Mazdak's religion, partly out of liking and sympathy,
and partly for the sake of agreeing with the king. From various
provinces and districts they came to the capital, and either openly
or secretly entered Mazdak's religion. The nobility, the peasantry
and the military for the most part had no great zeal for it, but out
of respect for the king they dared not say anything; of the priests
not one went over to Mazdak's religion; they said, 'Let us see what
[proof] he adduces from the Avesta and Zend.'

4 When Mazdak saw that the king had embraced his religion
and that people from far and near were accepting his invitation, he
introduced the subject of property, and said, 'Wealth must be
divided among the people, for all are God's slaves and children of
Adam. Whatsoever people may need, the expense must be met
from the communal funds, so that no man suffers neediness and
privation in any respect and all men are equal.' After he had convinced Qubad and his other adherents on this point and they had
agreed to the sharing of wealth, then he said, 'Your wives are like
your other possessions; they too should be regarded as common
property. If any man feels desire for a woman let him come together with her. There is no jealousy or intolerance in our religion
and nobody is deprived of the pleasures and lusts of the world.
The doors of desire and satisfaction are open for everybody.'
Then by reason of the sharing of women, people were more eager
to adopt his religion, especially the common people. And he laid
down the custom that if someone invited twenty men to his house
not only would he provide bread and meat and wine and minstrels
and other amenities, but all the guests would get up one by one
and make use of his wife; and they thought it no wrong. Their
custom was that whenever a man went into a room to have commerce with a woman, he put his hat on the door and then went
inside. If another person was seized with the same desire, on seeing the hat hanging on the door he turned back, knowing that
somebody was already engaged in that business within.

5 Then Nushirvan sent someone secretly to the priests and

said, 'Why do you stay thus silent and helpless? Why do you not say something about Mazdak and give some advice to my father and ask him why he has embraced this absurdity and been taken in by the deceit of this wicked imposter? Why, has this dog not ruined people's property, ripped the veils from their womenfolk, and made the common people masters of all? Very well, then let him be asked on what authority, at whose bidding he is doing all this. For if you remain silent, your property and your wives will be lost; and dominion and power will depart from our family. Arise and go before my father, and acquaint him of this matter and give him counsel. Then hold argument with Mazdak and see what proof he can produce.' And to the nobles and important people he sent secret messages saying, 'My father has been overcome by a vicious melancholy, and his wit has been impaired to such an extent that he cannot distinguish between good and evil; please consider how he may be cured. Beware of listening to Mazdak and acting upon his words; do not be deceived like my father; for this is a vain thing, and vanity does not endure, nor will it profit you in the future.'

6 The nobles were frightened at Nushirvan's words and threats, and although some of them had intended to go over to Mazdak's religion, because of Nushirvan's words they withdrew, saying, 'Let us see where Mazdak's affairs lead and what are the grounds for Nushirvan's assertion.' Nushirvan at this time was eighteen years old.

7 Then the priests agreed amongst themselves, and went to Qubad and said, 'From the time of Adam (upon him be peace) until the present we have never read in any history of such injunctions being given as these of Mazdak, nor have we heard of such things from any of the various prophets which have been in Syria. To us it appears as an abomination.' Qubad said, 'Speak to Mazdak and see what he says.' They called Mazdak and said, 'What justification have you for these statements of yours?' Mazdak said, 'Zoroaster commanded so, and thus it is written in the Avesta and Zend, but men have not known the interpretation thereof. If you do not believe me, ask the fire.' Again they went to the fire-temple and put their question to the fire. From the midst of the fire a voice came out, 'It is indeed as Mazdak says and not as you say.' Once more the priests returned abashed. The next day they saw Nushirvan and reported the matter. Nushirvan said,

'This Mazdak is succeeding because his religion is the same as the religion of the fire-worshippers in all but two respects.'

8 After a year had passed over these events, one day Qubad and Mazdak were talking; Qubad chanced to say, 'Have people been eager to come over to our religion?' Mazdak said, 'They would have come over one and all if Nushirvan had allowed them; but he has been obstinate and has not accepted the religion.' Qubad said, 'Do you mean that he is not of our faith?' He said, 'No.' Qubad said, 'Call Nushirvan.' Nushirvan was brought. Qubad said, 'Are you not a believer in Mazdak's religion?' He said, 'No, praise be to Allah.' He said, 'Why?' He said, 'Because he is an imposter and a cheat.' He said, 'Wherefore cheat? He makes the fire speak.' Nushirvan said, 'Four things are opposites of one another, and have no colour – water, fire, earth and wind. Let him make water, wind and earth speak as he did the fire, and then I will believe in him.' Qubad said, 'But all that he says comes from interpretation of the Avesta and Zend.' Nushirvan said, 'He who composed the Avesta and Zend did not say that wealth and wives were free to be shared, and in all these years no scholar has produced such an interpretation. Religion exists for the protection of wealth and wives; if these two become free, then what will be the difference between beasts and men, for it is of animals to be equal in feeding and coupling, not intelligent human beings.' Qubad said, 'That may be, but why are you opposing me, your father?' He said, 'I have learnt that from you, although it was never the custom before. When I saw you opposing your own father, I too opposed you. If you renounce that, then I will turn back from this.' Qubad and Mazdak in their conversation with Nushirvan eventually reached a point where they said plainly, 'Either you produce evidence to disprove this religion of Mazdak and to refute his arguments, or bring someone whose arguments are stronger and sounder than Mazdak's; otherwise we shall punish you as a warning to others.' Nushirvan said, 'Give me forty days' grace and either I will bring you evidence, or I will bring someone to answer Mazdak.' They said, 'Very well', and thereupon they all parted.

9 Having returned from his father's presence, Nushirvan the very same day sent a messenger with a letter to Pars, to the city of Gul[4] to a certain aged and wise priest who dwelt there, saying, 'Please come with all speed, for such-and-such has happened between the king, myself and Mazdak.'

10 When the forty days were up Qubad gave audience. He took his seat upon the dais; then Mazdak came and mounted the dais, and sat upon the throne. Qubad ordered Nushirvan to be brought in. Mazdak said to Qubad, 'Ask him what he has found to answer us.' Qubad said, 'Well then what have you found?' Nushirvan said, 'I am making my arrangements.' Mazdak said, 'The time for arrangements has passed; have him punished.' Qubad was silent. Mazdak gave a sign for attendants to seize Nushirvan. When they moved towards him, he laid his hand on the corner⁵ of the portico, and said to his father, 'Why are you in such haste to ruin your own house? The term has not yet expired.' They said, 'How so?' He said, 'I asked for forty days entire, and today is included in the forty until it is over. After that you know best; do whatever you will.' The commanders and priests shouted their assent and said, 'He speaks true; the agreement was for forty days, not forty less one.' Qubad said, 'Let him go for today.' They released him and he escaped from Mazdak's clutches.

11 Qubad then rose and left the audience-hall and the people dispersed; Mazdak returned to his house and likewise Nushirvan. Just then the priest whom Nushirvan had summoned from Pars arrived, mounted on a fast camel. By constant enquiry he reached Nushirvan's palace and dismounted and went straight inside. Softly he said to a servant, 'Go and tell Nushirvan that the priest from Pars has arrived and wishes to see him.' The servant quickly went into the room and told Nushirvan. Nushirvan soon ran out of the room and embraced the priest for joy, and said, 'O priest, imagine that I am just coming back from the other world'; and he told him of all the circumstances. The priest said, 'Do not be anxious, for everything is as you have said, and you are right and Mazdak is wrong. I will give answer to Mazdak as your representative, and I will make Qubad regret what he has done, and bring him back to the [right] road. But now please contrive for me to see Qubad, before Mazdak comes to know that I am here.' He said, 'That is easy; I will arrange for you to see the king tonight in private.' At the time of afternoon prayer Nushirvan went to his father's palace and requested an audience. When he saw his father, he pronounced his eulogy and then said, 'There has arrived from Pars a priest who will give answer to Mazdak, but he has besought me to request the king to hear what he has to say in private tonight, and see his proof; thereafter let the king

order whatever is appropriate.' Qubad said, 'Very well; bring him.'

12 Nushirvan returned, and when it was dark took the priest to his father. The priest blessed Qubad, and praised his forefathers; then he said to the king, 'This Mazdak has fallen into error; this task was not destined for him.' The king said, 'Why?' He said, 'I know him well, and I know the extent of his learning. He knows something about the science of the stars, but about their decrees he is mistaken. There are indications that in the present conjunction a man will appear who will lay claim to prophethood; he will produce a new book, and perform wonderful miracles, and cut the moon into two halves[6] in the sky; he will call the people to the way of The Good One, and found a holy religion to abolish the Magian religion and all other religions; he will promise paradise and threaten purgatory; he will protect people's property and wives by divine ordinances; he will shun the devil and consort with the angel [Gabriel]; he will destroy fire-temples and idol-temples, and his religion will spread through all the world and will last until the resurrection; heaven and earth will bear testimony to his prophethood. Now this Mazdak has conceived the fancy that he should be this person. But firstly this person will be an Arab: and Mazdak is a Persian. He will prohibit the people from fire-worshipping, and deny Zoroaster: while Mazdak actually follows Zoroaster and prescribes fire-worshipping. He will not allow a man to look at another's wife, nor to take a grain of another's property; for a single unlawful diram he will order hands to be cut off: but Mazdak has made wealth and wives common property. He will receive his orders from heaven, and speak from angelic inspiration: but this man speaks from the fire. He will bring a new book, but Mazdak still follows the Avesta and Zend. No, Mazdak's religion has no foundation. Tomorrow I will disgrace him in front of Your Majesty and prove that he is in error and is only intent on taking the kingship away from your house and wasting your treasure, and making you the equal of every mean fellow.' His words were pleasing and acceptable to Qubad.

13 The next day Qubad came to the audience-hall, and Mazdak sat upon the throne and Nushirvan stood in front of the dais, and the priests and nobles presented themselves. Then the priest from Pars said to Mazdak, 'Will you ask the first question or shall I?'

Mazdak said, 'I will.' The priest said, 'If you want yourself to be the questioner and me to answer, then come here where I am and I will go where you are.' Mazdak was ashamed, and said, 'The king himself seated me here; you ask and I will answer.' The priest said, 'You have instituted community of property; is it not so that those who build inns and bridges and perform good works do so for the sake of reward in the next world?' He said, 'Yes.' He said, 'If wealth is to be shared with everyone else, when people do good works, who will get the reward?' Mazdak was unable to answer. Again he said, 'You make wives common property; suppose twenty men lie with one woman, and the woman becomes pregnant, whose will the child be?' Mazdak failed to reply. Then he said, 'Your purpose is to ruin utterly the pedigrees and possessions of the people. The king sits upon this throne and is our ruler because he is the son of King Firuz and he inherited the throne from his father, just as King Firuz inherited it from his father. If ten different persons lie with the king's wife, then when a child is born, how shall they say whose child it is? Will the line of descent not be broken? When that happens will not the kingship leave this house? High and low rank depend upon riches or poverty; if a man is poor he is out of necessity compelled to enter the service and hire of a rich man; thus high and low rank are manifested. When all property is shared, differences of rank will disappear from the world; the meanest wretch will be equal to the king; in fact kingship will be nullified. You have come to annihilate the wealth and sovereignty of the royal family of Persia.' Mazdak could not say anything; he remained silent. Qubad said, 'Answer him.' He said, 'The answer is that you should instantly order his head to be cut off.' Qubad said, 'A man's head cannot be cut off without proof.' He said, 'I will ask the fire what it commands, for what I say is not from myself.' People had been much distressed for Nushirvan's sake; now they rejoiced that he had escaped death. Mazdak was angry with Qubad, because he had told him to kill the priest and kill Nushirvan, but he had not done so. Mazdak said to himself, 'My followers are now many amongst the peasantry and the army. I must arrange to remove Qubad from the scene; then I will kill Nushirvan and my other opponents.' So they settled that on the following day they would go to the fire-temple and see what the fire ordered; and they dispersed.

14 When night came on, Mazdak called two of his minions and

co-religionists and gave them gifts of money; and he promised to make them both generals. Then he made them swear not to say anything of this to anybody, and he gave them two swords, and said, 'Tomorrow when Qubad comes to the fire-temple with the priests and nobles, if the fire orders Qubad to be killed, you both straightaway draw your swords and kill him. Nobody else of course will come into the fire-temple armed.' They said, 'We obey.' The next day the nobles and priests went to the fire-temple, and Qubad likewise. Now the priest [of Pars] had told Nushirvan. 'Tell ten of your retainers to conceal swords beneath their clothes when they go with you to the fire-temple, in case Mazdak attempts some treachery.' Nushirvan did so, and went to the fire-temple. Whenever Mazdak intended to go to the fire-temple, he instructed his minion beforehand what to say from under the hole. So having told the minion what to say, he himself went to the temple. He said to the priest, 'You ask the fire to speak to you.' The priest put some questions to the fire, but he got no reply. Then Mazdak said to the fire, 'Judge between us, and bear witness that I am right.' From the midst of the fire the voice came, 'Since yesterday I have become weak; first strengthen me with the heart and liver of Qubad, so that I may tell you what to do. Mazdak is your guide to everlasting happiness.' Then Mazdak said, 'Strengthen the fire!' Those two men drew their swords and assaulted Qubad. The priest said to Nushirvan, 'Rescue him!' Nushirvan and his ten men drew their swords, intercepting those two persons and preventing them from striking Qubad; and Mazdak was all the time saying, 'The fire speaks at the bidding of The Good One.' The people then split into two parties; one party said, 'Let us throw Qubad dead or alive into the fire'; others said, 'Let us deliberate upon this until we can see more clearly.' At the close of the day they went back and Qubad was saying, 'Perhaps I have been guilty of some sin for which the fire wishes to use me as food; anyway I would rather be consumed in the fire of this world than in the fire of the next world.'

15 The next time that the priest was alone with Qubad he spoke about bygone priests and kings, and citing other religions as evidence, he argued that Mazdak was not a prophet, but the enemy of the royal family; the proof of this was that first he had tried to kill Nushirvan; when he was unsuccessful, he attempted to kill him, Qubad; why did he fancy that the fire had spoken; the

fire had never yet uttered a word, so why should it do so then; he would contrive to expose this fraud and shew the king whether it was the fire that spoke or someone else. He so affected the king that he repented of his deeds; but he added, 'Do not treat Nushirvan as a child, because he is in command of the whole world; whatever course he decides upon, do not swerve from it, if you want the throne to remain in your house; and do not reveal your secrets to Mazdak.'

16 Then the priest said to Nushirvan, 'I want you to try to allure one of Mazdak's closest servants, and tempt him with money to tell us the truth about the fire, so that I may remove all doubts from your father's mind.' Nushirvan induced someone to strike up a friendship with one of Mazdak's minions and by some device to bring the man to him; Nushirvan seated the man in a private place and laid a thousand dinars in front of him, and said, 'I am going to ask you something; if you speak the truth, I will give you these thousand dinars right away; and I will make you one of my intimates and promote you to high rank; if you lie, I will even now remove the head from your body.' The man was afraid and said, 'If I speak the truth, will you keep the promises you have made?' He said, 'Yes, and more.' He said, 'I will tell you.' Nushirvan said, 'Tell me what trick Mazdak has played to make the fire speak to him.' The man said, 'If I tell you this truly, can you protect me and my secret from Mazdak?' He said, 'I can.' He said, 'Know that near the fire-temple there is a piece of ground; Mazdak has bought this and surrounded it on all four sides by a high wall; from there to a point beneath the fire-temple he has driven a tunnel, ending in a small hole which opens into the middle of the fire. He always sends one of his minions into the tunnel, and instructs him to go underneath the fire, put his mouth to the hole and say such-and-such, so that whoever hears will think that it is the fire speaking.' When Nushirvan heard this he knew that the man was speaking the truth. He was glad and gave the man the thousand dinars.

17 When night came on, he took this man to his father, and made him repeat his words in front of his father. Qubad was amazed at the cunning and audacity of Mazdak; all doubts were completely removed from his mind. Straightaway the priest was brought in, and Qubad praised him and they explained everything to him. The priest said, 'I told Your Majesty that he was a fraud.'

Qubad said, 'Now we have found out. What is the best way to destroy him?' The priest said, 'He certainly must not get to know that you are aware of his deception and have recanted. It is better that you should hold another meeting, and I will dispute with him in front of everybody. In the end I will abandon the contest and confess defeat, and return to Pars. Thereafter you should do whatever Nushirvan sees fit so that this canker may be excised.' After a few days King Qubad commanded the priests and nobles to present themselves, and taking the side of the priest of Pars to dispute with Mazdak and look more closely into his claims.

18 The next day the meeting was held, with Qubad sitting upon the dais, and Mazdak on his throne. Everybody spoke in turn, and the priest of Pars said, 'What amazes me is the fire speaking.' Mazdak said, 'There should not be amazement at the mighty works of God. Do you not remember how Moses (upon him be peace) made a serpent out of a piece of wood, and caused twelve springs of water to flow from one piece of stone;[7] how he said, "I will drown Pharaoh with all his host", and he did so? God also made the earth obey Moses, so when Moses said, "O earth, swallow up Qarun", it swallowed him up; and Jesus (Allah's prayers be upon him) made the dead alive. All these things are not within the power of man; but they are in the power of God. I too am His apostle and He has made the fire obey me. If you do what I say and what the fire says, you will achieve salvation in both worlds; if you do not obey, you can expect God in His wrath to destroy you all.' The priest of Pars rose to his feet and said, 'I have no answer for a man whose words are from God and from the fire, and whose command the fire obeys; I retire from the contest in the face of one who can do something which I cannot. I am going; I cannot continue my presumption any longer.' So he straightaway departed, and took the road to Pars. Qubad left the audience-hall, and Mazdak went to the fire-temple to do seven days' homage to the fire. The other people returned home, and those persons who had been converted to Mazdak's religion believed in him all the more firmly, and they were delighted.

19 When it was night, Qubad called Nushirvan and said, 'The priest has gone, and he has left me in your hands, because you are capable of putting an end to this religion. Now what are your plans?' Nushirvan said, 'If your Majesty will leave this task to me and not talk about it with anyone but me, I will undertake to

prepare and execute suitable plans so that all trace of Mazdak and the Mazdakites will be removed from the world.' Qubad said, 'I shall not speak of this matter with anyone but you; the secret will remain with us alone.' Then Nushirvan said, 'Know that the priest of Pars has ostensibly confessed his defeat, and left for Pars, while Mazdak and the Mazdakites are encouraged and emboldened; they say there is nothing to stop them doing whatever they like to us. Now it is easy to kill Mazdak, but his followers are many. If we killed Mazdak, the Mazdakites would flee and disperse throughout the world; they would try to convert the people, and they would occupy mountain strongholds, and give trouble to us and our country. We must arrange matters so that all are destroyed and not one of them escapes from our swords.' Qubad said, 'What do you think is the best method?' Nushirvan said, 'What we should do is this: when Mazdak leaves the fire-temple and comes to see you, you should increase his rank and treat him with even greater respect; then one day when you are talking to him in private, tell him that since the priest of Pars withdrew and con-fessed defeat, I have become much more tractable; I am repentant and disposed to believe in him. See what he says.'

20 During that week, when Mazdak came to Qubad, Qubad treated him respectfully and humbled himself, and he spoke about Nushirvan in the terms they had agreed. Mazdak said, 'The majority of people look to Nushirvan and hang to his words and deeds. If he comes into this chosen religion, all the world will accept it. I hereby ask the fire to be my intercessor, and I pray The Good One to dispose Nushirvan to this religion.' Qubad said, 'Yes indeed, for he is my heir, and the army and the peasantry love him greatly. When he comes into this religion, the rest of the world will have no excuse. As soon as Nushirvan embraces our religion I swear by The Good One that just as Gushtasp built a golden kiosk in honour of Zoroaster on top of the cypress at Kishmar, so in your honour I will erect a stone tower in the middle of the Tigris, and place a golden kiosk on top of it, brighter than the sun.' Mazdak said, 'You give him counsel, while I pray; I am confident that The Good One will answer my prayers.'

21 When night came on, Qubad told Nushirvan all that had passed. Nushirvan said, 'After a week let my lord call Mazdak and say: Last night Nushirvan had a dream and he was afraid; in the early morning he came to me and said he had dreamed that a great

fire was attacking him and that he was seeking refuge; a handsome person appeared before him and he asked him what the fire wanted from him; he said the fire was angry with him because he had called it a liar; he asked him how he knew; he said that the angel was aware of all things. Then he woke up. Now he is going to the fire-temple, and is taking much musk and ambergris and aloes-wood to throw on the fire. For three days he is going to do service to the fire and homage to The Good One.' Qubad and Nushirvan said and did these things respectively; Mazdak was very happy.

22 One week after this event, Nushirvan told his father to tell Mazdak that Nushirvan had said to him, 'I am sure now that this religion is right, and that Mazdak is an apostle of The Good One. I would like to follow him, but I am afraid to do so because most of the people are opposed to his religion; we must not let them revolt and seize the country from us by force. I wish I knew how many people had embraced this religion and who they were. If they are many in number and powerful, of course that is good; but if not, I will wait until they gain strength and grow in number, and I will assist them with grants of arms and provisions. Then when we have complete power we will proclaim our religion and force the people to accept it.' [Nushirvan went on to Qubad,] 'If Mazdak says that his followers are many, tell him to make a register and write all their names in it, with the object of shewing it to me for my encouragement so that I may have no excuse for remaining aloof. By this means we shall come to know the number of the Mazdakites and who they are.' Qubad said the prescribed words to Mazdak. Mazdak was happy and said, 'A great many people have embraced this religion.' He said, 'Make a register and write their names in it so that Nushirvan will have no move[8] left.' Mazdak did so, and brought the register to Qubad. They counted the names; they came to 12,000, comprising townspeople, villagers and soldiers. Qubad said, 'Tonight I will call Nushirvan and present this register to him; if he comes over to our religion, I will instantly cause trumpets and drums to be sounded as a signal, and I will broadcast a rumour that a son has been born to me; when you hear the sound of trumpets and drums, you will know that Nushirvan has accepted our religion.'

23 When Mazdak had gone away and night had come on, Qubad called Nushirvan and shewed him the register, and told him of the signal he had arranged with Mazdak. Nushirvan said,

'Excellent; now have them sound the trumpets and drums, and tomorrow when you see Mazdak tell him that Nushirvan responded favourably and came over to our religion by virtue of his seeing the register and the number of people; tell him also that I said that had there been only 5,000 it would have been enough; since there are 12,000 men, even if the rest of the world were against us, there would be nothing to fear; hereafter whatever plans we make, Your Majesty, Mazdak and myself will all consult together. Then send someone to call me.'

24 When one watch of the night had passed Mazdak heard the sound of trumpets and drums: he rejoiced and said, 'Nushirvan has come over to our religion.' The next day Mazdak went to the audience-hall; Qubad sat on the dais and told Mazdak all that Nushirvan had said; Mazdak was glad. When they left the audience-hall, Qubad and Mazdak sat down in private together, and they sent someone to fetch Nushirvan. Nushirvan arrived and laid a multitude of gold and choice gifts before Mazdak, and scattered pearls as largesse. He apologized for past mistakes, and then they discussed all manner of things. Eventually Nushirvan spoke to his father as follows and they agreed on it: 'You are the lord of the world, and Mazdak is the apostle of The Good One. Grant me the command of our people's army, and I will see to it that in all the world there remains nobody who does not belong to our confession and religion; all will willingly and eagerly accept it.' Qubad and Mazdak said, 'Your wish is granted.' Nushirvan said, 'Then the best course of action is for Mazdak to send messengers to all districts and cities and villages to his adherents and tell them that three months hence on a certain day in such-and-such a week everyone from far and near must be present at our palace. From this day until that we shall be making arrangements and preparing necessary weapons and animals for them, but nobody shall know what our business is. On the appointed day we shall spread a feast with enough places for them all to sit down and room for more besides. Having eaten the food they will remove to another hall and there engage in a drinking party in which each person will drink seven cups of wine. Then fifty or twenty at a time we will invest them with robes of honour suited to each man, until all are invested. By nightfall whoever is fully armed, well and good; if anyone is not, they will open the armoury and give out weapons and chain-mail and cuirasses. That same night we shall go forth;

those who accept the religion will be safe; if anybody refuses we shall kill him.' Qubad and Mazdak said, 'There is nothing to add to this.' Having agreed on this they rose. Mazdak sent letters everywhere and warned all people far and near that on such-and-such a day of such-and-such a month they should be present at the court, fully armed and equipped; he told them to be confident, for everything was as they desired and the king was their leader.

25 On the appointed day all the 12,000 men arrived and went to the king's palace. There they saw such a feast prepared as nobody had ever seen before. Qubad sat on the dais, and Mazdak on the throne, while Nushirvan stood with loins girt as if to shew that he was the host. Mazdak could not contain himself for joy. Then Nushirvan seated everyone at the table in order of rank until all were sitting down. When they had finished the food, they moved from this hall to another; there they saw an assembly-room such as their eyes had never beheld before. Qubad and Mazdak again sat on dais and throne and all the guests were made to sit in order as before. Minstrels began to sing and cup-bearers took round the wine. After two rounds about two hundred pages and servants with pieces of brocade and linen wrappings on their arms came in and stood for a time on the edge of the throng. Then Nushirvan announced, 'Take the robes into the other hall, for it is crowded here; the guests will be taken there by twenties and thirties and have their robes put on; then they will pass from that hall to the polo-field, and wait there until all are robed. When all have been invested, the king and Mazdak will come on to the polo-field and cast an eye upon them and inspect them. Meanwhile I will have the armoury opened and weapons brought.' Now on the previous day Nushirvan had sent someone out into the villages and summoned two or three hundred casual labourers to come with spades, for the ostensible purpose of sweeping the palace and grounds and clearing away dirt and rubbish. When the men came from the villages he mustered them all on the polo-field and shut the gate tight. Then he said to them, 'During today and tonight I want you to dig 12,000 pits in this field, each one a yard and a half deep, and keep the spoil at the side of the pits.' He ordered the watchmen to detain them all in a certain yard when they had finished digging the pits and prevent any of them from going out. On the night [of the feast] he armed about four hundred men and stationed them on the polo-field and in a yard by the field and

instructed them as follows, 'Take each party of twenty of thirty men as I send them from the assembly-room to the [robing-]hall, and lead them from there into the yard and from the yard on to the field; strip them all naked and put them head first into the pits up to the navel with their legs in the air; shovel back the earth all around them and tread it down so that they are firmly planted in the pits.'

26 After the robe-bearers had gone from the assembly-room into the [robing-]hall, they brought in two hundred horses with gold and silver trappings, as well as shields and sword-belts. Nushirvan had them taken into the [robing-]hall. Then he picked the people in twenties and thirties, and sent them into the hall. From there they were taken through the yard on to the polo-field and put head-downwards into the pits, which were then filled with earth. Thus they destroyed them all. Then Nushirvan said to his father and Mazdak, 'They have all been invested with their robes and are standing ready on the polo-field. Come and inspect them for you have never seen such fine attire.' Qubad and Mazdak arose and went through the [robing-]hall and the yard on to the field. As far as he could see from end to end of the field Mazdak saw nothing but legs sticking up in the air. Nushirvan turned to Mazdak and said, 'For an army of which you are the commander what better kind of investiture could there be than this? You came only to despoil the people's property and wives, and take the kingship from our family.' They had made a high mound in front of the field and dug a pit in it. At Nushirvan's command they arrested Mazdak, took him on to the mound and placed him up to his chest in that pit, with his head outside and his feet inside. Then they poured plaster all round him so that he remained set in the plaster. Nushirvan said, 'Now look at your believers! gaze upon them!' and to his father he said, 'Behold the wisdom of the wise! The best thing for you now is to remain awhile indoors until the people and the army calm down, for this trouble arose through your weak-mindedness.' So he kept his father indoors. On his order the villagers who had been brought for digging the pits were released, and the gates of the polo-field opened for citizens and soldiers to see the sight, and they plucked Mazdak's beard and moustaches until he died. Then Nushirvan held his father in captivity, and having summoned all the nobility, he ascended the throne as undisputed sovereign, and began that

reign which was devoted to justice and generosity. This story has come down as a memorial of him.

Chapter XLV

On the emergence of Sinbad the Magian from Nishapur and his rising against the Muslims at Rayy

1 After these days no one of this sect dared to raise his head in the world. Now it so happened that Mazdak's wife, Khurrama bint Fada, had fled from Mada'in with two persons, and having arrived at the village of Rayy, with their help she began secretly to call people to her husband's religion, with the result that a considerable number of Zoroastrians adopted it. People gave them the name of the Khurrama-dins.[1] However, they dared not practise openly; they concealed the religion while constantly looking for an excuse to emerge and reveal it. In the year 137 after the flight of The Prophet (upon him be peace) when Abu Ja'far al-Mansur (Abu Dawaniq) slew Abu Muslim Sahib ad-Daula [The Master of the Empire] at Baghdad, there was in the city of Nishapur a Zoroastrian Mayor called Sinbad.[2] This man had been an old friend and servant of Abu Muslim, and the latter had promoted him and made him an army-commander. After the killing of Abu Muslim he emerged in revolt and came with an army from Nishapur to Rayy, and he stirred up the Zoroastrians of Rayy and Tabaristan, knowing that the people of Kuhistan and 'Iraq were fifty per cent Rafidis and Mazdakites. Pursuing his intention of preaching the religion openly, first of all he killed Ba 'Ubaida the Hanafite, who was the governor of Rayy on behalf of al-Mansur, and seized the hoards which Abu Muslim had laid up at Rayy. Having thus acquired some strength he sought to avenge Abu Muslim's blood; he claimed that he was Abu Muslim's apostle, and told the people of 'Iraq and Khurasan that Abu Muslim had not been killed, but

that when al-Mansur tried to kill him, he recited the greatest name of God, and turned into a white dove, and flew from his hands; he was now in a brazen fortress where he dwelt with the Mahdi[3] and Mazdak; soon all three would appear and their chief would be Abu Muslim with Mazdak as his vazir. He professed to have received messengers and letters from Abu Muslim.

2 When the Rafidis heard mention of the Mahdi, and the Mazdakites the name of Mazdak, a great multitude of Rafidis and Khurrama-dins gathered at Rayy, and Sinbad's affair grew in magnitude until eventually 100,000 people joined him, mounted and on foot. Whenever he was alone with Zoroastrians, he would say, 'According to one of the books of the Sasanians which I have found, the Arab empire is finished. I shall not turn back until I have destroyed the Ka'ba, for this has been [wrongly] substituted for the sun; we shall make the sun our *qibla* as it was in olden time.' And to the Khurrama-dins he would say, 'Mazdak has become a Shi'ite and his command is that you make common cause with the Shi'a.' By saying the former things to the Zoroastrians and the latter to the extreme Shi'ites and Khurrama-dins, he kept all three groups happy. He defeated al-Mansur's forces on several occasions and killed some of his generals; so after seven years al-Mansur appointed Jahwar 'Ijli to fight him. Jahwar summoned the troops of Khuzistan and Pars, and went to Isfahan; he also took with him auxiliaries from Isfahan, Arabs from Qum and 'Ijlis from Karaj.[4] Then he moved to Rayy and there he fought a fierce battle for three days with Sinbad. On the fourth day Sinbad was slain in single combat at the hand of Jahwar and all his company were routed, and dispersed to their homes. Then the Khurrama-din religion became mixed with Zoroastrianism and Shi'ism, and they held conversations in secret, and gradually grew more organized until they reached the stage where Muslims and Zoroastrians began to call the sect Khurrama-din. After Jahwar had killed Sinbad, he entered Rayy and slaughtered all the Zoroastrians, plundering their houses and carrying off their women and children into captivity.

On the risings of the Qarmatis [Carmathians] and Batinis and their evil doctrines (may Allah curse them)

1 The origin of the Qarmati religion was as follows.[1] Ja'far
as-Sadiq (may Allah be pleased with him) had a son whose name
was Isma'il; he died before his father leaving a son named
Muhammad; and this Muhammad lived until the time of Harun
ar-Rashid. Now one of the Zubairis[2] falsely suggested to Harun
ar-Rashid that [Musa ibn] Ja'far as-Sadiq[3] was plotting a revolt
and preaching in secret with the intention of seizing the caliphate.
Harun ar-Rashid brought [Musa ibn] Ja'far from Medina to
Baghdad and put him in prison, and during this confinement he
died, and was buried in the cemetery of the Quraish. Now this
Muhammad had a certain Hijazi page called Mubarak, and he was
calligrapher in the fine script known as *muqarmat*; for this reason
he used to be called Qarmatwaih. This Mubarak had a friend in
the city of Ahvaz whose name was 'Abd-Allah ibn Maimun al-
Qaddah. The latter was one day sitting with him in private and
said, 'Your master Muhammad ibn Isma'il was my friend and he
told me secrets which he did not tell you or anyone else.' Mubarak
was deceived and impatient to know what they were. Then 'Abd-
Allah ibn Maimun made Mubarak swear not to disclose what he
was going to tell him except to persons fit to hear it. He then made
several statements, introducing obscure words from the language
of the imams, mixed up with sayings of the naturalists and utterances of the philosophers, and consisting largely of mention of
The Messenger and talk of prophets and angels, the tablet and pen,
and heaven and the throne. After that they parted; Mubarak went
towards Kufa, and 'Abd-Allah to Kuhistan of 'Iraq; and they
sought to win over the people of the Shi'a.

2 This was at the time when Musa ibn Ja'far was in prison.
Mubarak carried on his activities in secret, and disseminated his
propaganda in the district around Kufa. Of the people who
accepted his teaching, the Sunnis call some of them Mubarakis
and others Qarmatis. Meanwhile 'Abd-Allah ibn Maimun preached
this religion in Kuhistan of 'Iraq. Incidentally he was a very clever

conjuror and used to practise this art, and Muhammad ibn Zakariyya [Razi][4] has mentioned his name in his book *Makhariq [al-Anbiya* 'Frauds of the Prophets'], including him among master conjurors. He then appointed a man called Khalaf to succeed him and said to him, 'Go in the direction of Natanz, for thereabouts in Rayy, Qum, Kashan and Aba the people are all Rafidis, professing Shi'a beliefs; so they will accept your teaching.' 'Abd-Allah himself departed towards Basra, fearing trouble.[5]

So Khalaf went to Rayy. In the district of Pashapuya there is a village which they call Kulain;[6] there he stayed and practised embroidery, at which craft he was expert. He remained there some time without being able to reveal his secrets to anybody, till at last by dint of a thousand wiles he managed to suborn a suitable person, and began to instruct him in the religion; he made out that the religion was that of The House [of The Prophet] and had to be kept hidden; and said, 'When the Qayim [Mahdi] appears the religion will be revealed, and the time of his coming is near. It behoves you to learn now, so that when you see him you will not be ignorant of the religion.' So the people of this village secretly began to learn the religion. One day the headman of Kulain was passing outside the village when he heard a voice coming from a ruined mosque. He approached the mosque and listened. This Khalaf was expounding his religion to one of the people. On returning to the village he said, 'O people, destroy his embroideries. Do not go near him. Judging by what I have heard, I am afraid that our village may suffer through his activities.' (Now Khalaf's speech was imperfect and he could not pronounce the letters *ṭā, rā* and *ḥā*.) 'I heard him say [in broken Arabic]: The hidden meaning of this chapter is mercy.'[7] When he knew that he had been discovered, he fled from Kulain and went to Rayy where he died. He had converted a few of the inhabitants of Kulain, men and women, and his son Ahmad ibn Khalaf took his place and continued to foster his father's religion. Nobody in the city of Rayy was aware of what was going on. Then Ahmad ibn Khalaf found a man named Ghiyath from the village of Kulain, who was well versed in literature and grammar; he made him his successor as propagandist.

3 This Ghiyath then embellished the elements of their religion with verses from the Qur'an, traditions of The Prophet, Arab proverbs, and various verses of poetry. He composed a book

entitled *Kitab al-Bayan* ['The Book of Explanation'] and in it he described in the manner of a lexicon the meaning of 'prayer', 'fasting' and other religious terms. Then he held argument with people of the Sunna, and news spread to Qum and Kashan and Aba that a man called Ghiyath had come forth from the village of Kulain as a missionary, and was giving glad tidings and teaching the religion of The House [of The Prophet]. The people of these cities flocked to Ghiyath and began to learn the new religion. Eventually the jurist 'Abd-Allah Za'farani was informed of this, and he knew that the religion was a heresy. So he urged the people of Rayy to attack and disperse the heretics. Ghiyath fled and went to Khurasan. Some of the people who adopted this religion were known by the Sunnis of Rayy as Khalafis, and others as Batinis. By the year 280[8] (from the hijra) the religion was widespread. This was the year in which a man called Sahib al-Khal ['the man with the mole'][9] led a revolt in Syria and captured most of that country. After Ghiyath had been forced to flee from Rayy and gone to Khurasan, he stayed at Marv-ar-Rud, where he proselytized the amir Husain ibn 'Ali. Husain was converted; his command extended over Khurasan, especially Taliqan, Maimana, Paryab, Gharchistan and Ghur. After adopting the new religion he converted a number of people in these districts.

4 Ghiyath then nominated a successor at Marv-ar-Rud to maintain the converts in the religion, while he himself returned to Rayy and began to preach again there in secret. Then he appointed as his lieutenant a man from the district of Pashapuya called Abu Hatim,[10] who was well versed in Arab poetry and strange tales, and together they began preaching [openly]. In Khurasan he had already promised that before long in such-and-such a year the Qayim (whom they call the Mahdi) would appear, and the Qarmatis had trusted in this promise. The people of the Sunna found out that Ghiyath had returned and was once more calling the people to the religion of the Seven. However, it chanced that the promised time for the coming of the Mahdi arrived, and he was proved false; moreover the Seveners criticized him on doctrinal grounds; for these two reasons they turned against him and renounced him The Sunnis also sought to kill him. He was obliged to flee and nobody knew where he went.

5 After that the Seveners of Rayy came to an agreement with one of the grandsons of Khalaf, and they combined under his

leadership. When he was about to die he named his son as successor, called Abu Ja'far The Elder; but he was overcome by melan-
cholia, so he appointed a man named Abu Hatim Laithi[11] to
deputize for him. By the time Abu Ja'far got better. Abu Hatim
had consolidated his position, and holding Abu Ja'far of no
account, had taken over the leadership. So the leadership passed
from Khalaf's family. This Abu Hatim sent missionaries abroad
into the districts on all sides of Rayy, such as Tabaristan, Gurgan,
Isfahan and Adharbaygan, and proceeded to convert the people.
The amir of Rayy, Ahmad ibn 'Ali, accepted his invitation and
became a Batini.

6 Then it happened that the Dailamites revolted against the
'Alavids of Tabaristan, saying, 'You say that ours is the true
religion, but Muslims keep writing to us from surrounding places
telling us not to listen to your words because they are irreligion
and heresy. Your argument is that true knowledge has gone from
our tribe. But knowledge does not go with lineage. If you learn,
you know; whoever learns, knows. Nor is knowledge inherited.
God (to him be power and glory) sent The Prophet (upon him be
peace) to all mankind alike; He did not distinguish some people
as noble in a religious sense, and others as common, for them to
say that His commands are this for the nobility, or that for the
commons. So it is clear to us that you are liars.' The amir of
Tabaristan was a Shi'ite, and he supported the 'Alavids; the
Dailamites defied him too and said, 'Go and fetch decrees and
documents from Baghdad and the cities of Khurasan and Transoxiana – and let some of us go with you – to the effect that your
religion is the pure Muslim faith, and that you are doing and saying
nothing but what God and The Prophet have commanded; then
we will accept you and embrace your religion; otherwise the
sword is betwixt us and you. We are mountain people and
foresters;[12] we understand but little of Islamic religious science.'
By chance Abu Hatim went at this time from Rayy to Dailaman,
and he visited the Dailamites, whose chief was Asfar[13] ibn Shiruy
Vardadavandi. He went to him and made an alliance with him,
vilifying the 'Alavids; he set about defaming them and declared
that their rule was not legitimate; one should be an 'Alavi in
religion, not in genealogy. He promised them, 'Soon an imam will
come forth from the Dailamites, and I know what his doctrine
and discourse will be.' The men of Dailaman and Gilan accepted

his teaching with alacrity, and his dealings with them prospered. This was in the days of Asfar ibn Shiruy and partly in the days of Mardavij ibn Ziyar. The wretched Dailams and Gils 'fled from the rain and resorted to the gutter': they sought the path of orthodoxy but they fell into the snare of heresy. For some time they continued their association with him.

7 When they saw that the period had elapsed in which he had promised that the imam would appear, they said, 'This religion is baseless; the wretched fellow seems to be an imposter.' They renounced him altogether, and renewed their devotion to the members of The Prophet's House (Allah pray for him). They attacked Abu Hatim with intent to kill him, but he fled, and in that flight he died. Whereupon the affairs of the sect of the Seveners degenerated into disorder and decay. Many of its adherents recanted, and went over to the Sunna in repentance. The Seveners remained in confusion for a while, but secretly they reorganized themselves and eventually settled down under the leadership of two men – 'Abd al-Malik Kaukabi and Ishaq; the latter lived at Rayy and the former at Girdkuh.

On the emergence of the Batinis in Khurasan and Transoxiana

8 The amir of Khurasan, Nasr ibn Ahmad, was led astray. When Husain ibn 'Ali Marv-ar-Rudi was on the point of death – the man who was converted Batini by Ghiyath – he handed on his mission in Khurasan to Muhammad [ibn Ahmad] Nakhshabi and made him his successor. This man was of that [brilliant] company of The Philosophers of Khurasan,[14] and he was a theologian. Husain enjoined him in his will to leave a deputy in that place and himself to cross the Oxus and go to Bukhara and Samarqand to convert the people of those cities, paying particular attention to the nobility at the court of the amir of Khurasan, Nasr ibn Ahmad; this would strengthen his position. So when Husain died, Muhammad Nakhshabi succeeded him and proselytized many of the people of Khurasan and they yielded to his invitation. There was a man called the son of Savada, who had escaped from the hands of the Sunnis at Rayy, and fled to Husain Marrudi in Khurasan; he was one of the leaders of the Batinis. Muhammad Nakhshabi made him his successor at Marv-ar-Rud, and himself crossed the river, and went to Bukhara. He found that the reputation of the sect was low

there, and he did not dare to come into the open. So he left there for Nakhshab, where he succeeded in converting Bakr Nakhshabi, who was a boon-companion of the amir of Khurasan and one of his relations. Now Bakr was a friend of Ash'ath who was the amir's private secretary and ranked as a boon-companion; he converted him too. Other converts were Abu Mansur Chaghani who was head of the military department and had married Ash'ath's sister, and Aytash who was the amir's private chamberlain and the friend of those just named.

9 This group then said to Muhammad Nakhshabi, 'There is no need for you to remain in Nakhshab; arise and come to Bukhara, the capital. We will see to it that in a short space of time we exalt your cause to the skies, and bring persons of reputation into this religion.' So he arose and went from Nakhshab to Bukhara where he joined this group in consorting with the notables and disseminating his propaganda amongst them. He made his converts swear not to say anything to anyone until he told them and made the word public. At first he was preaching the Shi'a religion; later he gradually shifted to Sevener doctrines, and into this sect he brought the mayor of Bukhara, the revenue officer and the leading citizens and merchants; also he converted Hasan Malik who was governor of Ilaq and one of the king's courtiers, and 'Ali Zarrad who was the private steward. Most of these whom we have mentioned were intimates or confidants of the king. When his following had increased, he had designs upon the king himself. He persuaded the courtiers constantly to speak favourably of him in front of Nasr ibn Ahmad in drunkenness and sobriety. They did this and took his part so well that Nasr ibn Ahmad became eager to see him. So they took Muhammad Nakhshabi before the amir of Khurasan, and extolled his learning; the amir received him gladly and treated him kindly. At every opportunity Muhammad brought a part of his teaching to the amir's attention, and whatever he said, the amir's intimates and companions who had embraced the religion added their approval and applause, saying, 'It is so.' Nasr ibn Ahmad treated him with increasing favour and could not bear to be without him. Eventually Nasr ibn Ahmad accepted his solicitation; Muhammad Nakhshabi then became so influential that he could appoint or depose ministers, and the king did whatever he said.

10 When Muhammad Nakhshabi's affairs reached this point he

made his propaganda public; his co-religionists rallied round him and they boldly proclaimed the religion; and the king himself supported the Seveners. Now the Turks and officers of the army were displeased that the king had become a Qarmati. (In those days anyone who embraced this religion was called a Qarmati.) So the learned men and judges of the city and neighbouring places got together and approached the commander-in-chief of the army, saying, 'Come to the rescue, for Islam has been corrupted in Transoxiana, and this wretched Nakhshabi has led the king astray and made him a Qarmati; he has misled many people and now his affairs have reached the point where he is preaching openly. We can no longer remain silent.' The commander said, 'I thank you: you go back and keep quiet; I hope that God will put matters right.' The next day he mentioned this subject to Nasr ibn Ahmad; but it did no good. Murmurs then arose amongst the troops and they said, 'We totally disagree with the course which the king has adopted'; and the army officers began to communicate with one another to see what to do about the matter. As they got to know one another's feelings it became clear that the troops and their leaders refused to acquiesce in the king's conduct, except one or two of the Turkish chiefs who had themselves been converted. Otherwise they were all wearers of turbans. In the end the army chiefs agreed that they did not want an infidel king: they would kill him and set up the army-commander in his place; they would swear not to go back on this decision. Both from religious principles and from personal ambition the commander-in-chief consented to this and said, 'First we must arrange that we chiefs meet together in a suitable place to come to an agreement, take oaths, and discuss how best we should deal with this matter without the king knowing.'

11 One of the army chiefs was an old man called Talan Auka; he said, 'The best plan is for you as commander-in-chief to submit to the king that the officers want you to give them a feast. Of course he will not say no. He will say, "If you have the wherewithal and can do it, proceed." Then you say that you lack nothing in the way of food and drink, but as regards mattresses, floor coverings and other furnishings and decorations such as are of gold and silver, you do not possess enough. The king will say, "Take whatever you need from my treasury, my cellar and my furniture store." Then you say that you are giving this feast to the

army on condition that when it is over they will go to Balasaghun to make holy war, because the infidel Turk has seized the province and the cries of the suffering people have exceeded all bounds; they must not have cause to think ill of the king. Then make preparations for the feast and invite the army to come on such-and-such a day; and borrow all the gold, silver, carpets, brocade and choice things which you can find in the king's treasury, cellar and furniture store, and take them to your house. On the appointed day when all the army has arrived at your house, close the house door in the excuse that it is getting crowded; then take the officers into one of the rooms to drink sherbet, and lay this matter before them. We who are at the root of the movement will of course be with you; those that are the branches will agree with us unanimously as soon as they hear our argument. We shall administer the oath and covenant to them all, and swear allegiance to you as king. Then we will come out of the room and proceed to the trays to eat. Having eaten the food we will go across to the drinking-hall where each one of us will drink three goblets of wine. All the gold and silver articles in that hall we will present to the officers. Then straightaway we will leave and go to the king's palace, seize the king and kill him. We will not spare a single one of his companions and co-religionists; we will kill them all and we will loot all the contents of his palace, treasury and stables. Then we will set you upon the throne; and we will tell the army to draw their swords, and fall upon towns and villages, and slaughter all the Qarmatis they can find, and burn their bodies and plunder their houses.' The commander-in-chief said, 'This is a good plan.'

12 The next day he said to Nasr ibn Ahmad, 'The officers and soldiers want me to give them a feast, and every day they are requesting me.' Nasr ibn Ahmad said, 'If you have the wherewithal to entertain them, do not fail to do so.' He said, 'Your slave has no shortage of food and drink, but carpets and furnishings and festive decorations, such as gold and silver, are lacking. Those who entertain should do it well or not at all.' Nasr said, 'You may take whatever you need of these things from my treasury, my cellar, and my furniture store.' The commander bowed and came out. The next day he invited all the army to come to his house on such-and-such a day. Then he took the gold and silver salvers and fine carpets and other things – all that was to be found in the king s treasury, cellar and stores; and he gave a feast

the like of which none had seen in those days. He received all the officers with their troops at his house, and according to plan he had the house door shut and took the nobles and officers into one of the rooms, and made them all swear oaths of allegiance.

13 Just as they came out of the room and went to the trays to eat, one of them got out of the house by way of the roof and straightaway informed Nuh ibn Nasr what the officers had just done. Nuh mounted immediately and rode at the gallop to his father's palace, and said, 'Why are you sitting there, when the officers of your army have this very hour sworn oaths and entered into a conspiracy with the commander-in-chief? As soon as they have finished eating they will go to the drinking-hall, and when each one has drunk three goblets of wine they are going to steal all the gold and silver brought from your treasury; then they will come out and rush headlong at our palace and kill you and me and everyone they can find. The purpose of this feast is to destroy us.' Nasr said to Nuh, 'Now what shall we do?' Nuh said, 'The best thing you can do is now, before they get up from eating and go to the drinking-hall, to send two private servants to whisper in the commander-in-chief's ear that the king says, "I hear that you have spared no pains and prepared a magnificent feast. Now I have in my possession a golden salver inlaid with jewels, such as no other king today possesses; it had been put somewhere outside the treasury, and I have just remembered it. Take this too, to provide the finest possible decoration for your feast; it is worth ten million dinars. Come quickly and I will hand it to you before the guests go into the drinking-hall." Undoubtedly in his greed of wealth he will come. As soon as he arrives we will chop off his head. Then I will tell you what to do.'

14 Immediately Nasr sent two private servants to deliver the message. The people were then busy eating. The commander-in-chief told one or two of his confederates why the king was calling him. They said, 'Go, and fetch that as well, for today it suits us to get all we can.' The commander went with all speed to the king's palace; there he was summoned into a room and the king straightaway ordered some pages to cut off his head and put it into a bag. Then Nuh said to his father, 'Mount, and let us go to the commander-in-chief's house taking the bag with us. There in front of all the officers you must abdicate the kingship and make me your successor; only so can I satisfy them and ensure that the kingship

remains in our family, for the troops will not put up with you any longer; and perhaps then you may die a natural death.' So they both mounted and rode swiftly to the commander-in-chief's house. The officers looked and saw the king come in at the door with his son. They all rose and went to greet him, and not one of them knew what was happening. They said, 'Perchance the king desired to join in the feast.' Nasr ibn Ahmad went and sat in his rightful place, with arms-bearers standing behind him; Nuh stood on his father's right hand and said, 'Pray be seated and finish your meal.'

15 So they ate the food and made general feasting. Then Nasr said, 'Know that I am aware of your conspiracy. When I learned of your design against me I was offended with you, and you who were offended with me will now be more so; hereafter you will have no confidence in me, nor I in you. If I have gone astray or adopted a heretical doctrine, or committed any other sin which has offended you, surely my son Nuh has no blemish?' They said, 'No.' He said, 'You are no longer fit to be my soldiers and I am not worthy to be your king. So I hereby nominate Nuh as my heir; he is now your king. Whether I am right or wrong, I shall now devote myself to regret and repentance before God. He who put you up to this has met with his just reward.' Then he told them to produce the commander-in-chief's head from the bag and throw it in front of the company. He himself descended from the throne and knelt on a prayer mat; while Nuh ascended the throne and sat in his father's place. When the officers heard and saw all this they were astonished, and could not find any excuse or pretext; they all fervently bowed their heads to the ground, and congratulated Nuh, throwing all the blame on the shoulders of the commander-in-chief and saying, 'We are all slaves under your command.' Nuh said, 'Know that in all respects I am Nuh, not Nasr. What is past is past. I now consider this mistake of yours as rectified. Through me all your desires will be fulfilled. Obey my commands and go and attend to your affairs.' He called for shackles and ordered that his father should be fettered, taken straight to Kuhandiz and incarcerated. Then he said, 'Come, let us go to the drinking-hall.'

16 When they had seated themselves in the drinking-hall and each one had drunk three goblets of wine, he said, 'You had planned that after drinking three goblets of wine you would plunder everything in this hall. So far from allowing plunder, I

now make you a present of everything. Take it all and divide it amongst yourselves, to each according to his station so that everyone receives a share.' So they picked up all the things and put them into sacks, which they sealed and handed over to a trusted person. Then Nuh said, 'If the commander-in-chief plotted mischief against us, he met with his just reward; and if my father deviated from the right path, he is now suffering his punishment. As for you, your scheme was that after enjoying this feast you would go to Balasaghun to wage war against the infidel Turks. But we should be warring against the infidels on our own doorstep. Arise! let us engage in holy war. Go and kill all those in Transoxiana and Khurasan who have become heretics and adopted this religion which my father adopted; and all their goods and riches are yours. I have just made you a present of all my father's property which was in this hall; tomorrow I will let you have what is in the treasury, for the chattels of the Batinis are only fit for plunder. Having finished this important work, we will turn to the infidel Turks. But first I wish you to bring forth Muhammad Nakhshabi with my father's confederates and behead them; then scour the city and the surrounding districts.'

17 Immediately they galloped off and brought Muhammad Nakhshabi, who was the propagandist, and beheaded him; also they executed Hasan Malik, Abu Mansur Chaghani and Ash'ath, together with several amirs who had become Batini. Then they ranged through the city and slaughtered all they could find of the heretics, and they recognized them because with the king's encouragement they had been openly discussing their doctrines and preaching in public. On the same day Nuh sent an amir with troops to cross the Oxus and go with speed to Marv-ar-Rud; first he was to capture the son of Savada and kill him; then they were to brandish their swords, and wherever in all Khurasan they found or heard of any of this sect among peasantry or soldiery they were to kill them all; and he commanded them to beware lest any Muslim should be slain by mistake, and he swore that if any Muslim were murdered he would kill the murderer and would not listen to any excuse. Then for seven days they ranged through Bukhara and its environs, killing and plundering, until the point was reached where not one of the heretics remained throughout Khurasan and Transoxiana; or if any were left they durst not shew themselves. Thus the sect remained concealed in Khurasan.

On the appearance of the Batinis in the lands of Syria and the West

18 Now we come to the story of Syria. When 'Abd-Allah ibn Maimun went to Basra, where he carried on his teaching secretly and also where he died, committing his unclean soul to hell, his son Ahmad departed and went to Syria, and from Syria to the Maghrib [N. Africa]. There his teaching failed to catch on. So he returned to Syria and dwelt in a city called Salami, working as a cloth merchant. There a son was born to him, and he called him Muhammad. When Ahmad died and his soul hastened to hell, his son was only small, so his brother Sa'id ibn al-Husain took his place and went towards the Maghrib, changing his name and calling himself 'Abd-Allah ibn al-Husain. He had a friend called Abu 'Abd-Allah Muhtasib;[15] he sent him as his lieutenant to the Bani Aghlab[16] and to the districts which they inhabited, to summon the people to this religion. The Bani Aghlab were mostly desert-dwellers and a great number of them accepted the religion. Then he gave the command that thereafter they were to operate with the sword, and kill everyone who was not of their faith. This they did, and a large company of the Bani Aghlab banded together and attacked towns and districts, plundering[17] and killing; they captured one city after another, until eventually they gained the mastery over most of the lands of the West. Now Zikrawaih,[18] the one known as Sahib al-Khal, was ruler over some of the towns of Syria; he was a Sunni and 'Ali Vahsudan Dailami was his general. He sent 'Ali with the Syrian army to make a surprise attack on Abu 'Abd-Allah Muhtasib. The latter fled but the Syrian army pressed home their attack and killed as many as they could of the Bani Aghlab and scattered the rest abroad. Abu 'Abd-Allah went to one of the towns of the Bani Aghlab where he put on a hood and lived as an honourable person[19] and was well treated by the people. Sahib al-Khal constantly sent messengers to them demanding that he should be handed over to him; but they made excuses and did not do so. Abu 'Abd-Allah was apprehensive lest the Bani Aghlab should defer to Sahib al-Khal and surrender him. So he went and lived on one of the islands belonging to the Bani Aghlab; there he built himself a house, and the Bani Aghlab used to send him alms. When he died his son succeeded him. The state of affairs in that part then remained unchanged for long periods.

On the appearance of the Batinis in the district of Herat and Ghur, and their destruction

19 In the year 295 (from the hijra) Muhammad ibn Harthama, the governor of Herat, informed Isma'il ibn Ahmad the Samanid (called The Just Amir) that in the foot-hills of Ghur and Gharcha a man known as Abu Bilal had appeared and had spread the doctrines of the Qarmatis; people of all classes had gathered about him and he had named his house Dar al-'Adl [The Abode of Justice]; many people from the country around Herat had gone to join him and were swearing allegiance to him; their numbers exceeded 10,000. He said, 'If Your Majesty neglects to deal with him the number of his followers will be doubled; then it will be a difficult business. They say that this Abu Bilal is the one who was a boon-companion of Ya'qub ibn Laith, and that he has succeeded him in the propagation of heresy.' When the amir Isma'il heard this, he said, 'I am given to understand that Abu Bilal's blood has come to the boil!' Then he gave orders to his chamberlain, Zakari, saying, 'Choose five hundred of the cleverest and bravest of all the pages; see that they are paid; make Tiqish their leader as he is an intelligent boy and let him be given 10,000 dirams; and let five hundred suits of mail be packed on mules. Tomorrow take them to Juy-i Muliyan[20] to parade before me for review.' The chamberlain Zakari did this.

20 Then the amir Isma'il ordered a letter to be written to Abu 'Ali Marrudi [at Marv-ar-Rud] saying, 'Give your men their pay, and come outside the city so that you are there before the pages arrive; then go with them to Herat and join forces with Muhammad ibn Harthama.' And to Muhammad ibn Harthama he wrote, 'Have your troops ready and wait outside the city until Tiqish and Abu 'Ali reach you.' He promised Tiqish that as soon as a report reached him from Muhammad ibn Harthama that he, Tiqish, had successfully accomplished his mission, he would give him a province. And to the rest of the pages he said, 'This is not the campaign against 'Ali ibn Sharvin, or 'Amr ibn Laith, or Muhammad ibn Harun, for in those cases we had large and well-equipped forces. For this operation I am relying on you. In the foothills of Herat a rebel has appeared and has spread the doctrines of the Qarmatis; the majority of his converts are shepherds and farmers.

If you are successful I will give you all robes of honour and presents, and raise your rank.' Then he appointed an experienced secretary to look after their administration.

21 As soon as they reached Marv-ar-Rud, Abu 'Ali joined them with his men. They garrisoned the ends of the roads so that the rebels should not get news of them. When they arrived at Herat, Muhammad ibn Harthama came out with his troops at once and blocked the roads so that no news reached Abu Bilal. Then they went up into the mountains, and after three days' march up hill and down dale and over difficult passes, they reached the rebels who were unsuspecting. They surrounded them unawares,[21] put them to the sword and killed them all. Abu Bilal, Hamdan, Abu Zaka' and ten other of their chiefs were taken prisoner. Within seventy days they returned to Bukhara. Abu Bilal was imprisoned at Kuhandiz and there he died. The other ten were sent to Balkh, Samarqand, Farghana, Khwarazm, Marv and Nishapur and other cities where they were hanged. Thus their substance was completely eradicated from Ghur and Gharcha. In this same year The Just Amir Isma'il died and his brother Nasr ibn Ahmad came to the throne – he whose story we have already related, how he had become a Batini.[22]

On the emergence of the Batinis in Khurasan and Transoxiana for the second time

22 After Nuh imprisoned his father he poisoned him, so that the officers of the army were completely rid of him, and Nuh reigned as king for many years. When Nuh died, his son Mansur succeeded him and followed in his father's footsteps. After fifteen years of his reign had passed, missionaries once more began preaching secretly in Khurasan and Bukhara, and again led the people astray. The majority of those who were converted were persons whose fathers and grandfathers had lost their lives because of this religion. Mansur was known in his time as The Righteous Amir; his vazir was Abu 'Ali Bal'ami; his commander-in-chief of Khurasan was Alptigin, Sabuktigin's master; Mansur ibn Bayqara was his great chamberlain; Abu Yahya ibn Ash'ath was governor of Farghana; Sarhang Husain, governor of Isbijab; Isma'il, governor of Chach; Abu Mansur 'Abd ar-Razzaq, governor of Tus; and Vushmgir, governor of Gurgan. Of the amirs who were resident

at the capital there were Babdah,[23] Nasr Malik, Hasan Malik, Abu
Sa'id Malik, Haidar Chaghani, Abu 'l-'Abbas Jarrah, Baktuzun,
Takinak, Khamartigin, and the like. In short Mansur ibn Bayqara,
Abu Sa'id Malik, Abu 'l-'Abbas Jarrah, Khamartigin, Takinak,
Abu 'Abd-Allah Jaihani and Ja'far secretly joined the Batinis.
The propagandists who converted this group were two: one
was Abu 'l-Fadl Zangurz Bardiji and the other was a one-
eyed man called 'Atiq. All the members of this company were
men on whom the business of the court, audience-hall and divan
depended, and in whose hands was the management of the
affairs of the whole country. Surreptitiously they put their co-
religionists into positions of power; and unless their work became
too much for them they did not delegate it to others. Officially
and unofficially they supported and assisted one another. If one of
them stumbled the rest stood by him and assisted him to discharge
his obligations. Thus their power and following increased daily,
and all over Khurasan and Transoxiana, wherever they were to be
found, they had become vociferous,[24] and with their help the
Batini propaganda was published and their doctrines were spread
abroad. People in far off places began to think that the whole
court had become Batini. Then Abu Mansur 'Abd ar-Razzaq also
joined the Batinis. The Batinis at the court wrote to The Wearers
of White[25] at Farghana, Khujand and Kasan urging them to
revolt, saying, 'Our arguments and yours are in origin the same.
We too are going to revolt, and our plan is first to capture the
king. Then we will join forces and conquer all the provinces on
this [north] side of the Oxus. Later we will attack Khurasan.'

23 The Batinis then united and with the co-operation of [Man-
sur] ibn Bayqara they proceeded to vilify Abu 'Ali Bal'ami the
vazir and the amir Baktuzun in front of the king. Both these men
were [orthodox] Muslims, and all the slave pages were under the
control of Baktuzun. Mansur ordered them both to be imprisoned
in Kuhandiz and fettered. This caused serious confusion in the
affairs of the country. When Alptigin saw that most of the nobles
and courtiers had adopted the religion of the Qarmatis and that
these two men, who were good Muslims and loyal to the king,
had at their instigation been imprisoned, he set out from Nishapur
to go to Bukhara and inform the king of these activities, and take
measures to deal with them. Abu Mansur 'Abd ar-Razzaq, who
was the amir of Tus, was something of a swashbuckler and he was

well provided with troops and equipment; he rushed out and blocked Alptigin's path so that he could not reach the capital without a battle. Alptigin got news of this; he changed his route, and went by way of Shir and Riza,[26] until he reached the bank of the Oxus and halted at Amuy [Amul]. Abu Mansur 'Abd ar-Razzaq turned back and despatched a letter to Mansur ibn Bay-qara and the rest of that group, saying that Alptigin had come to spoil their position. After consulting together they represented to the king that Alptigin was in rebellion against him, saying, 'He has never come to the court before although you have called him so many times. Now in defiance of you he has suddenly arrived at the bank of the Oxus and intends to cross without your summoning him.' The king sent Bik Arslan Hamidi and Hasan Malik with a force of men to the Oxus, and they took all the boats from the other side so that Alptigin could not cross.

24 When Alptigin saw that they would not let him cross, he wrote a letter submitting the reason for his coming, and saying, 'Most of your nobles, courtiers and officials have adopted the religion of the Qarmatis: both great and small have joined in it, and they are planning to revolt; while on their word you have imprisoned the two men who in all the country are your most orthodox and loyal subjects. I had come to take measures against them. If you listen to the Qarmatis rather than to me, you may take the consequences. I, your slave, have informed Your Majesty. Now I am going to Balkh.' He sent a similar letter to the judge of Bukhara and the religious leaders saying, 'The Qarmatis have become powerful and they are breaking out; the king is heedless; I have written to him; give him due counsel so that the faith and the kingdom may be saved.' And he went in the direction of Balkh. The letters arrived. The judge Abu Ahmad and the religious leaders of Bukhara were aware of the situation but dared not say anything about it just then, because the majority of the Qarmati company were of the king's select courtiers. They said, 'Maybe the king will not hear our word against them. Each one of them has a province and an army. They are rich and powerful; besides, they would become our enemies.'

25 One afternoon Abu Ahmad the chief judge went to the king's palace and requested a private audience; the king called him in and sat alone with him. Abu Ahmad said, 'Doctors of religion are always ready to give advice and counsel. Your father Nuh

(The Praised Amir – Allah have mercy upon him) used to meet
religious teachers every day and he never used to do anything
without consulting them. Consequently all crooked things were
by him made straight. Because you seldom sit with men of learning, all that your father made straight has in your time become
crooked.' He then shewed Alptigin s letter to the king; and he
also shewed him another letter written by the religious leaders, so
that the king should know that what he said was not from himself
alone. Then he personally warned the king and talked to him so
as to awaken him to the situation.

26 As it happened it was reported the next day that The Wearers
of White had revolted in Farghana and were killing all the Muslims they could find. The day after that news also came from the
Khurasan side that the Qarmatis were openly proclaiming the
Sevener religion in Taliqan and the foothills, and were committing
murders and other crimes. So Mansur (The Righteous Amir)
offered the vazirship to judge Abu Ahmad; he declined to accept,
saying, 'If I take the office of vazir, who else is there now to give
the king impartial counsel and advice? Besides interested parties
will say that the judge has done all this for the sake of the vazirship
not for the sake of the faith and the kingdom.' The king was
pleased with his words, and said, 'Then what is the best thing to
do about the vazirship?' He said, 'You have a vazir, who is not
only capable and worthy, but is a good Muslim and the son of a
vazir as well.' He said, 'Where?' He said, 'He is a prisoner in
Kuhandiz.' Mansur gave the command and Abu 'Ali Bal'ami and
Baktuzun were released from prison; and on the same day they
were fêted and reinstated in their posts with the utmost dignity
and ceremony. The next day the king, the vazir, the judge and
Baktuzun had a private meeting, and the king was made aware of
the state of affairs far and near. They decided that first they would
deal with the Muqanna'is of Farghana and Sughd, known as The
Wearers of White, and with the Qarmatis of Taliqan; then they
would attend to Abu Mansur 'Abd ar-Razzaq, and after that to the
nobles and courtiers.

27 The next day scholars bearing letters from religious leaders
in every city came to the vazir's court to complain to him and
request him to inform the king about the revolt of the Qarmatis.
Now Abu 'Ali deliberately delayed taking action with the result
that the scholars said, 'He would not be hesitating if he were not

in league with them.' Then Abu 'Ali spoke openly to the king, who ordered that a meeting should be held, attended by the Qarmatis on the one hand, and the scholars on the other; after debating the matter, they would abide by what they agreed to be in accordance with the precepts of the religious law of Islam. So the next day Abu 'Ali Bal'ami convened a meeting in the king's palace, and summoned Abu Ahmad Marghazi, the chief judge at the court, and all the religious leaders and notables; and they sent persons out to fetch the Qarmati leaders and as many of their spokesmen as could be recognized. So they debated and their doctrines were seen to be opposed to Islamic law. 'Atiq the one-eyed was beaten a hundred lashes and sent to Khwarazm where he died in prison; Abu 'l-Fadl Zangurz was also given a hundred lashes and banished with his wife and children to Amuy, and he died there. Then Baktuzun and Abu 'l-Qasim, who was the agent [accompanying the holy-warriors] of Pars and Khuzistan,[27] were sent to Taliqan with an army. Apart from the men they killed, they captured four hundred notable men who confessed to being Qarmatis and fined them 60,000 dinars, bringing 100,000 dirams to the treasury. Then another royal command was sent to the holy-warriors of Pars and Khuzistan, ordering the Qarmatis to be brought to the capital, where some of them were hanged and others were imprisoned for life.

28 When the operations in Taliqan were finished, Mansur appointed Ishaq Balkhi to go with Bik Arslan to Farghana, and he also sent the scholar Abu Muhammad with them to teach the rebels the religious law. So after the victory [at Taliqan] these men took an army to Farghana and defeated the other lot of rebels. Some were killed; others were fined; others confessed their folly and repented, and when they were introduced to Islam they accepted it and forsook the other religion. So the army returned to Bukhara bringing much booty. The scholar Abu Muhammad was asked, 'What kind of religion do those Muqanna'is practise?' He said, 'Such that they used not to hide their privy parts from one another, and did not refrain from mutual commerce; when a man was married, their chief was the first to lay hands upon the woman, afterwards the husband; they regarded wine drinking as lawful; they did not wash pollution from their bodies; they made free with their mothers, sisters and daughters; they repudiated the duties of prayer, fasting, alms, pilgrimage and holy war.'

29 When this business had been accomplished, The Righteous Amir Mansur had a private meeting with the vazir, the judge and Baktuzun to consider how to remove the courtiers, nobles and officials who had adopted the Qarmati religion, and how to bring about the downfall of Abu Mansur 'Abd ar-Razzaq and clear Khurasan, 'Iraq and Transoxiana completely of the Qarmatis. They decided that since the amir of Tus, Abu Mansur 'Abd ar-Razzaq, was the most powerful man in Khurasan at the time, because Alptigin had departed from Khurasan and settled at Ghaznain, first of all they must purge the capital, the king's abode, of the Qarmatis, and then deal with Abu Mansur and other places. So they appointed Nasir ad-Daula [Helper of the Empire] Abu 'l-Hasan Simjur as commander-in-chief of Khurasan, and summoned him with the whole army of Khurasan to the court. When he arrived at the capital they were able with his help to capture all the nobles and officials at the court who had become Qarmatis; they confiscated the whole of their property and then killed them all. After that they sent Abu 'l-Hasan Simjur with the Khurasan army to fight and capture Abu Mansur 'Abd ar-Razzaq. They sent letters to the border commanders including Vushmgir, instructing that the latter should bring his troops from Gurgan, and that the others should join forces with him and surround Tus, capture Abu Mansur, and kill all the Qarmatis they could find.

30 Abu Mansur was sick; when he saw that the armies had surrounded Tus, he made a sortie in the direction of Gurgan; Vushmgir intercepted him on the road, and from breakfast time until afternoon prayer a very fierce battle was fought. Abu Mansur was exhausted with weakness and sickness; he dismounted from his horse, laid his head on the bosom of a page, and thereupon expired. His troops then fled. Vushmgir ordered his head to be cut off. They continued to chase the fugitives, killing and taking prisoners until the evening prayer. They succeeded in recovering all Abu Mansur's stores and valuables; Vushmgir sent Abu Mansur's head and his treasure to The Righteous Amir at Bukhara along with 180 prisoners. Then in one direction Abu 'l-Hasan Simjur and in the other direction Vushmgir with his son Qabus traversed provinces and districts killing all the Qarmatis they could find. Eventually there remained not a single Batini in all Khurasan and Transoxiana; the religion collapsed completely and nobody took any more notice of it.

On the rising of Muhammad ibn 'Ali The Veiled 'Alavi to champion the Batini religion in Khuzistan and Basra with an army of negroes

31 In the year 255 Muhammad ibn 'Ali The Veiled 'Alavi led a revolt at Ahvaz. For several years he had been deceiving the negro slaves in Khuzistan and the people of Basra with propaganda and promises. He revolted at the promised time and all the negroes joined in league with him. First he took Ahvaz, then Basra and the whole of Khuzistan. All the negroes killed their masters and seized their wealth, wives and houses. Several times they defeated the forces of [the caliph] al-Mu'tamid, and for fourteen years four months and six days Muhammad ibn 'Ali ruled like a king over Basra and Khuzistan. In the end he was captured and all the negroes were killed; at the end of the month of Safar in the year 270 he was brought to Baghdad and put to death. His religion was in all respects the same as that of Mazdak, Babak, Abu Zakariyya,[28] the Khurrama-dins and the Qarmatis.

On the revolt of Abu Sa'id Jannabi and his son Abu Tahir in Bahrain and Lahsa

32 Then in the time of al-Mu'tadid was the revolt of Abu Sa'id al-Hasan ibn Bahram al-Jannabi in Bahrain and Lahsa. He summoned the people of those parts to the Sevener, or Batini religion as we call it, and led them astray. He gradually strengthened his position there, and when he had become established, he began to practise highway robbery and pillage the countryside. He also introduced community of property. He continued in this way for some time, and then a servant killed him. After that servants were not trusted in Bahrain and Lahsa. Abu Sa'id had a son called Abu Tahir. He took his father's place and for a time lived virtuously, knowing very little about the doctrines of the Seveners. Then he sent someone to their missionaries and asked for a copy of the final part of their book which they called *al-Balaghat as-Sabi'a* ['The Seventh Degree']. They sent him the book. He studied it and became one of those dogs. It seems that he invited all the men of Bahrain and Lahsa who were young and fond of arms to join him, saying, 'Come, I have a job for you.' The time of the pilgrimage was near. He gathered a vast crowd of men, marched

them off and led them to Mecca, just at the time of the pilgrimage, when pilgrims from all over the world had assembled. He ordered them to draw their swords and kill all they could find, laying hands on the people of Mecca and The Neighbours [of the sanctuary] in particular. They made a sudden attack and began killing. Seeing this the people fled into the sanctuary and protected themselves behind the chests[29] in which the Qur'ans were kept. The inhabitants of Mecca and those pilgrims who could fight took up arms and joined battle.

33 At this Abu Tahir interposed an envoy and said, 'We have come for pilgrimage not to fight. It was your fault for killing one of us without cause and breaking our *ihrām* [state of consecration], so that we were constrained to take up arms. If the report is spread about the world, that the people of Mecca are arming themselves and killing pilgrims, nobody will be eager to do the pilgrimage any more. The pilgrims' road will then be closed and you will get a bad name. You are spoiling our pilgrimage. Allow us to proceed.' The people of Mecca thought that perhaps he was telling the truth; it was possible that someone had quarrelled with their party, and drawn a weapon and hurt one of them. They agreed that both parties should sheathe their swords, and swear on the volume of the Qur'an and with irredeemable oaths that they would not fight again, and that the Meccans would go back and return the Qur'an-chests to the sanctuary, so that the pilgrims could visit the Ka'ba in safety and perform the rites. The Meccans and the armed pilgrims swore oaths and Abu Tahir and his men also swore as demanded and went back and put up their weapons. The Meccans retired and put the chests back in their place and the pilgrims entered upon the visitation and circumambulation of the Ka'ba.

34 When Abu Tahir saw that the armed men had dispersed, he ordered his comrades to take up their arms and fall upon the sanctuary and kill whomsoever they found inside or outside. So they made a sudden rush at the sanctuary, brandishing their swords and spears and killing everyone within reach. They killed all The Neighbours and an enormous number of other people lost their lives; in fear of the sword they were throwing themselves into wells and fleeing to the tops of the mountains. The raiders removed The Black Stone from its place, then went up on the roof of the building and tore down the golden gutters, saying, 'Since your

god goes to heaven and leaves his house on earth unattended, then let his house be plundered and destroyed.' Then they pulled down the covering, tore it up and carried it off as plunder, all the while saying in mockery [quoting from the Qur'an 3. 91], 'And he who entered it was safe', and [106. 4], 'He saved them from fear.' 'Since you had gone inside the house, why were you not safe from our swords?' and 'If you had had a real god he would have delivered you from the fear of our swords'; and suchlike blasphemies they uttered. They took captive the wives and children of the Meccans and led them away. Altogether about 20,000 men were killed apart from those whom they threw into wells alive; and they cast the bodies of the slain on top of those in the wells so that they too perished. They took 100,000 camels and an inestimable amount of gold, dirams, dinars, fine linen, musk, aloes-wood, ambergris and other precious things. When Abu Tahir returned to Lahsa he sent portions of the loot as gifts to his missionaries in various places. This catastrophe for Islam took place in the time of al-Muqtadir in the year 317 from the hijra.

35 Abu Tahir sent some gifts to the Maghrib to Abu Sa'id, who was a Jewish boy; one of the sons of 'Abd-Allah ibn Maimun al-Qaddah called Ahmad had married his mother, and brought up the boy, at the same time using him like his mother; he taught him the liberal arts, provided him with splendid adornments and made him his heir; he instructed him in his propaganda and gave him certain signs. Abu Sa'id arose and went to the West and stayed in the city of Sijilmas; there his affairs prospered and he forced his religion on the necks of the people by the sword. He claimed that he was the Mahdi and of the family of 'Ali; he imposed heavy taxes, made wine lawful, and permitted [commerce with] mothers, sisters and daughters; he openly cursed and ordered cursing of the Marwanids and 'Abbasids, and if we were to tell of all the innocent blood which he spilt and the wicked practices which he introduced, it would take too long and would not suit this abbreviated account. It is reported in the history books that the present occupants of the throne of Egypt [Fatimid caliphs] are descended from him.

36 When Abu Tahir Sa'id returned to Lahsa, they collected all the volumes of the Qur'an, the Torah, the Psalms and the Evangel that they could find and threw them into the desert. He used to say, 'Three persons have corrupted mankind – a shepherd, a

physician and a camel-driver;[30] I condemn the camel-driver more
than the others, who were mere conjurors, jugglers and cheats.'
He allowed [commerce with] sisters, mothers and daughters; he
broke The Black Stone in two, and put the pieces on the two sides
of a latrine pit; when he squatted over the pit, he put his feet one
on each half of the stone; he commanded public cursing of the
prophets. But his order that men should have commerce with
their mothers was intolerable to the Arabs; many of them ate
arsenic and brimstone, and died rather than lie with their mothers;
but the people of the Maghrib and those westerners[31] who were
more ignorant, all took to this practice quite naturally. He attacked the pilgrim caravan a second time, and again swore false
oaths and killed many people. But when the Muslims of Khurasan
and 'Iraq began planning to travel by sea as well as land, the ban-
dits were afraid and sent back The Black Stone; one day on entering the Central Mosque at Kufa people unexpectedly saw The
Black Stone lying there. They picked it up and having mended it
with an iron rivet, took it back to Mecca and put it in its place.
Then Abu Tahir brought Zakira, a Zoroastrian, from Isfahan to
Lahsa and set him up as king; this Zoroastrian set to and killed
700 of their leading men, and he was going to kill Abu Tahir and
his brother; but Abu Tahir was apprised of this, and killed him by
a trick, so regaining the ascendancy. But if we were to relate all the
crimes and seditions which this dog perpetrated in the lands of
Islam, it could not be contained in this book. This trouble lasted
until the time of ar-Radi; and it was in the time of ar-Radi that the
Dailamites rose to power.

37 This much has been related so that The Master of the World
(may Allah perpetuate his reign) may know what the religion of
these Batinis is, why their words and oaths are not to be trusted,
what crimes and evil works they have done against the Muslims
and the lands of Islam whenever they have had the opportunity,
what wicked people they are and what enemies of Islam and of the
state.

38 Muqanna' [The Veiled] Marghazi[32] also appeared in the
lands of Transoxiana at this time. He totally abolished the religious
law among his people, and at first he made the same claims as the
Batinis, such as Abu Sa'id Jannabi, Abu Sa'id Maghribi, Muhammad The Veiled 'Alavi and their missionaries. Muqanna' and the

two Abu Sa'ids lived at the same time and they corresponded with one another. Muqanna' worked a magic spell in Transoxiana and made the likeness of a moon to appear from a mountain; every day at the same time the moon would rise, and all the inhabitants of the district saw it; it lasted for a long time. He took the people of that province out of the bosom of Islam and the divine law, and when his position became strong he laid claim to divinity; then there followed a tale of bloodshed and crime; armies came from the frontier districts to support him, and for several years the Muslims were engaged in wars against him. If I were to narrate it all, it would come to twice as much as this; his story and the story of each one of these dogs that I have mentioned would make a very large, heavy volume, even if written in the *muqarmat* script. This much has been told of the story of Muqanna' in order that mention of him should not be omitted from our compendium.

39 Whenever the Batinis have appeared they have had a name or a nickname, and in every city and province they have been known by a different title; but in essence they are all the same. In Aleppo and Egypt they call them Isma'ilis; in Qum, Kashan, Tabaristan and Sabzvar they are called Seveners; in Baghdad, Transoxiana and Ghaznain they are known as Qarmatis, in Kufa as Mubarakis, in Basra as Ravandis and Burqa'is, in Rayy as Khalafis, in Gurgan as The Wearers of Red, in Syria as The Wearers of White, in the West as Sa'idis, in Lahsa and Bahrain as Jannabis, and in Isfahan as Batinis; whereas they call themselves The Didactics and other such names. But their whole purpose is only to abolish Islam, to mislead mankind and cast them into perdition.

Chapter XLVII

On the rising of the Khurrama-dins in Isfahan

1 Now your slave will compose a somewhat abbreviated chapter on the subject of the Khurrama-dins, so that The Master of the

World (may Allah perpetuate his reign) may be enlightened concerning them. Whenever the Khurrama-dins have arisen the Batinis have made common cause with them and strengthened them; and whenever the Batinis appear, the Khurrama-dins combine with them and assist them with men and resources; for the origin of these two religions is the same and they have but one object – to corrupt the faith.

2 In the year 162 in the days of al-Mahdi, the Batinis of Gurgan, known as The Red Banners, that is to say The Wearers of Red, gained great strength and joined forces with the Khurrama-dins, saying, 'Abu Muslim is alive! Let us seize the kingdom and give it back to him!' They made the son of Abu 'l-Mughra' (grandson of Abu Muslim) their leader and advanced as far as Rayy. Every unlawful thing they considered lawful; and they shared their wives with one another. Then al-Mahdi wrote letters to the governors of the frontier provinces, ordering them to join forces with 'Umar ibn al-'Ala', governor of Tabaristan, and go to war against the rebels. They attacked and routed them. Later at the time when Harun ar-Rashid was in Khurasan the Khurrama-dins revolted in the Isfahan district, coming from Paridan,[1] Kabala,[2] [Shahr-i] Babak[3] and other villages. A large mob came and joined them from Rayy, Hamadan and Dastaba.[4] Their total number came to more than 100,000. Harun sent 'Abd-Allah ibn Malik from Khurasan with 20,000 horsemen to make war on them. They took fright and went back to their places. 'Abd-Allah ibn Malik wrote a letter to Harun ar-Rsahid saying, 'Abu Dulaf is indispensable to us.' The reply came, 'Take your orders from him.' So the two joined forces. Once again the Khurrama-dins with the encouragement of the Batinis gathered into a large mob and set their hands to sedition and plunder. Abu Dulaf 'Ijli and 'Abd-Allah ibn Malik attacked suddenly and caught them unawares. They killed an enormous number of them and took their wives and children to Baghdad and sold them by auction.

On the revolt of Babak in Adharbaygan

3 Nine years after this Babak[5] came out in revolt from Adharbaygan. These Batinis attempted to join him; but they heard that forces had been sent in pursuit of them, so they were afraid and returned and dispersed. Then in the year 212 in the days of

al-Ma'mun the Khurrama-dins revolted in the districts of Isfahan, Punda,[6] Kabala and Karaj. The Batinis joined them and they aroused seditions; then they went to Adharbaygan and attached themselves to Babak. Al-Ma'mun sent Muhammad ibn Humaid Ta'i to make war on Babak and at the same time to repel the Khurrama-dins; he ordered him first to engage with Zurair ibn 'Ali ibn Sadaqa,[7] who had revolted and was wandering through Kuhistan of 'Iraq, pillaging the country and robbing caravans. Muhammad ibn Humaid went with speed; he asked for nothing from al-Ma'mun's treasury but equipped his troops from his own resources. He attacked Zurair, captured him and destroyed his followers. For this al-Ma'mun gave him Qazvin, Maragha and most of Adharbaygan. Then he made war on Babak and for a period of six months fierce battles took place between him and Babak. In the end Muhammad ibn Humaid was killed and he did not defeat them. Babak's fortunes rose high, and he sent the Isfahan Khurrama-dins back to Isfahan. Al-Ma'mun was extreme-ly vexed at the death of Muhammad ibn Humaid. He immediately nominated 'Abd-Allah ibn Tahir, governor of Khurasan, for the war against Babak and gave him the whole province of Kuhistan and all that had been liberated of Adharbaygan. 'Abd-Allah arose and went to Adharbaygan. Babak was unable to resist him; he fled into a secure fortress and the mass of the Khurrama-dins dispersed.

4 In the year 218 the Khurrama-dins of Pars, Isfahan and the whole of Kuhistan and Adharbaygan broke out in revolt because al-Ma'mun had gone to Rum. They had determined on a certain night, and under Babak's direction they revolted on that night in all the provinces and cities; they killed the tax-collectors every-where and slaughtered a great many of the Muslims, plundering their houses and carrying off their children as slaves. In Pars the Muslims gathered together and defeated the rebels, killing many and taking prisoners; but in Isfahan the Khurrama-dins banded together at Dar[8] and Paridan[9] under the leadership of a man called 'Ali ibn Mazdak. He mustered 20,000 men outside the gate of the city and went with his brother to Karaj. At that time Abu Dulaf was not there; his brother Ma'qil was at Karaj, and with only 500 horsemen he could not resist; so he fled and went to Baghdad. 'Ali ibn Mazdak captured Karaj, plundered the town and killed all the Muslims he could find; he carried off all the women and

children of the 'Ijlis. From there he went to Adharbaygan to join forces with Babak. The Khurrama-dins flocked to Babak from all sides; they came in 10,000s, 20,000s and 5,000s and they foregathered at a town called Sharistana[10] between Kuhistan and Adharbaygan. There Babak joined them.

5 Then al-Mu'tasim sent Ishaq with 40,000 horsemen to fight them; he attacked them suddenly and a battle ensued. In the end he defeated them thoroughly and Babak fled. Ishaq's army then laid about the Khurrama-dins with their swords. When they counted the casualties, those actually killed, apart from those who surrendered, came to 100,000 men. Another group had made for Isfahan and about 10,000 men under the brother of 'Ali ibn Mazdak occupied the houses of the city mayors; they had brought their wives and children with them. The amir of Isfahan, 'Ali ibn 'Isa, was away; the judge, Chaghan Bakira, with a party of nobles, mayors and citizens went out to fight them. They came upon them from three directions and defeated them; they took captive all their women and children, brought them to the city and kept them in slavery; any boys that were come of age they beheaded and threw into pits.

6 Six years after this al-Mu'tasim again attended to the matter of the Khurrama-dins, and he nominated Afshin[11] to make war against Babak. Afshin took troops and set out to meet him. The Khurrama-dins and Batinis from every place went to Babak's assistance. Altogether they were at war for two years, and several fierce battles were fought between Afshin and Babak, and vast numbers of men were killed on both sides. In the end Afshin devised a stratagem; he dispersed most of his troops by ordering them to strike their tents by night, retreat ten farsangs and remain there. Then Afshin sent an envoy to Babak saying, 'Send me a wise and experienced man, for I wish to say a few words which are for the benefit of both of us.' Babak sent him a man. Afshin said to him, 'Tell Babak that every work has an end; the head of a man is not a leek that it should grow again. Nearly all of my men have been killed; not one tenth remain. I have no doubt that it is the same on your side. Come, let us make peace. You be content with this province which you hold; rule it rightfully, while I go back and get the provincial charter from The Commander of the Faithful on your behalf and send it to you. If you do not accept my advice, come, let us contend with one another once and for all

to see whom fortune favours.' The envoy then left his presence; he looked all around to see the extent of Afshin's forces; what he saw were disencumbered as if they were on the verge of flight.

7 When the envoy came back to Babak, he delivered the message and reported on [what he had seen of] the paucity of the enemy's forces; spies brought back the same report. So they agreed to fight a great battle after three days. Afshin then sent a messenger to those dispersed troops, saying, 'On the night before the battle, come and conceal yourselves in the mountains and valleys on the left and on the right at a distance of one farsang or a half. When I take to flight and retire to a considerable distance from the camp, some of the enemy will pursue me, others will busy themselves with plundering the camp; you will then rush out from the mountains and block the road against them so that they cannot go back into the valley. Then I will come back.'

8 On the day of the battle Babak brought his troops out of the pass; they were more than 100,000 horse and foot. Afshin's army was contemptible in their eyes, judging from what they had seen from their camp; they did not see the extra troops. Then they joined battle and they fought fiercely on both sides and many men were killed. About noon Afshin took to flight and having retreated to a distance of one farsang from the camp, he said to his standard-bearer, 'Raise the standard and halt!' As his troops arrived at the spot they halted. Babak had told his men not to indulge in plunder, so that they might finally dismiss Afshin from their minds. All Babak's horsemen went with him in pursuit of Afshin; however, the foot-soldiers fell upon the camp and started to plunder. Then the 20,000 horsemen hurled themselves from behind the mountains to left and to right, and saw all the plain full of the Khurrama-din foot-soldiers. They blocked the road against them in the valley and set about them with their swords. Afshin came back with the 20,000 horsemen and Babak was caught in the middle. However much he strove he found no way of escape. Afshin closed in and took him prisoner. They went on charging and killing until afternoon prayer. More than 80,000 of the Khurrama-dins were killed there. Afshin left a page with 20,000 horse and foot to stay beneath Babak's fortress, and he himself took Babak and the other prisoners to Baghdad where they led him through the city for a spectacle.[12]

9 When al-Mu'tasim set eyes on Babak he said, 'O dog, why

did you stir up this trouble in the world and why did you kill so many thousand Muslims?' He made no reply. Al-Mu'tasim commanded his hands and feet to be cut off. When they had cut off one hand, he put the other one in the blood and rubbed it on his face making it all red with blood. Al-Mu'tasim said, 'Dog, what sign is this?' Babak said, 'There is wisdom in it.' They said, 'What wisdom is that, pray?' He said, 'You are going to cut off my hands and feet. Now it is blood that makes men's faces red; when the body loses blood, the face becomes yellow. When a man's hands and feet are cut off, the blood will not stay in his body; I am making my face red so that when my body loses blood, people will not say my face has turned yellow from fear.' Then on al-Mu'tasim's orders an ox was skinned, and the hide was brought as it was, fresh and with the horns. Babak was then put inside the skin with the horns protruding from behind his ears; and he was sewn up in it, and the skin dried up on him. Then he was hanged alive in that condition and he perished miserably.

10 The complete story of Babak from the beginning of his revolt until his capture would fill a very large volume. One of his executioners came to be captured, and he was asked how many persons he had put to death. He said, 'Babak had several executioners, but the number of Muslims that I have executed is 33,000 apart from those killed in battles by the other executioners.'

11 Al-Mu'tasim gained three victories and all three gave strength to Islam, the first was the conquest of Rum, the second was the victory over Babak and the third the victory over Mazyar the Zoroastrian in Tabaristan. If any one of these victories had not been won, it would have been a calamity for Islam.

The story of al-Mu'tasim's three victories

12 One day al-Mu'tasim was sitting at a drinking party, and judge Yahya ibn Aktham was present. Al-Mu'tasim got up and left the party and went into a room. After some time he came out and drank some wine. Again he got up and went into another room; yet again he got up and went into a third. After some time he came out and went to the bathroom and did a major ablution. He soon emerged and called for his prayer-mat; he performed two *rak'ats* of prayer and went back to the party. He said to judge

Yahya, 'Do you know why I said these prayers?' He said, 'No.' He said, 'It was a prayer of thanksgiving for one of God's benefits (to Him be power and glory) which he has vouchsafed me today.' Yahya said, 'O Commander of the Faithful, what benefit was that?' He said, 'In this hour I have deflowered the maidenhood of three maidens, all of them were daughters of my three enemies; one was the daughter of the king of Rum, the second the daughter of Babak, and the third the daughter of Mazyar the Zoroastrian.'

13 In the days of al-Wathiq the Khurrama-dins again revolted in the district of Isfahan, and they did much evil. They continued their insurrections until the year 300. They pillaged the town of Karaj for the second time, killed some people and were later subdued. Yarizadshah[13] revolted and took refuge in the mountains near Isfahan; the Khurrama-dins and Batinis gathered about him, and they began to attack caravans and plunder villages, killing old and young, and little children. He carried on his iniquities for thirty and odd years, and no army was able to resist him; they were powerless against the impregnable fastnesses which he held. At last he was captured and his head was hung up in Isfahan. On this victory they sent the glad tidings throughout the lands of Islam. However, if we mention everything, it will take too long and even then scarcely a thousandth part will be told. Whoever wishes to know about the revolts and seditions of the Batinis and Khurrama-dins should study Tabari's 'History', the 'History of Isfahan' and the 'History of the 'Abbasid Caliphs', so that it may be known to him.

14 Now the basis of the religion of the Khurrama-dins is that they reject all physical exertion as far as Islamic religious rites are concerned, such as standing straight [for prayer], performing prayer, fasting, going on the pilgrimage, making holy war against God's enemies, washing away pollution, forbidding wine, practising asceticism and abstinence – in fact they discard all obligatory observances; they spurn the religious law and follow not the way of Muhammad's people. When ever they hold a meeting or any group of them come together, they always commence the proceedings by bewailing the death of Abu Muslim Sahib ad-Daula, cursing his killer, and blessing Mahdi Firuz, son of Fatima the daughter of Abu Muslim, whom they call The Learned Boy (and in Arabic [al-]Fata'l-'Alim). From the foregoing it has been shewn

that the religions of Mazdak, the Khurrama-dins and the Batinis all have a common origin; the constant object of them all is to overthrow Islam. At first, in order to lure the Muslims, they display themselves as truthful, virtuous, abstemious and faithful to The Prophet's family (upon him be peace); having gained power and acquired followers, they try to overthrow and destroy Muhammad's people and Muhammad's religion. Even infidels shew greater mercy to Muhammad's people (upon him be peace) than they do.

15 We have related this account of their deeds and sayings, since they are digging a pit, and beating a drum once again.[14] There are persons who, having accepted their propaganda, are assisting their purposes, joining in their affairs, and supporting their schemes. Although the whole world belongs to The Master of the World (may Allah perpetuate his rule), and all its inhabitants are his slaves, they have made him greedy for the acquisition of wealth; they are depriving deserving people of their dues, and maintaining that this is economy; but you will never repair a shirt by cutting off the tail using it to patch the sleeves. One day The Master of the World (may his reign last for ever) will recall the words of his slave, when they begin to throw friends and nobles into this pit, when the sound of their drum reaches the ears of all, and when their evil practices and intrigues are exposed; in that critical situation will he know that all that his slave said was true, and that he never refused to offer any possible advice or goodwill, and always fulfilled his duties of service and loyalty to The Victorious Empire (may Allah strengthen its pillars). May God Almighty keep the evil eye and the hand of harm far from his life and his empire, may He never permit his enemies to attain their objects and desires, may He keep this court, audience-hall and divan provided with men of true faith, and never let there be any lack of loyal supporters of the dynasty; and may He every day grant him conquest of a kingdom.

Chapter XLVIII

Concerning treasuries and the procedures and arrangements for looking after them

1 Kings have always had two treasuries, the capital treasury and the expenses treasury. As revenue was acquired it was usually taken to the capital treasury, and seldom to the expenses treasury, and unless there was urgent necessity they did not allow disbursement from the capital treasury. When they did take anything out, they took it by way of a loan, and put an equivalent sum back later. If care is not taken in this way, the whole income of the st . _s will be dissipated on expenses, and if there comes some unexpected need for money, it will give rise to anxiety and there will be shortcoming and delay in meeting the commitment. It was always the practice that any money paid into the treasury such as revenue from provinces, should not be changed or encashed. Thus expenses were met at their due time, there was no failure or delay in the payment of awards, salaries and presents, and the treasuries were always replenished.

2 I heard that the amir Altuntash, who was the amir-chamberlain of Sultan Mahmud, was appointed to be Khwarazmshah, and was sent to Khwarazm. Now the estimate of the revenue of Khwarazm was 60,000 dinars; while the salaries of Altuntash's troops amounted to twice this figure. A year after Altuntash went to Khwarazm a person was sent to demand the revenue. Altuntash sent his own emissaries to Ghaznain and requested that the 60,000 dinars which were the burden [of taxation] of Khwarazm should be assigned direct to him for the payment of his troops instead of the money being sent from the divan. Shams al-Kufat Ahmad ibn Hasan Maimandi was vazir at that time; when he read this letter, he wrote an answer at once as follows, 'In the name of Allah The Merciful, The Clement; be aware that Altuntash cannot be Mahmud in any respect. Take the money which you have collected in taxes, and bring it to the sultan's treasury; having had the gold assayed and weighed, deliver it and take a receipt. Then ask for the salaries for yourself and your troops, and you will be given drafts upon Bust and Sistan;[1] go and collect the money and

bring it to Khwarazm. Thus will be maintained the difference between master and slave, between Mahmud and Altuntash, because the functions of the king and the responsibilities of the army are clear and distinct. The Khwarazmshah should refrain from futile talk; as for this request which he has made, either he must regard the sultan with the eye of contempt, or else he considers Ahmad ibn Hasan negligent, incompetent and ignorant. We did not expect this from the perfect intelligence and sound judgment of the Khwarazmshah, and everybody who heard about it was astonished. He must apologize for this mistake. It is a grave danger when slaves seek partnership in power with their masters.'

3 He sent this letter by hand of an army officer with ten pages to Khwarazm. So the 60,000 dinars were brought and delivered to Mahmud's treasury, and in exchange drafts upon the provinces of Bust and Sistan for oak-apples, pomegranate skins, cotton and suchlike were taken from the divan of Ghaznain. Persons went to those places, took the goods, sold them and brought 60,000 dinars back to Khwarazm from Bust.

4 The affairs of the kingdom have always been arranged and managed in this way, for the safeguarding of the interests of the country, for the preservation of the welfare of the peasantry and the prosperity of the treasury, and for the restraining of covetous hands from the revenue of the sultan and the property of the people.

Chapter XLIX

On dealing with complainants, giving answers and dispensing justice.

1 There is always a large crowd of complainants frequenting the court, and even when they receive the answers to their petitions they do not go away. Any stranger or envoy, arriving at the capital and seeing this clamour and tumult, will think that at this court

gross injustice is done to the people. These doors must be closed to such crowds, and all requests, whether from town or country, provided the population are sedentary,[1] should be collected and written down at their place [of origin]; five persons should then come to the court, state their case, explain the circumstances, hear the answer and receive the judgment. Having received the judgment they must go back at once so that there is no more of this unnecessary tumult and groundless clamour.

2 They say that Yazdijird Shahryar sent a messenger to The Commander of the Faithful 'Umar (may Allah be pleased with him) saying, 'In all the world there is no court more frequented than ours, no treasury more replete, no army more numerous; and nobody has such great resources as we have.' 'Umar replied, 'Yes, your court is crowded, but with complainants; your treasury is replete, but with ill-gotten wealth; your army is numerous, but disobedient; when your fortune is finished, wealth and resources are of no avail. All these facts indicate that your fortune is waning and your empire declining.' And so indeed it was.

3 In order that everyone should practise equity and cease to covet improper and impossible objects, the best method is for The Master of the World (may Allah perpetuate his reign) to give justice himself in person, as did Sultan Mahmud.

The story of Mas'ud ibn Mahmud and his debt

4 They say that a merchant came to Sultan Mahmud's court of complaints, and complained against Mahmud's son Mas'ud, imploring justice and saying, 'I am a merchant; I have been staying here for a long time and I want to return to my own city. I cannot go because your son has bought goods and materials from me to the value of 60,000 dinars, and he has not given me the money. I request you to send the amir Mas'ud with me to the judge.' Sultan Mahmud was vexed at the merchant's words and sent a harsh message to Mas'ud saying, 'I desire you either to pay this man his due, or else to go with him to the court of justice so that judgment may be given according to the provisions of Islamic law.' The merchant went to the judge's house and a messenger went to Mas'ud and delivered the message. Mas'ud was at a loss to know what to do. He said to his treasurer, 'See how much money there is in the treasury.' The treasurer went and looked, and came back

and said, 'I have only 20,000 dinars.' He said, 'Take it to the merchant, and for the rest ask for three days' grace.' And he said to the messenger, 'Tell the sultan that I have just given 20,000 dinars on the spot, and I will pay the rest after three days. I am standing here with my cloak on and my loins girt, waiting for the sultan's command.' The messenger went and came back with another message from Sultan Mahmud saying, 'Go to the court of justice or else pay the merchant his money; and know for sure that you will not see my face until you pay him in full.' Mas'ud dared not say anything further, so he sent people in all directions to ask for loans. By the time of afternoon prayer the 60,000 dinars had been paid to the merchant. When reports of this reached distant parts of the world, merchants from China, Cathay, Egypt and 'Aden set out for Ghaznain bringing all the choicest goods in the world.

5 But as the kings of this age, if they command the merest servant or groom to be present at the court of law with the civil governor of Balkh or the mayor of Marv, the man will disobey the order and will not care two grains for the king's word.

6 The governor of the city of Homs wrote to 'Umar ibn 'Abd al 'Aziz saying, 'The city wall of Homs is in ruins and it must be built up. What is your command?' 'Umar replied, 'Let the city of Homs be protected by a wall of justice, and let the road be purged of fear and violence; then there is no need for bricks and mortar, stones and lime.'

7 God (be He exalted) commands David [Qur'an 38. 25], 'O David, I have made you a viceroy upon earth; judge between the people with equity.' (Which being translated means: O David, We have made you Our viceroy upon earth, so that you may look after Our servants, and not allow one to do wrong to another; every word that you say, say it with justice; every work that you do, do it with righteousness.) [And the Qur'an 39. 37 says:] 'Will not Allah suffice His slave?'

8 Muhammad The Elect (may Allah pray for him) says [in Arabic], 'He who appoints a governor over the Muslims, knowing that there is amongst the people a better man than that, has betrayed Allah, His prophet and the whole body of Muslims.' (Which being translated means: Good, pious and honest men should be put in charge of affairs, so that they will not trouble

God's servants, but rather have compassion upon them; if a man is appointed who is not so, a treachery will have been committed against God and His prophet.)

9 This world is the journal of kings. If they are good, they are blessed and well remembered; if they are evil, they are cursed and ill remembered; as 'Unsuri says:

If you make the firmament your throne you will be famous;
If you make your girdle of the Pleiades you'll be renowned;
See that when your fame is won that fame is pure and sound;
Take care that when you are renowned your renown is good.

Chapter L

On keeping account of the revenue of the provinces and the method of doing it

1 Accounts of the revenue of the provinces are always kept, shewing income and expenditure; the advantage of this is that a salutary watch can be kept upon spending; any items which need to be reduced (and the money not spent) can then be cancelled. If someone has something to say concerning income and proposes an increase, his words should be heard, and if what he says has some justification, the money should be raised; thus if it appears that there is any extravagance or waste of money, by this means it can be checked, and thereafter the true state of affairs will not remain concelead.

2 Now as regards following a middle course in finance and other affairs, the king must be just in every case, he must follow ancient customs and institutions which good kings have laid down; he must not initiate evil laws, nor assent to heresy. It is obligatory for the king to investigate the actions and transactions of tax-collectors, to know about income and expenditure, to look after the revenue, and to build treasuries and storehouses for the

purpose of strengthening the state and resisting enemy attack. He should not be so close-fisted that people will brand him as miserly or worldly; on the other hand he should not be so extravagant that people call him a spendthrift and a wastrel. When giving largesse he should have regard to the rank of each recipient; if ten dinars is a suitable bounty for a man, he should not give a hundred; nor should he give a thousand dinars to one who is fit to receive a hundred; for this is detrimental to the dignity of notable men, and besides people will say that the king is ignorant of men's worth and rank, and is ungrateful for the services and skills of his subjects; then for no cause people will be offended and become less diligent in their work.

3 Furthermore the king should so wage war against his enemies that there remains room for peace and so make peace as to leave scope for war; with friends and foes he should so make contracts that they can be broken, and so break them that they can be mended. He should not drink wine for the sake of intoxication. Let him not be constantly jocular, nor altogether austere. If occasionally he occupies himself with entertainment, hunting and drinking, let him also sometimes devote himself to thanksgiving, almsgiving, nocturnal prayer, fasting and charitable works; then he will possess both worlds. In all things he should take the middle course, for The Prophet (upon him be peace) said [in Arabic], 'The best of things is the middle of them.' (That is to say: the middle course in affairs is right for it wins the most approbation.) In every work let him observe the portion due to God (to Him be power and glory); then he will suffer no misfortune. Let him be industrious and zealous in obeying the commands of The Truth and in performing his religious duties; then God Almighty will give him success in all his religious and secular affairs, and cause him to gain his ends in both worlds and attain all his desires.

Colophon [in Arabic]

It was completed by the help of Allah Almighty and His enabling grace in the middle of the month of Shawwal in the year six hundred and seventy-three at the hands of His weak, poor, sinful servant, confessing his guilt, needing Allah's mercy, Husain ibn Zakariyya ibn al-Hajji Husain ad-Dihistani, may Allah pardon him and his parents and all faithful people until the Resurrection day, and may Allah bless our master, The Seal of the Prophets, Muhammad The Elect, and all his Family, his Companions and his Followers, and grant them abundant salvation. May Allah furnish the owner of it with lifelong happiness, through Muhammad and his Family. And the praise be to Allah.

Notes

Prologue
1 MS *hsyn* (with three dots under *s*; pointed to be read Hussain). All other sources give Nizam al-Mulk's name as Ḥasan; the mistake probably arose from the ancient practice of decorating undotted *s* with a subscript hook or three dots below; this can cause misreadings, such as *sy*.
2 MS *hsyn*.
3 Probably Sultan Muhammad, who ruled from 498/1105 to 511/1118.

Chapter I   On the turn of Fortune's Wheel
1 Mythical progenitor and primordial king of the Turkish race.
2 i.e. in addition to the five prescribed times of prayer.

Chapter II   On the extent of God's grace towards kings
1 The translation into Persian corresponds exactly to the Arabic.
2 MS *y'*. Persian *tā* with the meaning 'even' occurs several times in the *Kimiyā-yi Saʿādat* of Ghazzālī, and I believe it should be restored here; cf. page 73, line 4.
3 Baghdad was not yet founded as a capital city in the time of ʿUmar b. al-Khattab, but there had long been a settlement there.

Chapter III   On holding court for the redress of wrongs
1 i.e. Persian 'Iraq: see Le Strange, *Lands*, 185.
2 'Esoterics': a term of reproach applied by the Sunnis to the Ismaʿilis and Qarmatis; see *World-Conqueror*, 641.
3 MS *sbʿyʾn*.
4 Persian *ʿayyārī* 'knight-errantry' or 'chivalrous brigandage'.
5 The North African capital of the Fatimid (Ismaʿili) caliphs, which was founded in 308/921, whereas Yaʿqub began his advance on Baghdad in 261/875.

Chapter IV   On tax-collectors and the affairs of vazirs
1 Klausner (*Seljuk Vezirate*, pp. 15ff.) describes the Saljuq system of civil administration, while Bosworth (*Ghaznavids*, pp. 55–97) and Muhammad Nazim (*Sultan Mahmud*, pp. 126–50) give the comparable Ghaznavid system.
2 The author confused, perhaps by way of a visual pun, the archaic word *ravishn* 'conduct' with *raushan* 'bright'; both words appear the same in unpointed Arabic script.
3 The second half of the proverb is corrupt in the MS. This story is also found (ascribed to the legendary king Gushtasp) in the *Naṣīhat al-Mulūk* of Ghazzālī; the translation represents an amended text (*har ki bi nān khiyānat kunad bi jān andar mānad*), based on verses occurring there (*Counsel for Kings*, 94). The story ends at this point

in *Naṣiḥat* with the execution of Rast-ravishn, and probably this is how it was found in the 'Collections of Tales' to which Ghazzali refers and the sequel was invented by Nizam al-Mulk, suggested to him by 'the daily lists of prisoners'.

4 Persian *majlis*; cf. pp. 215–16. The words *majlis* and *majlis-khāna* are found in old books apparently meaning 'tray' or 'salver', and generally described as made of gold and silver: in *Tarikh-i Baihaqi* (539–40) 380 such trays are said to have been set out at the coronation of Sultan Mas'ud in 429/1037–8, and filled with aromatic substances; see also *World-Conqueror*, 500. The *Tarikh-i Tabaristan* (46) records that a second/eighth century king of Tabaristan possessed 2,000 silver trays, used for displaying presents; there the Persian word is *ṭabaq*. Perhaps *majlis-khāna* originally denoted the store room in which the trays were kept, and was extended to apply to the trays themselves, just as later *tūp-khāna* came to mean artillery.

Chapter V   On assignees of land and the peasantry
1 Persian *iqṭāʿ*: see Lambton, in *CHI* v, 231ff.
2 Persian *sim az miyān mī-barand*; cf. page 119, line 29.
3 Persian *parvāna-hā-yi dihlīzī*.

Chapter VI   On judges, preachers and censors
1 The festival of the autumn equinox.
2 The festival of the vernal equinox, starting the Persian new year.
3 'Father of sixths (of a diram)', nickname of the caliph al-Mansur, referring to his noted parsimony.
4 The duties of the censor (*muḥtasib*) are described in detail in the *Maʿalim al-Qurba*.
5 The notion of a great warrior being equal to 1,000 ordinary men must have been proverbial, since in the early stages of the Arab conquest an Iranian veteran called Hazar Savar (Thousand Knights) was killed in battle; see *CHI* iv, 7.
6 The lacuna in the Nakhjivani MS begins here.

Chapter VII   On obtaining information about tax-collectors
1 A famous mystic of the fourth/tenth century, who lived and preached at Nishapur in Khurasan: see *Kashf al-Mahjub*, 162.
2 Abu 'Ali Muhammad ibn Ilyas (if the author means him) was amir of Kirman in his day, but not of Khurasan; see Bosworth, 'The Banū Ilyās', and cf. page 65, line 12.
3 See Lane-Poole, *Dynasties*, 286 note.
4 A famous ascetic and teller of traditions: see *Kashf al-Mahjub*, 97.
5 *Rakʿat* is a cycle of prayers and prostrations; each of the five daily prayers consists of a prescribed number of *rakʿats*.
6 The lapse into the first person is noteworthy.
7 In the *Tarikh-i Guzida* (319) an expedition to Constantinople to

rescue a captive Muslim woman is similarly introduced as an example of al-Muʿtasim's zeal for Islam; this is a legend which grew out of his conflict with the emperor Theophilus; in 223 838, assisted by al-Afshin (see page 234, line 22), he personally directed the campaign to ʿAmmuriya (Amorium), but he never reached, much less sacked, Constantinople. The ʿAmmuriya campaign is described in detail by Tabari in *The Reign of al-Muʿtasim* (regarding the legend see page 59, note 293; Nizam al-Mulk's story may derive from Tabari's mention of a Muslim captive on page 67, note 334).

Chapter VIII   On enquiry into religion
1 Son of the caliph ʿUmar and a famous teller of traditions.
2 A celebrated scholar of tradition and a contemporary of the first ʿAbbasid caliphs.
3 A famous lawyer and ascetic, contemporary of the Umayyad caliph ʿUmar b. ʿAbd al-ʿAziz: see *Kashf al-Mahjub*, 86.
4 Persian *farr-i ilāhī*: see page 117, line 9 (note 15).

Chapter X   On intelligence agents and reporters
1 The lacuna in the Nakhjivani MS ends here.
2 'Plaster Convent': see Le Strange, *Lands*, 208.
3 See Le Strange, *Lands*, 317, 323; C. E. Bosworth, 'The Kūfichīs or Qufs in Persian History', *Iran* XIV (1976), 9–17.
4 This amir of Kirman was not a contemporary of Sultan Mahmud.
5 'The coast of India begins with Tiz, the capital of Makran'; Biruni's *India* I, 208. Tiz was a great port in the middle ages; it is now in ruins; see Le Strange, *Lands*, 329.
6 See *Mirror for Princes*, 134.
7 According to Juvaini (*World-Conqueror*, 642) the Rāfiḍīs were a subdivision of the Shiʿa, being the followers of Muḥammad Bāqir the fifth imam, and this is how the name can be understood here and on page 188. The author's definition of Rafidis is on pages 162–4, where he equates them with the Qadaris (Muʿtazilites), a sect who rejected the doctrine of predestination, belonging to early orthodox Islam, and believed in human free will. However, the name was also used as a general pejorative term for Shiʿites, as appears from pages 97 and 160.
8 MS *tyr* = *tīr* (later MSS *nyzh* = *naiza*); a similar expression (with *yak naiza* 'one spear') is used by Ghazzāli (*Kimiyā-yi Saʿādat*, 189.19; 219.17). According to al-Bīrūnī in his *Tafhīm* (Persian version quoted in Dihkhudā, *Lughat-nāma*) the word *tīr* 'arrow' (in the subsidiary sense of 'portion') was used for a twenty-fourth part of a day and night, and this may be the intention here, i.e. 'two hours after sunrise'. However, in view of the parallel usage with *naiza*, we probably have to do with some quite unscientific and imprecise way of telling the time in the early hours of sunlight.
9 See *Chahar Maqala*, translation, 26, 10.

10 Sayyid Abu'l-Faḍl Naṣr b. Aḥmad was appointed governor of Sistan by Sultan Mahmud of Ghazna in 421/1030; he remained in this capacity under the Saljuqs and died in 465/1073; see *Tarikh-i Sistan*, 362–83.

Chapter XI On honouring the sublime commands and edicts
1 MS *y*'; see page 12, line 28.

Chapter XII On sending pages from the court
1 Persian *ghulām*. Ghulams were a 'pampered class' of boy-slaves: see Muhammad Nazim, *Sultan Mahmud*, 139. English 'page' corresponds in several respects and this rendering has been adopted consistently here.

Chapter XIII On sending spies for the good of the country
1 A Persian MS gloss adds: 'for the sake of his recovery'.
2 MS *'wky'n*: later MSS *₊'wky'n*, read as *nāvakiyān*. ('Abbās Iqbāl read *yāvagiyān* 'irregulars'.)
3 See Le Strange, *Lands*, 259.
4 MS *mgwy* = *ma-gūy*.

Chapter XIV On constant employment of couriers
1 MS *prndk'n* = *parandagān*.

Chapter XV On messages
1 MS *prw'nh'* = *parvāna-hā*: in the Syriac 'Song of the Pearl' *parvānak* is mentioned as a member of the king's retinue in Parthian times; *Mafātīḥ al-'ulūm* (s.v. *furāniq*) defines the word as 'the bearer of letter-pouches'; in the present context the word may refer to bearers of verbal orders or more likely to the actual orders, which is the usual Persian meaning; cf. page 40, line 4.

Chapter XVII On boon-companions and intimates
1 Persian *kāhil būda-and*.

Chapter XIX On solitaries
1 MS *₊yẓb'y rmh* = *naiza-hā-yi rumḥ* (later MSS *naiza-hā-yi Khaṭṭī*).

Chapter XXI On ambassadors and their treatment
1 Internal evidence of the authorship of the book.
2 It was on this expedition in 465/1072 that Alp Arslan met his death.
3 See Barthold, *Turkestan*, 314–16; Bosworth, *Dynasties*, 111; Shams al-Mulk was the brother of Tarkan Khatun, Malikshah's wife (*Rahat as-Sudur*, 133), and he was the patron of 'Umar Khayyam in the beginning of his career (*CHI* IV. 659).
4 See page 66, line 5.
5 Since the time of Harun ar-Rashid, Sunni practice had been to wear rings on the left hand, and wearing them on the right was a sign of

Shi'ism. In the time of the Prophet rings were worn on the right hand; changes were made by the first Umayyad caliph Mu'awiya to the left, by the first 'Abbasid as-Saffah to the right, and finally by ar-Rashid to the left (*Safinat al-Baḥār,* siv. *khātam*).

6 The Jikil (or Chigil) tribe formed the nucleus of the Qarakhanid army, and all eastern Turks were called Jikil by the Turkmans of the Saljuq empire (Barthold, *Turkestan,* 254, note 6, 317, note 2).

Chapter XXIII On settling the dues

1 This word (in Arabic *al-'ashrīniyya*; see *Mafātīḥ al-'ulūm*) has not been satisfactorily explained; the Persian form suggests a payment 'by twenties'. Barthold (*Turkestan,* 230, n. 11) thought that it might be based on the fact that the total sum paid to the army of Khurasan in Samanid times was 20 million dirams.

Chapter XXVI On keeping Turkmans in service

1 See Lambton, *Landlord and Peasant,* 56.

Chapter XXVII On organizing the work of slaves

1 Persian *bandagān,* 'unskilled slaves', as distinct from ghulams who were trained slaves.
2 Persian *zaḥmat mi-kunand*: see *Raḥat as-Sudur,* 503 (glossary).
3 Persian *tir andākhtan.*
4 Errors in the numbering of chapters began when scribes numbered this subheading as chapter 28.
5 Zandana (adj. Zandanījī or Zandanīchī), a town in the district of Bukhara, was noted for its textiles; see Le Strange, *Lands,* 462; *History of Bukhara,* 15; *Raḥat as-Sudur,* 504 (glossary).
6 See *Hudud al-'Alam,* 111, 347.
7 These events took place on the death of 'Abd al-Malik: see *Tarikh-i Guzida,* 384. 'Abd al-Malik is also left out of the author's reckoning at page 156, line 13 and page 221, line 26.
8 Persian *vakil-darān.*
9 In the *Zain al-Akhbar* of Gardizi this amir is named *bbd'ḥ* = Babdāḥ (see p. 222), and in the *History of Bukhara* he is named Ash'ath b. Muhammad.
10 The discrepancy between the plan and the action is in the text.
11 Shīr is an eastern Iranian form corresponding to Persian *shāh*; see *CHI* iv, 171; *Hudud al-'Alam,* 109.
12 Alptigin took Ghazna from the local ruler, the Lavik, in 351/962; see *CHI* iv, 165.
13 Persian *khusur,* restored from corruptions in later MSS; our MS has *jnz*; cf. page 162, line 36.
14 Muhammad Nazim, *Sultan Mahmud,* 115 and App. M gives an account of the expedition to Somnat.
15 Nizam al-Mulk supports the old Iranian belief, which goes right back to the Avesta, in the *farr-i kayāni* 'regal charisma or aura',

mysteriously vested in a person, an animal (as in the story of Ardashir Papakan) or an object (e.g. a ring).

Chapter XXVIII On the conduct of private and public audiences
1 Persian *tīr andākhtan.*

Chapter XXIX On rules for drinking parties
1 Persian *sīm az miyān bi-barand;* cf. page 33, line 7.

Chapter XXXIII On reprimanding those in high positions
1 MS ₓ*rk'ny* read as *barakānī (barakān-i* or *barakanī-ī?): barakān* and *barakānī* are given in old dictionaries as *gilīm-isiyāh* 'black blanket'; but in a verse of the Ghaznavid poet Mas'ūd Sa'd Salmān *barakān* is coupled with *aṭlas* 'satin'; it must therefore have been a fine kind of cloth (later MSS have *dastār-ī,* '*amāma*).
2 MS *dst'r = dastār.*

Chapter XXXV On setting a good table
1 The khans Turkistan (known as Qarakhanids or Ilak Khans) gave occasional trouble to the Saljuqs and ultimately became their vassals; cf. page 96, n. 3. Malikshah invaded Transoxiana in 481/1088–482/1089, and besieged Samarqand, because religious leaders had complained about Ahmed Khan and called for intervention; they said the ruler was oppressive; maybe he had already displayed those Isma'ili leanings for which he was later deposed and executed; see Barthold, *Turkestan,* 316–17 and *CHI* v, 66, 79, 92. *Rahat as-Sudur* records two journeys to Samarqand and Uzand, in 471/1078(128.5) and 481/1088(129.10–130.2), placing the siege of Samarqand and the deportation of the Khan in the earlier one.
2 'Ali is not mentioned by name in the Qur'an, but several verses are regarded (not only by Shi'is) as referring to him. Tabari commenting on Qur'an 5.55–6 quotes the story of 'Ali's gift to the beggar and indeed interprets the verses as designating 'Ali for the caliphate. According to Ṭabari, Qur'an 2.275 refers to 'Ali's generosity.
3 'Unsuri (died 431/1039–40) was poet laureate at the court of Sultan Mahmud of Ghazna.

Chapter XXXVI On acknowledging the merits of worthy servants
1 Ibn Khurdadbih, the third/ninth-century Persian author of the oldest Arabic geographical work, also wrote a book on music from which this anecdote may have been taken.
2 MS *drm*(!)

Chapter XXXVIII On the inadvisability of hastiness in affairs
1 This is a sure reference to the famous mystic, 'Abd-Allah Ansari (396/1006–481/1088), who was known as 'the old man of Herat'; see *Chahar Maqala,* trans., 163 (note XXXI).
2 MS *mkrky* (later MS *mkrk*); the reading here is adopted on the authority of *Rahat as-Sudur* (117.3), which records that Bikrak was a chamberlain of Alp Arslan.
3 MS *ṭlx;* this unusual spelling of Persian *talkh* occurs in a MS of Asadi, *Lughat-i Furs,* s.v. *frž(farazh).*

Chapter XXXIX   On commanders of the guard

1 A pious ejaculation (in Arabic) equivalent to 'Bless my soul!' or the like.

2 Ḥamza b. 'Abd al-Muṭṭalib, an uncle of The Prophet, was killed at the battle of Uḥud.

3 Persian *du-mūy* 'having two (colours of) hair'.

Chapter XL   On shewing mercy to the creatures of God

1 As the author takes up his pen again, probably in 484/1091, the year before his death, the ideas and even the very words of chapter I return to his mind.

2 Persian *farẓandān-i rūẓgār*; this is evidently a translation of the Arabic *abnā' ad-daula*, a name given to the Khurasani troops who supported the 'Abbasid revolution, and also to their descendants; see *CHI* iv 91.

3 MS *byftr* read as *bī ḥaṣr* (later MS *bī andāẓa*).

4 See *Hudud al-'Alam*, 361–2.

5 The name of the horse on which the prophet Muhammad ascended to heaven.

6 MS *ḥryr w knry w ṭrqwb*; *knry* (*kbry* in a later MS) is read (following the suggestion of Professor Sir Harold Bailey) as *kabaẓī* 'cotton goods' from Uighur Turkish *kabaẓ* 'cotton'; see Paul Pelliot, *Notes on Marco Polo* (Paris, 1959), 433 ff. *Ṭarqū* (*ṭarghū*) is given in dictionaries as a kind of red silk; the *b* here possibly arises from confusion with Qurqūb (see *Ḥudūd al-'Alam*, 131 and Asadi, *Lughat-i Furs*, s.v *mānā*, where the best reading is *qurqūb-u šūštar* – '[the silken stuffs of] Qurqūb and Shūshtar').

7 At this point in the previous text and translation came a passage (of the length of one page of the present book), now confirmed as a spurious interpolation, in which there were references to the death of Malikshah, to some of his successors and to Nizam al-Mulk in the third person.

Chapter XLI   On not giving two appointments to one man

1 Cf. *Mirror of Princes*, 139.

2 MS *š''ym*.

3 These places were noted for their fanatical Shi'ite population; see Le Strange, *Lands*, 209–11, and *Rahat as-Sudur*, 30. 20.

4 MS *'lhy* read as *ābajī*; although *dihkhudā* means 'village headman', it is probably a proper name here, especially since Ābajī is a surname form meaning 'belonging to Āba'.

5 MS *š''yst*.

6 There was a lawyer of the Hanafi school called Mushattab ibn Muhammad Farghani, who was contemporary with Nizam al-Mulk.

7 Lūkar or Laukar was a village near Marv; see Le Strange, *Lands*, 406. The judge may be identified with the contemporary philosopher Lukari; *CHI* v, 288.

8 MS *qdḥy knd y'ny škstky*.

9 Persian *khusurān*.

10 A quotation (of little relevance but evidently suggested by the words *bā mā-st*) from the contemporary poet Hakim Sana'i (ghazal 25; trans. Arberry, *Immortal Rose*, 5). Sana'i (quoted again on p. 164), at first a panegyrist of the later Ghaznavids, subsequently devoted himself to mysticism; he died in 525/1131.

11 This is probably a reference to Nizam al-Mulk's rival Taj al-Mulk, who was patronized by Tarkan Khatun, wife of Malikshah: see *Rahat as-Sudur*, 133–4.

12 Persian *sutūdān* (lit: 'bone-repository').

13 See Le Strange, *Lands*, 216, 217 note.

14 Persian *bi du pūshish*.

15 Persian *kūkh-i*.

16 MS *dwry = daur-i*.

17 The Arab general whose forces defeated the Persians at the battle of Qadisiyya; he was appointed by 'Umar to be the first governor of the newly founded town of Kufa; see *CHI* IV.

18 In the previous text and translation Nizam al-Mulk himself came at the end of this list; this is now seen to have been a spurious addition, though it is still surprising that he should have mentioned his old enemy Kunduri.

19 This story with almost identical wording is found in the opening pages of an earlier book, the *Tarikh-i Baramika* 'History of the Barmakids', and this is undoubtedly the source from which our author drew it; the important difference is that there the vazir is Barmak not Ja'far; Nizam al-Mulk has gratuitously altered the name and thereby perpetrated an anachronism, probably for no other reason than to introduce a more celebrated name.

20 Nau-bahār, meaning 'new *vihāra*', was in fact a Buddhist monastery: see Barthold, *Turkestan*, 77; R. W. Bulliet, 'Naw Bahār and the survival of Iranian Buddhism' *Iran*, XIV (1976), 140–5.

21 No doubt Nizam al-Mulk is referring to Malikshah's small son Mahmud, whom Tarkan Khatun wished to be heir, against the advice of Nizam al-Mulk; see *CHI* V. 77, and *Rahat as-Sudur*, 134.

Chapter XLII   On those who wear the veil
1 It is wheat in Islamic tradition rather than an apple.

Chapter XLIII   On heretics
1 MS *nhnbn = nihunban*.

Chapter XLIV   On the revolt of Mazdak
1 Persian *mūbad-mūbadān*: cf. page 43, line 9.
2 MS *xl'ft* read as *khilāf* with later MSS.
3 The direction to which Muslims turn in prayer, i.e. towards Mecca.
4 This is evidently a variant form of the name Gūr or Jūr (later Firūzābād): see Le Strange, *Lands*, 255–6.

5 MS *kwšh* = *gūsha*; later MSS have *d'rbzyn* = *dārbazīn* 'balustrade'.
6 See Qur'an 54.1.
7 See Qur'an 2.60.
8 MS *d'yš* = *dāy-ash*: Persian *dāv* (variant *dāy*) means 'a move or throw in a game', and by extension 'claim, pretension' (cf. modern *dāv-ṭalab* 'candidate'); later MSS have *bahāna(-ash)*.

Chapter XLV   On the emergence of Sinbad
1 A parallel passage in the *Mujmal at-Tavarikh* (p. 354) confirms the name of Mazdak's wife and also the form Khurrama-din rather than Khurram-din.
2 MS *synb'd*; see *CHI* IV. 494.
3 'The divinely guided', the twelfth imam of Twelver Sh'ism who went into occultation in about 260/873 and is expected to return and fill the world with justice; see *CHI* IV. 516.
4 MS *krh*: see Le Strange, *Lands*, 198.

Chapter XLVI   On the rising of the Qarmatis and Batinis
1 See Stern, 'Early Isma'ili missionaries' for a commentary on this chapter.
2 This would have been Bakkār b. 'Abd-Allāh b. Mus'ab b. Thābit b. 'Abd-Allāh b. Zubair, who was sent as governor to Medina by Harun ar-Rashid for the express purpose of harassing 'Alids. According to some sources the accuser was Muhammad b. Isma'il.
3 The erroneous omission of the name Musa is found in all MSS and may have been a slip on the part of the author; cf. para. 2 below, and see *World-Conqueror*, 644.
4 The great physician known in Europe as Rhazes; see *CHI* IV.
5 MS *'kft* = *āgaft*.
6 Fashāfūya (as it is now) is a district S. of Rayy and W. of Varāmīn; the village still exists.
7 MS *hδ' h'b h'tnh 'lwhmh*.
8 MS *dwyst w hšt'd*.
9 See page 219, line 21.
10 This must surely be Abū Ḥātim Aḥmad b. Ḥamdān Rāzī, the noted Isma'ili philosopher; see *CHI* IV.
11 MS *ky*ty* (later MS *kynty*) read as Laithi (letter *l* with *fatḥa* mistaken for *k*); there is some confusion about the nomenclature of Abu Hatim, and this is probably the reason why our author makes it appear that there were two persons of this name (see Husain Hamdani's introduction to his edition of Abu Hatim's *Kitāb az-Zina* (Cairo, 1957), p. 26); in addition to the general surname (*nisba*) Rāzī (of Rayy) Abu Hatim had (according to Ḥāfiz 'Asqalānī, *Lisān al-Mīzān*, no. 523) two particular surnames, Laithi (family) and Warsāmī (presumably place: Varsām might be expected to be a village in the district of Fashafuya, but it has not been found).
12 Persian *bīsha-parvar*.

13 MS *sy'r* (for *sh'r* = Sapār < Asfār?).
14 See Browne, *Literary History* I. 365–6.
15 Abu 'Abd-Allah Muhtasib played the same part in the foundation of the Fatimid state as Abu Muslim had played in the 'Abbasid revolution; he was put to death by the first Fatimid caliph in 289/910; see *World-Conqueror*, 649.
16 The name belongs to a dynasty, not a tribe; see Bosworth, *Dynasties*, 24.
17 Persian *mi sitadand*.
18 MS *zkrw* (a later MS *zkrwk*). Sahib al-Khal ('the man with the mole') was actually the nickname of Zikrawaih's son, Husain, and he was a Qarmati, active in Syria at the end of the third/ninth century.
19 MS *'dly*: *'adl* (pl. *'udūl*) is an Islamic legal term for a person of good reputation, whose testimony is assumed to be true; see also pages 51 and 77.
20 See *History of Bukhara*, 27; *Chahar Maqala*, trans., 121 (note XVI).
21 A few words have been supplied from later MSS.
22 The author has confused the Nasr ibn Ahmad who was Isma'il's brother and predecessor on the Samanid throne with the Nasr ibn Ahmad who was his grandson and succeeded him next but one.
23 MS *✶nd'j*: see page 110, line 35 (note 9).
24 MS *syhy* read as *ṣaiḥī*; this word is not in any dictionary, but if correct, it could have been coined by the author from Arabic *ṣaiḥa* 'a shout', with particular reference to Qur'an 50.41–2.
25 Persian *sapīd-jāmagān*; see *CHI* v. 500 and Browne, *Literary History* I. 318.
26 MS *syrwrzh*. The seventh/thirteenth-century geographer Yaqut describes Shīr as a small town two days' journey from Sarakhs by camel in the direction of Herat; he gives Riza as a place near Herat, adding that there are many places of this name in Iran.
27 We may suppose that a contingent of holy-warriors (*ghāziyān*) from Fars and Khuzistan (then under Buyid rule) were operating in Samanid territory (Taliqan or Tayiqan of Tukharistan; see Le Strange, *Lands*, 428) and that a Samanid agent (*vakīl*) was appointed to accompany them and oversee them.
28 Possibly this is the man named as Ibn Abi Zakariyya by Biruni (*Ancient Nations*, 196); see Browne, *Literary History* I. 359.
29 In ancient times books were usually kept in chests.
30 viz. Moses, Jesus and Muhammad.
31 MS *'hl myrb w 'hl 'z✶y'n*: out of several possible readings I have chosen *va ān gharbiyān*, on the authority of later MSS.
32 See *CHI* IV.

Chapter XLVII   On the rising of the Khurrama-dins
1 MS *bryd✶n* (one later MS *bw✶dn*) read as Parīdan (modern Farīdan), a place between Gulpaygan and Shahr-i Kurd.
2 MS *k'blh*: *Rahat as-Ṣudūr* (287.3) states that Kābala (Kāpula?) was near the castle of Farrazīn; Farrazīn (modern Farzīn) can still be seen

to the west of Arāk (formerly Sultanabad), lying to the north of the road to Burujird (see *Nuzhat al-Qulub*, trans. 73; *World-Conqueror*, 382; Le Strange, *Lands*, 198).

3 MS *f'bk*: a similar spelling is found in *Hudud al-'Alam*, 129.

4 MS *dstbyh*: this can hardly be other than the district of Dastabā (spelt *dstby* by the Arab geographers) between Rayy and Hamadan; see Le Strange, *Lands*, 220.

5 See *CHI* IV.

6 MS *ₓr₊dh* (later MSS *bwydh, rwndh*) tentatively read as Pūnda, which could be an earlier form of Pūda, now a large village to the south of Isfahan.

7 This person appears to be related to, or confused by the author with, Ṣadaqa b. 'Ali b. Ṣadaqa, known as Zuraiq, who according to Tabari, so far from being a rebel, was governor of Armenia for al-Ma'mun and is listed by Tabari, along with Muḥammad b. Ḥumaid (al-Ṭūsī in Tabari), among the generals defeated by Babak; see *The Reign of Mu'tasim*, 56.

8 MS *d'r*: surely modern Dārān, which is not far from Farīdan.

9 MS *brndyn* read as Parīdan again.

10 *Mujmal at-Tavārikh* (p. 356) says 'at the village of Shahristana'; Tabari (*The Reign of al-Mu'tasim*, 2) says 'in the district of Hamadan'; Shāristāna (being an alternative or erroneous form in our text) can thus be identified as the village of the Shahristāna, still existing and situated 20 km NNW of Tūysirkān.

11 Afshin was the title of the local rulers of Ushrusana; the Afshin Khaidhar (or Haidar) entered the service of al-Ma'mun with a corps of his own subjects; he held several governorships under al-Mu'tasim; see *The Reign of al-Mu'tasim*.

12 Babak's fortress was at Badhdh in Arran and it was captured in 222/837. Babak's execution took place at Samarra.

13 MS *b'ryzds'h* (later MSS *b'z br b'ds'h*): a proper name must be contained here, but until confirmation is found in some other source we cannot be sure how to read it; Bār-Īzad-shāh ('Lord-God-king') is hardly likely, but with a slight mutation Yār-Īzad-shāh ('Friend-of-God-king') becomes a possible reading. Since Tabari's 'History' and the 'History of Isfahan' are mentioned at the end of this paragraph, and as names ending in -shāh are especially common in Kurdistan and Dailaman, this may well represent the first name of al-Lashkarī, 'chief of the Dailamites', whose career, according to those authorities, bears some resemblance to the account given here; 'in 319/931 he attacked Isfahan, promising his followers the sharing out of estates and farms and licence to molest women and children; he was killed at the castle of Mārbīn and his head was sent to the city; a long poem in Arabic was composed to celebrate this event'; see Browne, 'History of Isfahan', 665, *Mahāsin Isfahān* of Māfarrūkhī (Arabic text composed in 421/1030), 38 (later Persian translation, 84), and the chronicles of Tabari and Ibn al-Athir under the year 319. Nizam al-Mulk may have adapted this story to make a

dramatic tail-piece to his account of the Khurrama-dins and indeed to the whole section of the book dealing with heretics and beginning with chapter XLIII; or he may have derived his version, with the problematical name, from one of the lost histories of Isfahan, listed by Hajji Khalifa.

14 MS *dygrb'r*.

Chapter XLVIII   On treasuries
  1 See Bosworth, *Ghaznavids,* 83. Compare the well-known story of Nizam al-Mulk paying boatmen on the Oxus by drafts on Antioch, which in *Rahat as-Sudur* (128. 15) is related to Malikshah's campaign of 471/1078.

Chapter XLIX   On dealing with complainants
  1 Persian *ḥāḍir*.

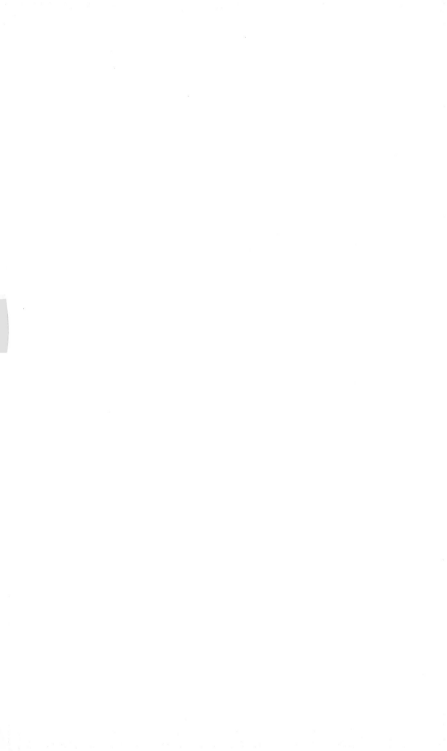

Index

INDEX

Printed in Great Britain
by Amazon

72274207R00169